# COMPUTER-AIDED INNOVATION (CAI)

T0180630

# IFIP – The International Federation for Information Processing

IFIP was founded in 1960 under the auspices of UNESCO, following the First World Computer Congress held in Paris the previous year. An umbrella organization for societies working in information processing, IFIP's aim is two-fold: to support information processing within its member countries and to encourage technology transfer to developing nations. As its mission statement clearly states,

> IFIP's mission is to be the leading, truly international, apolitical organization which encourages and assists in the development, exploitation and application of information technology for the benefit of all people.

IFIP is a non-profitmaking organization, run almost solely by 2500 volunteers. It operates through a number of technical committees, which organize events and publications. IFIP's events range from an international congress to local seminars, but the most important are:

• The IFIP World Computer Congress, held every second year;
• Open conferences;
• Working conferences.

The flagship event is the IFIP World Computer Congress, at which both invited and contributed papers are presented. Contributed papers are rigorously refereed and the rejection rate is high.

As with the Congress, participation in the open conferences is open to all and papers may be invited or submitted. Again, submitted papers are stringently refereed.

The working conferences are structured differently. They are usually run by a working group and attendance is small and by invitation only. Their purpose is to create an atmosphere conducive to innovation and development. Refereeing is less rigorous and papers are subjected to extensive group discussion.

Publications arising from IFIP events vary. The papers presented at the IFIP World Computer Congress and at open conferences are published as conference proceedings, while the results of the working conferences are often published as collections of selected and edited papers.

Any national society whose primary activity is in information may apply to become a full member of IFIP, although full membership is restricted to one society per country. Full members are entitled to vote at the annual General Assembly, National societies preferring a less committed involvement may apply for associate or corresponding membership. Associate members enjoy the same benefits as full members, but without voting rights. Corresponding members are not represented in IFIP bodies. Affiliated membership is open to non-national societies, and individual and honorary membership schemes are also offered.

# COMPUTER-AIDED INNOVATION (CAI)

*IFIP 20th World Computer Congress, Proceedings of the Second Topical Session on Computer-Aided Innovation, WG 5.4/TC 5 Computer-Aided Innovation, September 7-10, 2008, Milano, Italy*

*Edited by*

**Gaetano Cascini**
*University of Florence*
*Italy*

Springer

*Computer-Aided Innovation (CAI)*

Edited by Gaetano Cascini

p. cm. (IFIP International Federation for Information Processing, a Springer Series in Computer Science)

ISSN: 1571-5736 / 1861-2288 (Internet)

ISBN: 978-1-4419-3519-9          eISBN: 978-0-387-09697-1

Printed on acid-free paper

9 8 7 6 5 4 3 2 1

springer.com

# IFIP 2008 World Computer Congress (WCC'08)

## Message from the Chairs

Every two years, the International Federation for Information Processing hosts a major event which showcases the scientific endeavours of its over one hundred Technical Committees and Working Groups. 2008 sees the 20th World Computer Congress (WCC 2008) take place for the first time in Italy, in Milan from 7-10 September 2008, at the MIC - Milano Convention Centre. The Congress is hosted by the Italian Computer Society, AICA, under the chairmanship of Giulio Occhini.

The Congress runs as a federation of co-located conferences offered by the different IFIP bodies, under the chairmanship of the scientific chair, Judith Bishop. For this Congress, we have a larger than usual number of thirteen conferences, ranging from Theoretical Computer Science, to Open Source Systems, to Entertainment Computing. Some of these are established conferences that run each year and some represent new, breaking areas of computing. Each conference had a call for papers, an International Programme Committee of experts and a thorough peer reviewed process. The Congress received 661 papers for the thirteen conferences, and selected 375 from those representing an acceptance rate of 56% (averaged over all conferences).

An innovative feature of WCC 2008 is the setting aside of two hours each day for cross-sessions relating to the integration of business and research, featuring the use of IT in Italian industry, sport, fashion and so on. This part is organized by Ivo De Lotto. The Congress will be opened by representatives from government bodies and Societies associated with IT in Italy.

This volume is one of fourteen volumes associated with the scientific conferences and the industry sessions. Each covers a specific topic and separately or together they form a valuable record of the state of computing research in the world in 2008. Each volume was prepared for publication in the Springer IFIP Series by the conference's volume editors. The overall Chair for all the volumes published for the Congress is John Impagliazzo.

For full details on the Congress, refer to the webpage http://www.wcc2008.org.

*Judith Bishop, South Africa, Co-Chair, International Program Committee*
*Ivo De Lotto, Italy, Co-Chair, International Program Committee*
*Giulio Occhini, Italy, Chair, Organizing Committee*
*John Impagliazzo, United States, Publications Chair*

# WCC 2008 Scientific Conferences

| | | |
|---|---|---|
| **TC12** | **AI** | Artificial Intelligence 2008 |
| **TC10** | **BICC** | Biologically Inspired Cooperative Computing |
| **WG 5.4** | **CAI** | Computer-Aided Innovation (Topical Session) |
| **WG 10.2** | **DIPES** | Distributed and Parallel Embedded Systems |
| **TC14** | **ECS** | Entertainment Computing Symposium |
| **TC3** | **ED_L2L** | Learning to Live in the Knowledge Society |
| **WG 9.7**<br>**TC3** | **HCE3** | History of Computing and Education 3 |
| **TC13** | **HCI** | Human Computer Interaction |
| **TC8** | **ISREP** | Information Systems Research, Education and Practice |
| **WG 12.6** | **KMIA** | Knowledge Management in Action |
| **TC2**<br>**WG 2.13** | **OSS** | Open Source Systems |
| **TC11** | **IFIP SEC** | Information Security Conference |
| **TC1** | **TCS** | Theoretical Computer Science |

**IFIP**
- is the leading multinational, apolitical organization in Information and Communications Technologies and Sciences
- is recognized by United Nations and other world bodies
- represents IT Societies from 56 countries or regions, covering all 5 continents with a total membership of over half a million
- links more than 3500 scientists from Academia and Industry, organized in more than 101 Working Groups reporting to 13 Technical Committees
- sponsors 100 conferences yearly providing unparalleled coverage from theoretical informatics to the relationship between informatics and society including hardware and software technologies, and networked information systems

*Details of the IFIP Technical Committees and Working Groups can be found on the website at http://www.ifip.org.*

# Contents

# Preface

Computer-Aided Innovation (CAI) is emerging as a strategic domain of research and application to support enterprises throughout the overall innovation process.

The 5.4 Working Group of IFIP aims at defining the scientific foundation of Computer Aided Innovation systems and at identifying state of the art and trends of CAI tools and methods.

These Proceedings derive from the second Topical Session on Computer-Aided Innovation organized within the 20th World Computer Congress of IFIP. The goal of the Topical Session is to provide a survey of existing technologies and research activities in the field and to identify opportunities of integration of CAI with other PLM systems.

According to the heterogeneous needs of innovation-related activities, the papers published in this volume are characterized by multidisciplinary contents and complementary perspectives and scopes.

Such a richness of topics and disciplines will certainly contribute to the promotion of fruitful new collaborations and synergies within the IFIP community.

Gaetano Cascini

Florence, April 30th 2008

# CAI Topical Session Organization

**The IFIP Topical Session on Computer-Aided Innovation (CAI)**

is a co-located conference organized under the auspices of the
IFIP World Computer Congress (WCC) 2008 in Milano, Italy

**Gaetano Cascini**
CAI Program Committee Chair
gaetano.cascini@unifi.it

**CAI Program Committee**
A. Albers, Germany
T. Arciszewski, USA
M. Ashtiani, USA
G. Cascini, Italy
D. Cavalucci, France
U. Cugini, Italy
S.K. Cho, USA
R. De Guio, France
J. Gero, Australia
N. Khomenko, Canada
N. León, Mexico
G. J. Olling, USA
P. Rissone, Italy
C. Rizzi, Italy
R. Tan, China
R. Vidal, Spain

# IFIP WORLD COMPUTER CONGRESS 2008

# COMPUTER-AIDED INNOVATION:
# THEORY AND PRACTICE

**Keynote Speech**

# The future of Computer Aided Innovation

N. Leon Rovira

Tecnologico de Monterrey, CIDYT-CIII
Ave. Eugenio Garza Sada # 2501
Col. Tecnológico, Monterrey, NL, CP. 64839, Mexico
http://cidyt.mty.itesm.mx

## Summary

The technological evolution is also the history of the human being in an eternal fight to dominate his surroundings as part of his own evolution. With the technological evolution humans unfolded the capacity of producing useful objects for satisfying their needs. Nowadays the transition from resource-based products to knowledge-based products is compelling the New Product Development process to be more innovative and efficient, making innovation processes even more challenging.

The development of a new category of tools known as CAI (Computer Aided Innovation) is an emergent domain in the array of CAx technologies. CAI has been growing in the last decade as a response to a higher industry demand regarding reliability of new products not only regarding engineering and design solutions but also concerning success rate of new products, processes and services being launched into the market.

Scientists, engineers, academics and managers all over the world are joining in an effort for clarifying the essential factors characterizing these new arising tools for bridging the gap between the traditional methods and current trends in search of efficient innovation. The goal of these emerging CAI tools is to assist innovators, inventors, designers, process developers and managers in their creative stage, expecting changes in paradigms through the use of this new category of software tools. Although some initial ideas and concepts of CAI focused on assisting product designers in their creative stage, a more comprehensive vision conceives CAI systems beginning at the creative stage of perceiving business opportunities and customer demands, then continue assisting in developing inventions and, further on, providing help up to the point of turning inventions into successful innovations in the market.

CAI therefore stands out as being a break from the usual trends that is challenging the previous standards, with the aim to support enterprises throughout the complete innovation process.

As Product Life Cycle Management tools are being integrated with knowledge management methods and tools, new alternatives arise regarding the Engineering and Manager Desktop. It is expected that changes in innovation paradigms will

Please use the following format when citing this chapter:

Leon Rovira, N., 2008, in IFIP International Federation for Information Processing, Volume 277; *Computer-Aided Innovation (CAI)*; Gaetano Cascini; (Boston: Springer), pp. 3–4.

occur through the use of Computer Aided Innovation methods and tools, which structure is partially inspired by modern Innovation Theories as TRIZ, QFD, Axiomatic Design, Synectics, General Theory of Innovation, Mind Mapping, Brain Storming, Lateral Thinking, Technology Maps and Kansei Engineering, among others.

Additionally the use of evolutionary algorithms, especially genetic algorithms and neural networks together with modern modeling and simulation techniques are creating the foundation for enhanced virtual reality environments, which allow reducing the risk of failure in new product development. On the other side the expanded use of new information technologies and methods, such as semantic web, data mining, text mining and theory of chaos have augmented the capability of predicting the future in many fields. Especially the use of these tools for weather predicting techniques has been the basis for reducing the likelihood of false predictions.

This paper starts from the state of the art of Computer Aided Innovation tools and methods for projecting the next steps of these emerging techniques. The latest trends are presented and analyzed and conclusions are derived regarding the future of these emergent tools. Following directions are being researched:

- CAI and Market: the role of computer aided innovation tools.
- CAI and New Product Development:
  - o Supporting the innovation activity with computer tools and methods.
  - o Supporting the Engineer's Desktop focusing on end-to-end product creation process with methods and tools to ensure the feasibility and success of innovations in all stages of the new product development process
- CAI and innovation methodologies
- CAI and patents analysis
- CAI and prototype testing
- Organizational, technological and cognitive aspects of the application of CAI methods and tools
- Evaluation of the effectiveness and efficiency of CAI methods and tools
- Theoretical foundations of CAI

# IFIP WORLD COMPUTER CONGRESS 2008

# COMPUTER-AIDED INNOVATION: THEORY AND PRACTICE

**Podium Presentations**

# Optimization with Genetic Algorithms and Splines as a way for Computer Aided Innovation

## Follow up of an example with crankshafts

**Albert Albers[1], Noel Leon Rovira[2], Humberto Aguayo[3], and Thomas Maier[4]**

[1] Director of IPEK, Institute of Product Development, Universität Karlsruhe (TH), Germany, Email: albers@ipek.uni-karlsruhe.de

[2] Professor CIDT, Director Research Program Creativity and Innovation in Engineering, ITESM, Campus Monterrey, Chairperson WG5.4 Computer Aided Innovation IFIP. Mexico, Email: noel.leon@itesm.mx Phone: +52 81 81582012.

[3] Center for Innovation in Design & Technology (CIDT), ITESM, Mexico, Email: haguayo@itesm.mx

[4] IPEK, Institute of Product Development, Universität Karlsruhe (TH), Germany, Email: maier@ipek.uni-karlsruhe.de

**Abstract:** This paper describes the conceptual foundations to construct a method on Computer Aided Innovation for product development. It begins with a brief re-cap of the different methodologies and disciplines that build its bases. Evolution-ary Design is presented and explained how the first activities in Genetic Algo-rithms (GAs) helped to produce computer shapes that resembled a creative behavior. A description of optimization processes based on Genetic Algorithms is presented, and some of the genetic operators are explained as a background of the creative operators that are intended to be developed. A summary of some Design Optimization Systems is also explained and its use of splined profiles to optimize mechanical structures. The approach to multi-objective optimization with Genetic Algorithms is analyzed from the point of view of Pareto diagrams. It is discussed how the transition from a multi-objective optimization conflict to a solution with the aim of an ideal result can be developed means the help of TRIZ (Theory of In-ventive Problem Solving), complementing the discipline of Evolutionary Design. Similarities between Genetic Algorithms and TRIZ regarding ideality and evolu-tion are identified and presented. Finally, a brief presentation of a case study about the design of engine crankshafts is used to explain the concepts and methods de-ployed. The authors have been working on strategies to optimize the balance of a crankshaft using CAD and CAE software, splines, Genetic Algorithms, and tools for its integration [1] [2].

**Keywords:** Genetic Algorithms, Splines, imbalance, TRIZ

*Please use the following format when citing this chapter:*

Albers, A., Leon Rovira, N., Aguayo, H. and Maier, T., 2008, in IFIP International Federation for Information Processing, Volume 277; *Computer-Aided Innovation (CAI)*; Gaetano Cascini; (Boston: Springer); pp. 7–18.

# 1. Introduction

Computer Aided Innovation builds its bases on software tools used for a large number of applications: from modeling activities and optimization tasks, to performance's simulation of a product. But the addition of new tools is intended to extend the support to the creative part of the design process. This support allows the designer to improve the performance of their concepts, allowing computers to take part on the generation of variants, and on the judgment, by simulation, of these variants. Genetic Algorithms, CAD/CAE, Splines and TRIZ are all software tools that can nurture the knowledge of designers to generate new solutions, based on many separate ideas, suggesting entirely new design concepts. Methods for structural and topological optimization, based on evolutionary design, are used to obtain optimal geometric solutions. They are evolving to configurations that minimize the cost of trial and error and perform far beyond the abilities of the most skilled designer. Next is presented a brief description of the methods and tools that lead to our strategy of Computer Aided Innovation.

## 1.1. Evolutionary Design

A relatively new area of development called Evolutionary Design [3] is being object of intensive research. Peter Bentley describes that Evolutionary Design has its roots in computer science, design and evolutionary biology. It is a branch of evolutionary computation that extends and combines CAD and analysis software, and borrows ideas from natural evolution. Evolutionary Computation to optimize existing designs (i.e. perform detailed design or parametric design) was the first type of evolutionary design to be tackled. A huge variety of different engineering designs have been successfully optimized, using these methods. Although the exact approach used by developers of such systems varies, typically practitioners of evolutionary optimization usually begin the process with an existing design, and parametrize those parts of the design they feel need improvement. Different brands of Evolutionary Design derive: Evolutionary Optimization, Creative Evolutionary Design and Conceptual Evolutionary Design. Evolutionary Optimization places great emphasis upon finding a solution as close to the global optimal as possible perhaps more than any other type of evolutionary design. Creative Evolutionary Design is concerned with the preliminary stages of the design process. But generating creative designs could only be possible by going beyond the bounds of a representation, and by finding a novel solution which simply could not have been defined by that representation. In Conceptual Evolutionary Design, the relationships and arrangements of high-level design concepts are evolved in an attempt to generate novel preliminary designs. Generative (or conceptual) Evolutionary Designs using computers to generate the form of designs rather than a collection of predefined high-level concepts has the advantage of giving greater freedom to the computer. Typically such systems are free to evolve any form capable of being represented, and the evolution of such forms may well result in the emergence of implicit design concepts. Genetic Algorithms, an evolutionary computational tool, is selected to be integrated as part of our strategy.

## 1.2. Genetic Algorithms

Genetic Algorithms are global optimization techniques that avoid many of the shortcomings exhibited by local search techniques on difficult search spaces [4]. A GA is an iterative procedure which maintains a constant-size population $P(t)$ of candidate solutions. During each iteration step, called a generation, the structures in the current population are evaluated, and, on the basis of those evaluations, a new population of candidate solutions is formed. The initial population $P(O)$ can be chosen heuristically or at random. The structures of the population $P(t + 1)$ are chosen from $P(t)$ by a randomized selection procedure that ensures that the expected number of times a structure is chosen is approximately proportional to that structure's performance relative to the rest of the population. In order to search other points in the search space, some variation is introduced into the new population by means of idealized genetic recombination operators. The most important recombination operator is called crossover. Under the crossover operator, two structures in the new population exchange portions of their internal representation. The power of GA's derives largely from their ability to exploit efficiently this vast amount of accumulating knowledge by means of relatively simple selection mechanisms. Termination of the GA may be triggered by finding an acceptable approximate solution, by fixing the total number of structure evaluations, or some other application dependent criterion. In addition, a number of experimental studies show that GA's exhibit impressive efficiency in practice. While classical gradient search techniques are more efficient for problems which satisfy tight constraints, GA's consistently outperform both gradient techniques and various forms of random search on more difficult (and more common) problems, such as optimizations involving discontinuous, noisy, high-dimensional, and multimodal objective functions.

The class of GA's is distinguished from other optimization techniques by the use of concepts from population genetics to guide the search. However, like other classes of algorithms, GA's differ from one another with respect to several parameters and strategies:

1) Population Size (N): The population size affects both the ultimate performance and the efficiency of GA's. GA's generally do poorly with very small populations, because the population provides an insufficient sample size for most representations.

2) Crossover Rate (C): The crossover rate controls the frequency with which the crossover operator is applied. In each new population, $C * N$ structures un-

dergo crossover. The higher the crossover rate, the more quickly new structures are introduced into the population.

3) Mutation Rate (M): Mutation is a secondary search operator which increases the variability of the population. After selection, each bit position of each structure in the new population undergoes a random change with a probability equal to the mutation rate M.

4) Generation Gap (G): The generation gap controls the percentage of the population to be replaced during each generation. That is N * (G) structures of P(t) are chosen (at random) to survive intact in P(t + 1).

5) Scaling Window (W): When maximizing a numerical function f(x) with a GA, it is common to define the performance value u(x) of a structure x as u(x) = f(x) - fmin, where fmin is the minimum value that f(x) can assume in the given search space.

6) Selection Strategy (S): A good strategy assures that the structure with the best performance always survives intact into the next generation. In the absence of such a strategy, it is possible for the best structure to disappear, due to sampling error, crossover, or mutation. The optimization systems of our interest are described in the next section.


## 1.3. Design Optimization Systems

The evolution of Product Development tools has been characterized by different trends; the analysis of these trends offers useful hints for the prediction of next generation systems. In mechanical design, optimization tasks are used for structural optimization, which deals with the development of mechanical structures. For example, when minimizing the weight of the wing of an airplane or optimizing the shape of a crankshaft, restrictions have to be included to guarantee the stability of the structure (ex. stresses or natural frequencies). The objectives of structural optimization are: minimizing stress or weight; maximizing lifespan, stiffness or first natural frequency. Any of those under different constrains as: maximum deflection, maximum stress, target weight (volume), target stiffness (displacement) and durability. The choice of design variables ranges from geometrical parameters, control points of spline functions, position of nodes, shell thickness, beam cross-section, angle of fibers from compound materials, etc. As design variable restrictions we have: upper and lower limit of the design variables (fixations, limitations), discrete and continuous. Also symmetrical conditions and constraints for manufacturing conditions (drilling, casting or forging) are possible. Particularly, two kinds of structural optimization are frequently used: Topology Optimization and Shape Optimization.

Topology Optimization consists on determining an optimal material distribution of a mechanical product. A basic FE model is created and analyzed in a design area with given boundary conditions. The aims are commonly to maximize stiffness or maximize the natural frequency of a product. The constraints of the design are: the fixations, material volume and maximum displacement allowed. The design variables are the material density of the elements, which are counted commonly in hundreds of thousands; this means a huge amount of design variables. The goal is, given a predefined design domain in the 2D/3D space with structural boundary conditions and load definitions, to distribute a given mass, which is a given percentage of the initial mass in the domain such that a global measure takes a minimum (maximum) value.

Shape Optimization consists of changing the external borders of a mechanical component. The aims are: minimizing the stress or the volume or maximizing the natural frequency. Constrains to the design are: fixations, restrictions for displacement of component borders. The design variables of the product are, for geometric models: length, angle and radii measurements; for FE model: node coordinates.

Each optimization method uses a strategy to obtain the optimum of the objective function. The choice of the optimization method and the strategy depends mainly on the properties and number of the variables, the objective functions and constrains and how these are used in the optimization. Specific criteria for optimization problems are: the number of variables (often a huge number of them); characteristics of the objective function (continuous, discontinuous, linear/quadratic/arbitrary, etc.); characteristics of restrictions (none, several, etc). Moreover, the external conditions for choosing an optimization method rely on the required accuracy (improvement or exact optimum); efficiency of the algorithm; computing time and memory space; user friendliness and complexity of the problem formulation.

In order to further develop the optimization systems it is required to add new concepts into the previous paradigms. A new kind of parameterization is inferred by taking the characteristics of last optimization methods. In order to obtain a similar behavior within a CAD model, the geometry of the product is described in terms of Splines. The "splining" approach extends these features, allowing the introduction of innovative concepts.

## *1.4. Design optimization of splines shapes*

A great variety of different engineering designs have been successfully optimized using Evolutionary Design, i.e. antennas and aircraft geometries. Although the methods used by developers of such systems varies, one of these types of evolutionary design that has potential to be classified as generative or creative is the splined shape approach [5]. The splining of the shapes and its control points, codified to be interpreted by Genetic Algorithms, are the basis for an evolutionary designed shape. Practitioners of evolutionary optimization using splines usually start the process with an existing design, and then parameterize the control points of the splines that embody those parts of the design they feel need improvement. Moreover, the concept can be extended to reach the whole structure of the product and even the functional structure. The control points are encoded as genes, the alleles (values) from which parameters are described, are evolved by an evolutionary search algorithm, i.e. Genetic Algorithms. Three main genetic operators act on the "genes" of the geometry, as known: selection, crossover and mutation. Crossover allows the geometrical characteristics of selected splines (compared from a fitness function) be merged in pairs and extend its properties to next generations. The designs are often judged by making an interface of the system to simulation or analysis software, which is used to obtain a fitness measure for each design.

## 2. Evolutionary Design transition to Computer Aided Innovation

In the previous section a brief explanation of the methods and tools that conducted our research work to the development of our framework on Computer Aided Innovation was presented. Starting from the Evolutionary Design approach, and particularly on Genetic Algorithms, the concept of splining applied to the structural optimization of products was explained. The last element to be considered is the analysis of conflicts during optimization that prevent a design to reach the Ideal Solution

### 2.1. Multi-objective Optimization and conflicts in product development

Genetic Algorithms, are well suited to searching intractably large, poorly understood problem spaces, but have mostly been used to optimize a single objective. They all describe a scalar value to be maximized or minimized. But a careful look at many, if not most, of the real-world GA applications reveals that the objective functions are really multi-attribute. Many optimization problems have multiple objectives. Historically, multiple objectives have been combined ad hoc to form a scalar objective function, usually through a linear combination (weighted sum) of the multiple attributes, or by turning objectives into constraints. Typically, the GA user finds some ad-hoc function of the multiple attributes to yield a scalar fitness function. Often-seen tools for combining multiple attributes are constraints, with associated thresholds and penalty functions, and weights for linear combinations of attribute values. A few studies have tried a different approach to multi-criteria optimization with GAS: using the GAs to find all possible trade-offs among the multiple, conflicting objectives. Some authors propose to perform a set of mono-objective optimization tasks to reveal conflicts [6]. These solutions (trade-offs) are non-dominated, in that there are no other solutions superior in all attributes. In attribute space, the set of non-dominated solutions lie on a surface known as the Pareto optimal frontier. The goal of a Pareto is to find and maintain a representative sampling of solutions on the Pareto front. Hence, the term "optimize" is referred to find a solution, which would give the values of all the objective functions an "acceptable trade off" to the designer [7]. Moreover, computer geneticists have faced the concept of the ideal [8]. They named it the ideal point. The Pareto diagram (used mainly in multi-objective optimization processes) shows a boundary that divides the region of feasible solutions from the point where the ideal solution lies. When there is a set of optimal solutions lying on a line that prevent the functions to reach the "ideal" at the same time, because of constraints in the solution space, it becomes an unrealistic goal to reach the ideal point.

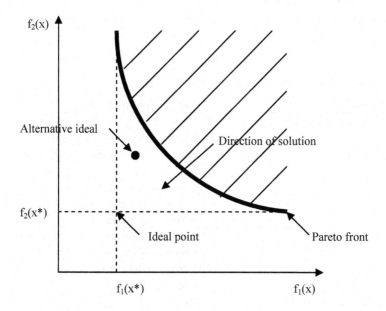

Figure 1. Pareto diagram and the concept of ideal

According to traditional TRIZ theory, the reach of an Ideal Final Result is encouraged and TRIZ presents tools for identifying technical and physical contradictions underlying in a technological system. TRIZ general solutions (i.e. inventive/ separation principles, Standard Solutions, etc.) are proposed to overcome the conflict and let the product evolve, according to the "laws of technical evolution" [9]. It is a natural convergence direction to merge Evolutionary Design (based on laws of biological evolution) with TRIZ (based on laws of technical evolution) inside a computer framework aimed to Computer Aided Innovation.

GAs can extend its paradigm of multi-objective optimization by taking advantage of the inventive principles, letting the operators be not only the basic "mutation" and "crossover" but new operators or "agents" capable to modify the way the algorithms perform on the CAD geometry [10]. In this way, CAD systems could develop new configurations and alternative modifications to the geometry, in order to reach the ideal point or the "Ideal Final Result". The solution can reach a level of detail that derives in the possibility that the designer be inspired by these suggestions, selects the most suitable solution and implements it. In other words the designer could be presented a set of alternative modifications, defined automatically on the base of the selected principles that may be applied based on the concept of "Cataclysm Mutations" [11]. Cataclysmic mutations with similar pattern are now being studied in Evolutionary Algorithms as tools for finding innovations [12][13]. From the TRIZ inventive principles, those that have a geometric interpretation can be added to form the extended cataclysmic operators. See table 1.

Table 1. Genetic interpretation of TRIZ inventive principles

| TRIZ principles | Genetic Interpretation |
|---|---|
| Segmentation, combination | Divide two genotypes and combine alternate parts (Crossover, simple) |
| Asymmetry | Break symmetrical genotypes (Crossover, simple) |
| Merging | Join genotypes (Crossover, simple) |
| Nesting | Place part of a genotype inside another (Crossover, nesting) |
| Another dimension | Create genotypes from different parameters (Crossover, nesting) |
| Homogeneity | Turn a genotype homogeneous (Crossover, nesting) |
| Discarding and recovering | Break and rebuild genotypes (Crossover, nesting) |
| Inversion | Turn around a genotype (Inversion, genetic) |
| Extraction | Extract a gen in a genotype (Mutation) |
| Feedback | Return fittest genotypes (Selection) |
| Copying | Take a copy of fittest genotypes (Selection) |

The level of impact from the different operators can vary from a slow and steady accumulation of changes (the way an optimization algorithm normally performs), to a sudden disturbance in the nature of the system (or cataclysm). The most important effect is creating a jump in the phase transition. More suggestions can be enriched by means of guidelines, provided by the inventive principles that can be associated to the genetic operators. As result, the algorithm should be capable of applying the agents according to the conflict that is being faced.

## 2.2. Follow up of crankshaft example

In an attempt to exemplify the concepts deployed, the development of an engine crankshaft is conducted by making automatic changes in the geometry of its counterweights. In order to make geometry modifications to our case study, the geometry of the counterweights was transformed from simple lines and arcs to spline curves. Splines allow smooth shape changes via the coordinates of its control points. That smooth shapes benefit the material fluency during the manufacturing process. The variation of these control points results in a balance response of the crankshaft. The x and y coordinates of the control points can be parametrically manipulated by the Genetic Algorithm. Figure 2 shows how the splines substitute the original profile of the crankshaft. It is possible to see how close the spline is to the original profile.

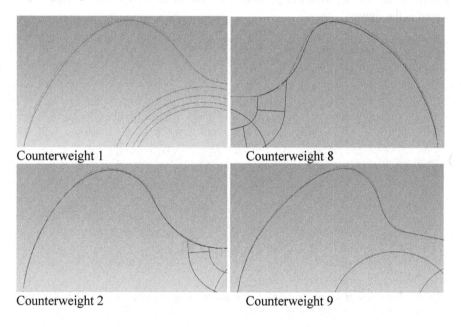

Counterweight 1                     Counterweight 8

Counterweight 2                     Counterweight 9

Figure 2. Splinization approach applied to a Crankshaft; the original profile consists of arc and line segments.

The selected Genetic Algorithms that were applied are from the DAKOTA toolkit from Sandia Laboratories. It was developed an interface programmed in Java language to link the GAs to the CAD geometry. The optimization loop runs fully automated so the computer generates shapes in every generation. Some of the genetic operators are described next.

It was used an initial population size of 50 individuals, because the number of genes were 32 (8 in each of the 4 counterweights) and it allows a good representation of the chromosomes in every generation. A crossover rate of 0.8 was selected, that was a number of 40 individuals out of 50 to be crossed over and have a wide amount of new shapes. A mutation rate of 0.1 allowed exploring the solution space for local optima not possible to find by conventional methods.

The results from the first attempts show that the imbalances from both sides of the crankshaft are in conflict each other. These conflicts are then aimed to be resolved by "innovation agents". Further development of the algorithms can only be achieved by its integration with Innovation methods. The resulting systems are of a parametric shape and topology innovative configuration. Some features need to be added to the system in order to work in an "out of the paradigm" way, leading to solutions that were not considered before. In order to have a visual impression about the way the algorithm is performing, some of the counterweights are presented in the figure.

Figure 3. Representations of the crankshaft's counterweights (external ones, 1 and 9, are transparent to let visualize the others, 2 and 8)

The shapes are presenting some notches that are not suitable for forging, but the direction of solution is cataclysmic. An open minded designer should be able to recognize that the paradigm is challenged and a new concept can be derived. This is the intention of these systems, as mentioned at the beginning of the paper, presenting to the designer challenging alternatives. Finally, these proposals are solution triggers that inspire him, but they are not substituting its role in selecting the most suitable solutions and implement them properly.

## 3. Conclusions

This paper started with a brief recap of the different methodologies and disciplines that build the bases for developing a conceptual framework on Computer Aided Innovation. The area of Evolutionary Design is presented and explained how the first activities in Genetic Algorithms helped to produce the first computer shapes that resembled a creative behavior. Some of the genetic operators are explained as a background of the creative operators that are intended to be developed. A summary of some Design Optimization Systems is explained as also its use of spline profiles to optimize mechanical structures. The transition from a multi-objective optimization conflict to a solution with the aim of an ideal result is developed means the help of TRIZ. The innovative operators are analyzed to find relation with the genetic operators and turn into a "cataclysmic similar" set of new principles. Finally, an example of the development of an engine crankshaft is shown, with some preliminary results that may help to embody the complete framework of Computer Aided Innovation. Activities to be continued in the future are the definition of additional fitness functions not only in CAD but in CAE simulation (forging simulation), in order to control "strange" shapes. Also, objective functions and restrictions are going to be added by the use of forging simulation and stress analysis during geometry variations, resulting on what is pretended to be an integration of different systems running totally or partially automatic.

As a final reflection, it can be said that creativity and innovation can be structured to an objective methodology, and taken away from the individual's subconscience. Inventive principles suggest a series of recommendations to change the direction in which solutions are searched. These recommendations can be regarded as a knowledge database, which can be used to feed the cataclysmic similar transformation of genotypes during an evolution for optimization, allowing it to trespass the barriers of contradictions or constraints.

Experience and judgment can make a good design. When evaluating a fitness function, the genetic algorithms rely only in the last of these two characteristics (judgment) based on evaluation and comparison against certain criteria. The first one (experience) can be added from the substantial knowledge of designers into the genetic algorithms by means of the incorporation of inventive principles as cataclysm genetic operators.

## 4. Acknowledgments

The authors acknowledge the support received from Tecnológico de Monterrey through Grant No. CAT043 to carry out the research reported in this paper.

# References

1. Aguayo-Téllez H. et al.: Comparison of Strategies for the Optimization/Innovation of Crankshaft Balance. In Trends in Computer Aided Innovation, pp. 201-210, Springer, USA (2007).

2. Aguayo-Téllez H. and Leon-Rovira N.: Computer Aided Innovation of Crankshafts Using Genetic Algorithms, in Knowledge Enterprise: Intelligent Strategies in Product Design, Manufacturing, and Management, pp. 471-476, USA: Springer Boston, (2006); http://dx.doi.org/10.1007/0-387-34403-9_64.

3. Bentley P.: Evolutionary Design by Computers, Morgan Kaufmann, (1999).

4. Goldberg D.E.: Genetic Algorithms in Search, Optimization and Machine Learning, Addison-Wesley Longman Publishing Co. USA Inc. (1989).

5. Leon-Rovira et al.: Automatic shape variations for optimization and innovation, in Trends in Computer Aided Innovation, pp. 179-188, USA, (2007); http://dx.doi.org/10.1007/978-0-387-75456-7_18.

6. Cugini, Cascini, Ugolotti: Enhancing interoperability in the design process, the PROSIT approach, in Trends in Computer Aided Innovation. USA, (2007); http://dx.doi.org/10.1007/978-0-387-75456-7_19.

7. Coello C.A.: An empirical study of evolutionary techniques for multi-objective optimization in engineering design, USA, Tulane University, (1996).

8. Coello C.A.: An updated survey of GA-based multi-objective optimization techniques. ACM Computing Surveys, vol. 32, pp. 109-143 (2000).

9. Altshuller G., Shulyak L.: 40 Principles: Triz Keys to Innovation. Technical Innovation Center, USA, Inc (1997).

10. Leon-Rovira N. et al.: Optimization vs. Innovation in a CAE environment, in IFIP world computer congress 2004, France: (2004).

11. Zhang Y., Liao M., and Ren Z.: Cataclysmic Genetic Algorithm for Reactive Power Dispatch Comparing with an Interior-Point Algorithm, M.H. Hamza, USA, (2005); http://www.actapress.com/Abstract.aspx?paperId=22063.

12. Dubrovsky O., Levitin G., Penn M.: A Genetic Algorithm with a Compact Solution Encoding for the Container Ship Stowage Problem, Journal of Heuristics, vol. 8, pp. 585-599, (2002).

13. Levitin G., Rubinovitz J., and Shnits B.: A genetic algorithm for robotic assembly line balancing, European Journal of Operational Research, vol. 168, pp. 811-825, (2006).

# Methodology development of human task simulation as PLM solution related to OCRA ergonomic analysis

M. Annarumma[1], M. Pappalardo[2], and A. Naddeo[3]

[1] University of Salerno, Fisciano (SA), Italy, maannarumma@unisa.it
[2] University of Salerno, Fisciano (SA), Italy, mpappalardo@unisa.it
[3] University of Salerno, Fisciano (SA), Italy, anaddeo@unisa.it

**Abstract:** In the current demanding global marketplace, ensuring that human fit, form and function are comprehensively addressed, is becoming an increasingly important aspect of design and, in particular, obliges the most important automotive industries to develop more flexible assembly lines and better methods for PLM solution. In the meantime, designers attempt to elaborate product development methodologies that conform health and safety standards while still maximizing the productivity. The aim of this work consists in developing a methodology based on preventive ergonomics and feasibility analyses of assembly tasks, simulating a work cell, in which acts a digital human model (manikin), in order to maximize human safety and performance and analyze manikin interaction in the virtual environment. In ergonomic analyses the OCRA protocol will be used, evaluating different involvement degrees of upper limb segments. The methodology is carried out by ergonomic tool of DELMIA software, using Digital Human Models technology.

**Keywords:** PLM solution, ergonomic analysis, OCRA protocol, Digital Human Models

## 1. Introduction

The actual manufacturing processes are designed in order to produce a given good but, often, have a limited flexibility, in particular from the point of view of ability to meet meaningful variations of productivity in rapid way and result being equal. The products increasing proliferation and the need to fit in real time the manufacturing on variations of volumes required by the market (without resorting to hard-working actions for rearrangements of men, means and materials, with heavy impact on costs, process stability, quality) represents a competitiveness decisive factor.

*Please use the following format when citing this chapter:*

Annarumma, M., Pappalardo, M. and Naddeo, A., 2008, in IFIP International Federation for Information Processing, Volume 277; *Computer-Aided Innovation (CAI)*; Gaetano Cascini; (Boston: Springer), pp. 19–29.

In fact, each product variation can imply changes that become: different and more flexible working place organizations, different assembly procedures, different methods and tools to be used in operations and even different tasks subdivisions among the workers in the working places.

The manufacturing process planning is fundamental [1], since it allows to define and to verify product assembly sequences [2], to create the assembly line layout, to assign the time needed for each operation, to verify lines performances also in terms of productivity and use of the resources, to carry out the lines balancing and to analyze production costs.

In order to assist the manufacturing process planning, studies and software tools was developed, allowing the whole manufacturing process simulation with Virtual Manufacturing techniques [3] (DELMIA, VIS FACTORY, UGS, etc).

Subsequently, verifying new types of accidents or work diseases, it realizes the importance of the working place ergonomics [4], [5] considered as "respect of the ergonomic principles in the working place conception, in the tools choice and in the definition of work and production methods, also in order to attenuate the monotonous and repetitive work".

For this reason, there was the need to introduce in virtual environments biomechanical digital models able to simulate the man from a cinematic and dynamic point of view [6].

Since the '70 years many studies were addressed to the biomechanical models development. The first notable results were gotten by Chow and Jacobson (1971), which developed a theory for the human movements optimal control; Seireg and Arvikar (1975), whose results were taken by Rohrle (1984), studied the optimal distribution problem of the muscular strength in the hip, knee and ankle articulations during the walking; Marshall (1986) developed optimization criterions for the mass centre trajectory computation; Bean, Chaffin and Schultz (1988) proposed a linear programming method for the muscular strengths computation in a muscular-skeletal system.

In the last years DHM (Digital Human Modelling) software has been developed, provided with digital biomechanical models, for instance Jack (UGS), Ramsis (TechMat) and Delmia (Dassault Systemes) [7], which allow to simulate human movements by specific tools.

By these softwares it is possible to create specific virtual environments with CAD data available, in which to insert the manikins; in such way the operator can be simulated during the productive task carrying out in his working place. This approach allows effecting all the necessary analyses before the productive line realization, reducing both design variation costs and execution times.

## 2. Description of the approach to development methodology

The approach followed for developing this methodology is based on the Virtual Manufacturing technologies. These tools allow to reach totally virtual factory, constituted by virtual models of men, tools and materials, that can be analyzed their continuous interactions. The virtual tools seem the ideal environment to solve the problems related to manufacturing high variability/flexibility, since they allow, if opportunely developed, to study changes needed for the line organization, in order to reach optimal operating solutions.

The developments needed to reach the target concern, in particular, the "integrated" methodologies availability for the virtual simulation and the Working Place "Ability" optimization, considering the whole of factors that affect the whole working place performances: man, means of work, material handling, safety and ergonomics.

In order to achieve this goal a preliminary work of a virtual work-cell reproduction was carried-out. This means to collect product and process CAD models by the Product Data Management (PDM) and to arrange them according to the real lay-out and situation which will be effectively reproduced into the plant. Tools and methods typically used in computer graphics applications must be applied on the CAD models in order to have a realistic simulation.

Subsequently, several factors that characterize product process performances was integrated, both in terms of productivity, machineries and manpower output, both in terms of ergonomic analyses on human factors as: postures, movements, cinematic potentiality of the human body, efforts feasibility, tools accessibility, breaks management within the work shift and additional factors that take into account working environment characteristics.

The whole of these factors, opportunely weighed according to examined context characteristics, can be used as assessment and designing procedure of working configurations.

Using Virtual Engineering, the need to evaluate human factors (HF) in real life, forces the introduction of virtual manikins in virtual environments already carried out for product and process prototypes, and that has developed the "Digital Human Modelling" (DHM) [8-9-10]. These human models are digital biomechanical models, able to simulate the man from a cinematic and dynamic point of view.

### 2.1 Aims of the work

The aim of this work consists in developing a design methodology founded on ergonomics and feasibility preventive analyses of work tasks, by simulating a work-cell, in which acts a digital human model.

Combining process and ergonomic analyses and analyzing the relationship between workers and other entities within the simulation, with the evaluation of manikin interaction in the virtual environment, thanks to Digital Human Models (DHM) technology, it possible to improve product development process and maximize human safety and performance in designing step.

OCRA (OCcupational Repetitive Actions) protocol was used in ergonomic analyses; OCRA's index consider time and posture factors, in order to evaluate different involvement degrees of human upper limbs.

The OCRA index is the ratio between the Actual number of Technical Actions carried out during the work shift (ATA) and the Reference number of Technical Actions (RTA) (for each upper limb) which is specifically determined in the examined scenario.

Subsequently, an analysis of **postures** (the type of quantitative and qualitative joint involvement, the static or dynamic component of movement) will make it possible to obtain a general estimation of the degree of repetitiveness and of the duration of single joint movements within the sequence of technical actions.

Figure 1: OCRA ergonomic evaluation tool

| SHIFT DURATION | 480 | | | |
|---|---|---|---|---|
| Breaks (min) | 30 | | | |
| Non repetitive work time (min) | 15 | | | |
| Work time considered as recovery (min) | 0 | | | |
| | | | | |
| **Total repetitive work net time in the shift** | **435** | | | |
| | | | | |
| | A | B | C | D |
| | 100% | | | |
| Repetitive work net time for each task | 435 | 0 | 0 | 0 |
| No. of units per shift | 5220 | | | |
| No.hours without recovery period | 5 | | | |
| | | | | |
| Recovery multiplier (R$_{CH}$) | 0,45 | | | |
| | | | | |
| ACTION FREQUENCY CONSTANT | 30 | | | |

Figure 2: OCRA ergonomic evaluation tool zoom top

| LEFT | A | B | C | D |
|---|---|---|---|---|
| Force multiplier (Fo$_H$) | 0,92 | | | |
| Posture multiplier (Po$_H$) | 0,70 | | | |
| Additional multiplier (Ad$_H$) | 0,85 | | | |
| Repetitiveness multiplier (Re$_H$) | 0,70 | | | |
| Reference No. Of techical actions without R$_{CH}$ | 5011 | | | |
| **CYCLE TIME (sec.)** | **5.0** | **#DIV/0!** | **#DIV/0!** | **#DIV/0!** |
| TOT.NO.OF TECHNICAL ACTIONS OBSERVED in each ta: | 10440 | #DIV/0! | #DIV/0! | #DIV/0! |
| **frequency (No.of technical actions per mir** | **24** | **#DIV/0!** | **#DIV/0!** | **#DIV/0!** |
| No. of technical actions in the cycle | 2,0 | 0,0 | 0,0 | 0 |
| TOT.NO.OF ACTUAL TECHNICAL ACTIONS (ATA) | 10440 | | | |
| TOT.NO.OF. RECOMMENDED TECHNICAL ACTIONS (R | 2255 | | | |
| Duration multiplier (Du$_H$). | 1,0 | | | |
| **OCRA INDEX LEFT** | **4.6** | | | |

| Forecast of VMSDs | min | AVERAGE | max |
|---|---|---|---|
| | 10.0 | 11.1 | 12.1 |

Figure 3: OCRA ergonomic evaluation tool zoom right

| RIGHT | A | B | C | D |
|---|---|---|---|---|
| Force multiplier (Fo$_H$) | 0,94 | | | |
| Posture multiplier (Po$_H$) | 0,60 | | | |
| Additional multiplier (Ad$_H$) | 0,85 | | | |
| Repetitiveness multiplier (Re$_H$) | 0,70 | | | |
| Reference No. Of techical actions without Rc$_H$ | 4379 | | | |
| CYCLE TIME (sec.) | 5,0 | #DIV/0! | #DIV/0! | #DIV/0! |
| TOT.NO.OF TECHNICAL ACTIONS OBSERVED in each task | 10440 | #DIV/0! | #DIV/0! | #DIV/0! |
| frequency (No.of technical actions per minu | 24 | #DIV/0! | #DIV/0! | #DIV/0! |
| No. of technical actions in the cycle | 2,0 | 0,0 | 60,0 | 0 |
| TOT.NO.OF ACTUAL TECHNICAL ACTIONS (ATA) | 10440 | | | |
| TOT.NO.OF. RECOMMENDED TECHNICAL ACTIONS (RT/ | 1971 | | | |
| Duration multiplier (Du$_H$). | 1,0 | | | |
| OCRA INDEX RIGHT | 5.3 | | | |

| Forecast of VMSDs | min | AVERAGE | max |
|---|---|---|---|
| | 11,4 | 12,7 | 13,9 |

| da 0 a 2,2 | ACCEPTABLE |
|---|---|
| da 2,3 a 3,5 | VERY LOW |
| da 3,6 a 9 | PRESENT |
| oltre 9 | HIGH |

Figure 4: OCRA ergonomic evaluation tool zoom

For these reasons, the methodology was developed integrating design/ simulation tools, which exactly allows simulating and analyzing the work environment with digital human models that carry out manual assembly tasks. In this way, designers are assisted and guided in the context of a product/service, before it exists and throughout its entire lifecycle.

Therefore, an ergonomic evaluation tool, based on the OCRA protocol, as shown in figures 1,2,3,4 has been implemented and integrated inside the DHM software used for carrying out the simulation, recognizing several human postures and making ergonomic assessments founded on other standard protocols, by own specific tools.

The tool gives a final validation of the task. Input data which can be acquired during the simulation are:

- numerical manikin body information (angles and postures);

- task and single movement times.

The Computer Aided Innovation consists in using both posture recognition and all ergonomic evaluation tools within a Product-Process-Resources (PPR) data collaboration system, that's ensuring that human factors become an intuitive component in the manufacturing design process, so having several advantages:

- to improve simulation reliability: experts are supported, in real time, during the simulation because they can define the best movement for the worker, cutting down or changing incongruous postures;

- to improve the analysis performance: according to analyzed task, the expert can evaluate the most meaningful index between all the available ones;

- to ensure conformance to relevant health and safety standards;

- to reduce analysis time: critical postures are recognized at once, reducing subjective interpretations;

- to accelerate time to market;

- to reduces design timeframe and associated costs.

This complete integration with PPR data system allows companies to share their best practices and ensure everyone has access to the right information at the right time, optimizing workplaces and work cell design and increasing productivity.

## 2.2 Application on case study

In order to validate the methodology, the work present an application of the method to an interesting case study, by a simulation of an assembly task inside the car-body, that suggests new solutions, carrying out a more ergonomic and efficient task.

First of all, the virtual work cell has been built, therefore 3D models of the car and the assembly line have been collected and merged.

Then, a digital human model has been put into the virtual environment simulating the assembly task, in order to evaluate the situation using the classical approach.

The ergonomic study has been conducted on an operator employed in an operation frequently carried out during the dashboard assembly inside the car's cabin.

In figure 5 is shown an axonometric sight of the virtual work place with the digital human model.

The manikin's movements have been evaluated and the most critical postures, as shown in figure 6, during the simulation have been analyzed with ergonomics indexes, above all with OCRA index. According to this kind of analysis, a different approach to the work place improves the user's comfort thanks to a more comfortable arms movements.

In addition to analysis tools provided in Delmia software, a form for the OCRA index evaluation has been developed, integrated in the software and which can be recalled by the menu of Delmia tools, appearing to screen as a dialogue box, in which can be input data drawn by the simulation's observation, and allowing automatic assessment of the aforesaid ergonomic index.

It should be underlined that the OCRA index "critical values" and its association with the occurrence of Upper Limbs Work-related Musculo-Skeletal Disorders (UL-WMSDs), reported in figure 7, should be used as an help to better frame the risk assessment and more effectively guide any consequent preventative actions, rather than rigid numbers splitting results between "risk" or "no risk".

In our case (OCRA_dx = 0.9, OCRA_sx = 0.6), the dashboard assembly operation, under examination, represents a not very critical example from the ergonomic point of view: it doesn't require great strength, and upper limbs' postures are not at risk considerably. These factors, with a good organization of the work shift, allow to say that UL-WMSDs occupational diseases are not forecasted.

The innovation introduced by this tool, in comparison with the classical manual compilation of the form, consists in the followings advantages:

- the index evaluation is simplified by surveys of numerical data on manikin postures, avoiding uncertain situations and minimizing evaluation errors from the operator;

- automatic assignment of indicative values of risk situations, beginning from times of duration of critical postures.

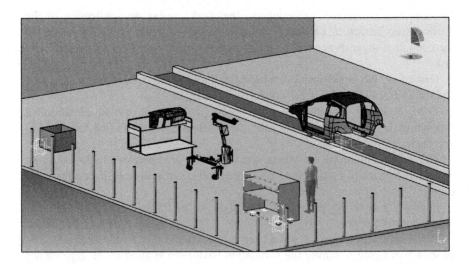

Figure 5: Assembly line

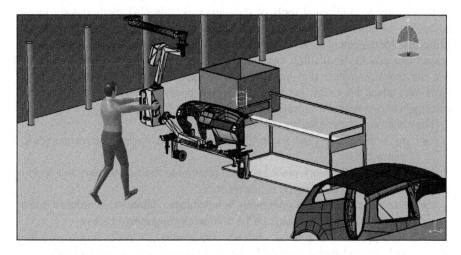

Figure 6: Critical posture

| AREA | OCRA INDEX VALUES | RISK LEVEL | CONSEQUENCES |
|---|---|---|---|
| GREEN | ≤ 2,2 | NO RISK (UL-WMSDs (PA) forecast is not significantly different from the one expected in the reference population). | Acceptable, no consequences. |
| YELLOW | 2,3 – 3,5 | VERY LOW RISK (UL-WMSDs (PA) forecast is higher than previous but lower than twice the one expected in the reference population). | Advisable to set up improvements with regard to structural risk factors (posture, force, technical actions, etc.) or to suggest other organizational measures. |
| RED | > 3,5 | RISK (UL-WMSDs (PA) forecast is higher than twice the one expected in the reference population. The higher the index, the higher the risk). | Redesign of tasks and workplaces according to priorities is recommended |

Figure 7: OCRA Method: Final assessment criteria

## 3. Conclusions

Manufacturing organizations today continue to design and develop machines, vehicles and products that are capable of performing better, faster and longer. An increasingly design consideration is to ensure that these technological innovations are being designed from the perspective of people who actually build, maintain and operate them. Therefore, manufacturers must consider these human factors early in the product life cycle.

The power of this methodology is notable and its application could occur in any step of the product/process development.

In addition to traditional tools of data analysis, this CAI methodology takes advantage of simulation tools of the product development process for Product Lifecycle Management (PLM) solutions and human factors evaluation tools, geared towards understanding and optimizing the relationship between humans and the products which they manufacture, install, operate and maintain. These tools take place as a link between the virtual product and the virtual factory, assuring a two-way communication between them.

The obtaining advantages are the following:

- to analyze the task feasibility in relation to operator anthropometric characteristics;
- to analyze the work place layout in relation to the task to carry out and to operator anthropometric characteristics;
- to store sequences of operations in a dedicated database, in order to make analyses in different steps of the product development process;
- to support the ergonomic indexes computation, in order to evaluate the risk due to Loads Manual Moving and Manual Assembly operations or to not comfortable postures;
- to carry out training phase on the ground of the optimised methods by the use of movies simulated and by the workers involvements in simulated tasks.

Using these analyses and evaluations it is possible to obtain indications for modifying the design in process development step.

Therefore this method allows a significant saving in terms of time and costs in design process, providing the enterprise with an important competitive lever.

# References

1. Laring J., Christmansson M., Dukic T. et al.: Simulation for Manufacturing Engineering (ViPP), Digital Human Modelling for Design and Engineering Symposium, Iowa City (Iowa), 14-16 June (2005).
2. Miller D. M., Park Y.: Simulation and Analysis of an Automotive Assembly Operation, Southern Automotive Manfacturing Conference & Exposition, Nashville (Tennessee), 11-13 August (1998).
3. DELMIA WORLD NEWS, Managing Change Across Virtual Design and Manufacturing, Delmia World News, n. 14 (2007).
4. Di Pardo M., Riccio A., Sessa F.: Intelligent Design of Ergonomic Workplace, CRF, ELASIS, Proceedings of IPMM, in The 6th International Conference on Intelligent Processing and Manufacturing of Materials, Salerno, 25-29 June (2007).
5. Temple R., Adams T.: Ergonomic Analysis of a Multi-Task Industrial Lifting Station Using the NIOSH Method. Journal of Industrial Technology, vol. 16(2), (2000).
6. Gu E. Y., Oriet L. P.: Proactive Ergonomic Verification Through Human Biodynamic Modeling and Digital Simulation, Southern Automotive Manufacturing Conference and Exposition Birmingham, Alabama, 28-30 September (1999).
7. http://www.delmia.com.

8. Albers K. M., Abshire K. J.: Virtual Human Modeling for Manufacturing and Maintenance, in Digital Human Modeling for Design and Engineering Conference and Exposition, Dayton (Ohio), 28-29 April (1998).
9. Geyer M., Rösch B.: Human Modeling and e-Manufacturing, Digital Human Modeling for Design and Engineering Conference and Exposition, Arlington, Virginia, 26-28 June, (also SAE Paper n. 2001-01-2119) (2001).
10. Stephens A., Godin C.: The Truck that Jack Built: Digital Human Models and Their Role in the Design of Work Cells and Product Design, in Digital Human Modelling for Design and Engineering Conference, Lyon (France), 4-6 July (2006).

# Measuring patent similarity by comparing inventions functional trees

**Gaetano Cascini**[1] **and Manuel Zini**[2]

[1] University of Florence, Italy, gaetano.cascini@unifi.it
[2] drWolf srl, Italy, mlzini@drwolf.it

**Abstract:** The estimation of the conceptual distance between patents is a critical issue for Computer-Aided patent portfolio analysis systems, an emerging class of computer tools for supporting R&D analyses and decisions, patent infringement risk evaluation, technology forecasting. The aim of the present work is the introduction of an original algorithm for patent comparison: since typical text analyses are biased by the writer's style, the inventions similarity is here estimated by comparing the components and their hierarchical and functional interactions automatically extracted by means of a custom software tool. The whole procedure is clarified with an exemplary application in the field of electric current circuit breakers.

**Keywords:** Patent mining, document similarity, plagiarism

## 1. Introduction

Computer-aided patent portfolio analysis is an emerging topic in the scientific community and attracts interests from several disciplines, since it deals with economical, technical, management, life science issues [1-4].

Indeed, computers have been used for patent searches and analyses since the '90s, but most of the applications were limited to statistical computations by means of bibliometric methods. Indeed, these techniques are still adopted as a relevant source of information [5]. This is mainly due to a heritage of traditional practices when statistical techniques were adopted to examine the effect of technology development in economic, national and international contexts or to plan a corporate technology activity at a corporate level [2].

The introduction of text-mining algorithms has created new opportunities for identifying complex relationship among patent documents. Besides, up to now, the researchers in this field have dedicated major attention to Information Extraction purposes in order to capture relevant information from patents, while still limited

*Please use the following format when citing this chapter:*

Cascini, G. and Zini, M., 2008, in IFIP International Federation for Information Processing, Volume 277; *Computer-Aided Innovation (CAI)*; Gaetano Cascini; (Boston: Springer), pp. 31–42.

studies exist about patent comparison and trend extraction, except applications of general purpose clustering algorithms [6].

Nowadays, computer-based systems for patent analysis are assuming more and more specialistic roles and will cover soon a wider range of application areas like:

- generation of new research directions for biomedical studies [1];
- comparison of the morphology portfolio of different technologies [2];
- evaluation of the R&D landscape and business opportunities [3];
- evaluation of the risk of patent infringement [4].

All the above mentioned activities require the estimation of the conceptual distance between patents, but all the approaches proposed so far are based on keywords comparisons (e.g. co-occurrences of terms and/or multi-words), while the nature of patent contents is poorly taken into account. An even more critical issue is the dependence of these techniques to the language style of the writer; as a result, very often it happens that patents of the same inventor or company are clustered together despite their different contents, while conceptually close inventions are considered distant from each other just because they adopt a different terminology.

In the present paper the authors, also thanks to previous experiences in the field of plagiarism detection, propose a novel technique for assessing patent similarity as a means for avoiding the impact of the language style on patent comparison.

In the next chapter we report a brief survey of plagiarism detection techniques; then the third section describes the proposed algorithm also resuming some previous works relevant for the present application. Then an exemplary application of the proposed similarity metric is shown, by comparing the results of the automatic analyses performed by means of a prototype software to the results obtained by humans in the field of electrical circuit interruption devices. Finally, in chapter five, the discussion is focused on the capabilities and the sore points of the proposed technique.

## 2. State of the art techniques for plagiarism detection

Plagiarism is a growing problem and has recently received a lot of attention. The increase in availability of material in digital form has made plagiarism much easier.

However, the use of digital media also means that there are greater opportunities to trace plagiarism by means of dedicated software tools. Automated plagiarism detection as a subject has not yet achieved the same degree of scientific maturity as other subjects in the Text-Mining field, but a growing number of publications [7], websites and recently available products on this matter [8, 9] indicates that both the scientific and the industrial communities have started to recognize and acknowledge the existence of a recent problem which is yet awaiting its systematic solution [10].

There are several approaches to automatically identify plagiarism in different types of documents. The SCAM tool developed by Shivakumar [11] is based on building unions of word sets and counting domain-specific keywords in them. Plagiarism is then revealed via unexpected or otherwise suspicious occurrences of such keywords.

In some works, plagiarism detection has been regarded as a special case of duplicate document detection, which is both a necessary and difficult task in the management of large scale and very large scale databases (possibly multi-media databases). A variety of data mining methods and text-based techniques for such purposes have been proposed and investigated [12].

Comparing whole document checksums is simple and suffices for reliably detecting exact copies; however, detecting partial copies is subtler; in some works, for example in [13], an approach based on multiple fingerprints evaluation is used to detect partial copies. These techniques mostly rely on the use of k-grams, i.e. contiguous sub-strings of characters with length k. The process requires to divide a document into k-grams, and extract a hash value from each one [14, 15]. The result of this process is a fingerprint that represents the document in each of its sub-parts of length k, further exploited for comparison. Such a procedure, however, does not take into account the behavioral pattern of the plagiarist. In [16], the edit distance is introduced as a similarity metric between chunks of text.

In [17] an hypothetical behavioral pattern of the plagiarist is taken into account. The authors hypothesize that the behavior of the plagiarist consists in the repetition of three prototypical actions: insertion, deletion and substitution. This actions can be performed at any level of the document structure, phrase, paragraph or chapter. Distance between documents is then evaluated recursively exploiting the Levensthein edit distance [18].

All this approaches take into account plagiarism as an operation on text to be considered a mere sequence of characters, with no attempt to capture the likely semantic nature of plagiarism.

The main limit of plagiarism detection algorithms, as a means for identifying similar inventions and patent infringements, is their focus on the language of the description instead of the structure of the invention. Still some lessons learned can be readapted to the specific situation.

In facts, an acknowledged measure of similarity is expressed in the form

$$SIM_{ij} = \frac{keywords_{ij} + keywords_{ji}}{keywords_i + keywords_j} \tag{1}$$

where $keywords_{ij}$ is the number of occurrences of keywords of the document $i$ found in the document $j$ and $keywords_i$ is the overall number of keywords extracted from the document $i$.

An exemplary attempt to reuse in a novel form such a typical plagiarism assessment metric is proposed in [4], where the authors measure patent similarity by comparing the number of shared SAO triples (Subject Action Object), instead of the keywords alone. The main advantage of the SAO-based approach is that patents are compared in terms of functions delivered by the elements of the invention and general terms are filtered out.

Nevertheless, we observe that while taking into account syntactical information this comparison is still too dependent on the mere text and, as such, it depends more on the writer's style than on the actual 'semantics' of the described invention.

In this paper we propose an alternative approach which is not based on text comparison but on the comparison of the structural and functional architecture of the invention disclosed in a patent.


## 3. A new approach to measure patent similarity

As discussed above, the main limit of the traditional techniques for estimating the conceptual distance between two patents is the dependence on the language style of the inventor.

In order to clarify this concept let's consider the following excerpts:

- US4,713,635: "For example, the barrier portion or insert 107 includes a rib or tongue 109 that is aligned with rib or tongue portions 111, 113, and 115."
- US4,056,798: "One end of the cradle 48 forms a tongue member 50 which is releasably secured within an apertured latch 52 of the trip mechanism 42. [...] This deflection causes the bimetal element to engage a hook-shaped projection 66 of the latch 52, pulling the latch 52 to the right and causing the tongue 50 of the cradle 48 to be disengaged from the latch 52."

In both patents, a *tongue member* is a feature of the disclosed invention and can be considered as a subsystem of a further element of the invention (the *barrier portion 107* and the *cradle 48* respectively). The property of being a subsystem is expressed by means of totally different locutions: <component i> "includes" <component j> and <component i> "of the" <component j>. It is worth to notice that the adoption of a SAO-based comparison criterion does not allow to identify this kind of similarity, whatever is the richness and quality of its synonyms list. Similar remarks can be applied also to functional and positional interactions.

In the present paper the authors suggest to evaluate the similarity between two patents by comparing their functional tree [19], i.e. the hierarchical architecture of the invention's components and their functional interactions. In facts, working with the functional tree allows to identify conceptual similarities like the example presented above and to limit the influence of the language style. Moreover, the algorithm described hereafter allows to focus the comparison on a subset of components and/or interactions according to the peculiarity score proposed in [20].

## 3.1 Previous works: automatic functional analysis of patents and extraction of invention peculiarities

The authors are working on the development of new techniques and algorithms for patent analysis and comparison [19-23]. As a result of these previous experiences a prototype software system (named PatAnalyzer) has been developed with the following functionalities:
- identify the components of the invention;
- classify the identified components in terms of detail/abstraction level and their compositional relationships in terms of supersystem/subsystem links;
- identify positional and functional interactions between the components both internal and external to the system;
- build a thesaurus of "alternative denominations" of the functional elements identified in a given set of patents (hereafter called *project*);
- identify the most relevant components of each patent for a given *project* according to a ranking criterion which combines the detail level of the description with the *Inverse Document Frequency*, i.e. the "rarity" of each synset of the Thesaurus.

In Figure 1 the exemplary results related to the patent US6,064,024 are shown: the conceptual map visualizes the components of the inventions, their hierarchical and functional interactions, as well as their relevance score by means of a color code.

It is worth to notice that the score assigned to the components of each invention allows to select a subset of sentences from the description and the claims of the patent where the top-ranked components are mentioned. In [20] it was demonstrated that such a subset of sentences is sufficient for a "person skilled in the art" for understanding what the core of the patent is about.

In this paper, the top-ranked components and their hierarchical and functional relationships are adopted as a means to compare the inventions of a given *project* in order to estimate their similarity, as described in the following paragraph.

## 3.2 Comparing the functional tree of two inventions

In this work it is assumed that two technical systems belonging to the same field of application, sharing the same components, structured with the same architecture and characterized by the same functional interactions are conceptually identical. As a consequence, the similarity between two patents is estimated by comparing their components, hierarchical relationships and functions.

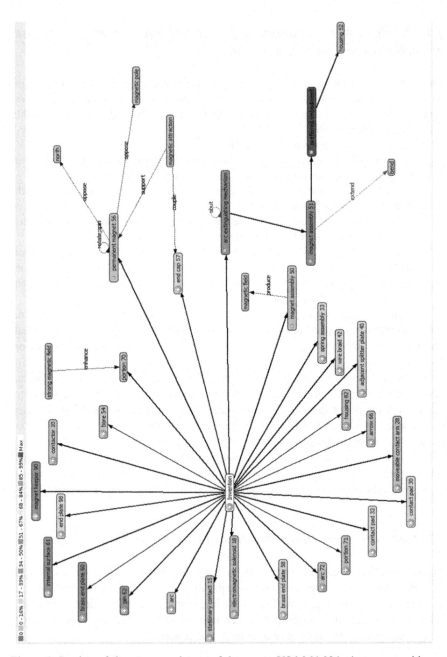

Figure 1. Portion of the conceptual map of the patent US6,064,024: the arrows with no label represent hierarchical relationships (the component at the tip of the arrow is a subsystem of the components at the tail of the arrow); labeled arrows represent functional and positional interactions; the colors highlight the relevance score of each component.

Such a comparison is made also taking into account the alternative denominations of each component, by means of the Thesaurus built according to the rules defined in [20]. More precisely, while comparing the functional trees of two inventions, two nodes are considered equivalent if they belong to the same synset in the Thesaurus of the *project*.

Then the following formula is applied:

$$SIM_{ij} = \alpha \frac{\left|\Gamma(i) \subset \Gamma(j)\right| + \left|\Gamma(j) \subset \Gamma(i)\right|}{\left|\Gamma(i)\right| + \left|\Gamma(j)\right|} + \beta \frac{\left|C(i) \subset C(j)\right| + \left|C(j) \subset C(i)\right|}{\left|C(i)\right| + \left|C(j)\right|} \qquad (2)$$

where $\Gamma(i)$ is the set of hierarchical and functional interactions belonging to the $i$-th patent; $\Gamma(i) \subset \Gamma(j)$ stands for the hierarchical and functional interactions of the $i$-th patent appearing also in the functional tree of the $j$-th patent; $C(i)$ is the list of components belonging to the $i$-th patent; $\alpha$ and $\beta$ are coefficients to weight the mutual relevance of interactions and components.

It is worth to note that the formula (2) can be applied to the whole set of components and interactions extracted from each patent or to a subset of top-scored components and their interactions. Thus, three parameters must be arbitrarily set to evaluate the similarity between two patents: $\alpha$, $\beta$ and $\gamma$, where the latter represents the threshold score for components selection ($\gamma = 0$ means that the whole hierarchical/functional tree is considered to estimate the patent similarity, while $\gamma = 1$ means that only the component with the highest score and its interactions are taken into account).

Whatever is the value assumed by $\alpha$, $\beta$ and $\gamma$, the similarity matrix of a given *project*, built in analogy of the incidence matrix proposed in [24], is a symmetric square matrix $N \times N$ ($N$ being the number of documents analyzed in the *project*) constituted by the similarities of each patents' pair. In other words each cell $(i, j)$ contains the estimated similarity among the $i$-th and the $j$-th patent.

The rules to define the most suitable values for $\alpha$, $\beta$ and $\gamma$ are still under validation; nevertheless some general directions have already been developed and are briefly discussed in section 5.

## 4. Exemplary application: electrical circuit interruption devices

In order to clarify the procedure described in section 3.2 and to demonstrate its capabilities this chapter reports an exemplary application in the field of electrical circuit interruption devices.

On the base of a previous experience with ABB SACE (www.abb.com), an evolutionary analysis of electrical circuit breakers has been made at the MTI Lab of the University of Florence. A set of 85 patents (ABB *project*) was selected as a combination of two citation trees, i.e. the patents cited from US6,064,024 and US6,373,016 following backward citations up to three levels from the source patent. Figure 2 shows a portion of the citation tree related to the former patent: each arrow represents a backward citation.

In order to perform such an evolutionary analysis each patent has been analyzed by a technician and a summary has been extracted in the form Problem-Solution (figure 2, close up). In other words, the citation trees have been manually translated into a Problem-Solution tree which can be used with similar purposes of the OTSM-TRIZ Problem Flow Network proposed in [25].

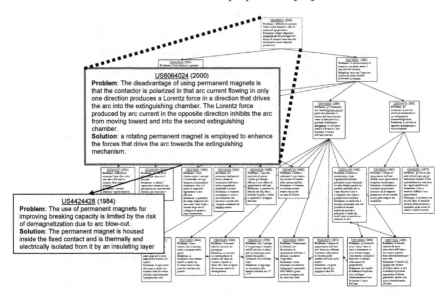

Figure 2. Excerpt from the Patent Citation tree and close up on the Problem-Solution notations associated to a pair of citing-cited patents.

The details of this evolutionary analysis are outside the scopes of the present paper and will be presented in a next publication. Besides, such an extensive analysis carefully operated by humans constitutes a valuable resource to validate the proposed similarity score.

According to the above mentioned procedure, the 85 patents have been processed by PatAnalyzer, thus producing a corresponding number of conceptual maps (as the functional tree shown in figure 1) and related relevance scores. Moreover the analysis has generated a thesaurus specifically dedicated to the ABB *project* (figure 3). The similarity matrix (figure 4) has been calculated assigning the same weight to components and interactions (i.e. $\alpha = 1$, $\beta = 1$) and discarding those components with a score lower than one fifth of the maximum score of the entire project (i.e. $\gamma = 0.2$). The whole computation (functional tree identification, thesaurus generation, definition of the similarity matrix) has required less than 60 minutes on a standard laptop.

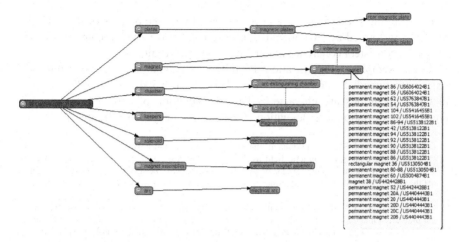

Figure 3. Portion of the Thesaurus graph of the ABB project: the arrows point from hypernyms to hyponyms, (red) dashed lines represent alternative denominations. The box in the right-low corner lists the patents containing the selected word/multi-word.

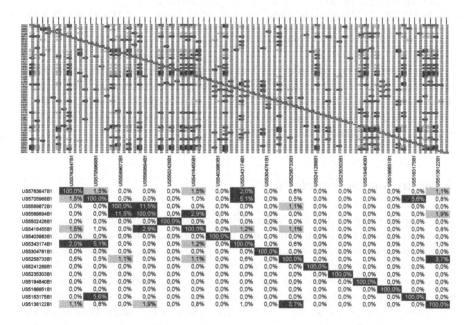

| | US5763847B1 | US5705968B1 | US5589672B1 | US5569894B1 | US5502428B1 | US5416455B1 | US5403983B1 | US5343174B1 | US5304761B1 | US5258733B1 | US5241289B1 | US5235303B1 | US5194840B1 | US5166651B1 | US5163175B1 | US5138122B1 |
|---|---|---|---|---|---|---|---|---|---|---|---|---|---|---|---|---|
| US5763847B1 | 100,0% | 1,5% | 0,0% | 0,0% | 0,0% | 1,5% | 0,0% | 2,0% | 0,0% | 0,6% | 0,0% | 0,0% | 0,0% | 0,0% | 0,0% | 1,1% |
| US5705968B1 | 1,5% | 100,0% | 0,0% | 0,0% | 0,0% | 1,0% | 0,0% | 5,1% | 0,0% | 0,5% | 0,0% | 0,0% | 0,0% | 0,0% | 5,6% | 0,8% |
| US5589672B1 | 0,0% | 0,0% | 100,0% | 11,5% | 0,0% | 0,0% | 0,0% | 0,0% | 0,0% | 1,1% | 0,0% | 0,0% | 0,0% | 0,0% | 0,0% | 0,0% |
| US5569894B1 | 0,0% | 0,0% | 11,5% | 100,0% | 0,0% | 0,0% | 0,0% | 0,0% | 0,0% | 0,0% | 0,0% | 0,0% | 0,0% | 0,0% | 0,0% | 1,9% |
| US5502428B1 | 0,0% | 0,0% | 0,0% | 0,0% | 100,0% | 0,0% | 0,0% | 0,0% | 0,0% | 0,0% | 0,0% | 0,0% | 0,0% | 0,0% | 0,0% | 0,0% |
| US5416455B1 | 1,5% | 1,0% | 0,0% | 2,9% | 0,0% | 100,0% | 0,0% | 1,2% | 0,0% | 1,1% | 0,0% | 0,0% | 0,0% | 0,0% | 0,0% | 0,8% |
| US5403983B1 | 0,0% | 0,0% | 0,0% | 0,0% | 0,0% | 0,0% | 100,0% | 0,0% | 0,0% | 0,0% | 0,0% | 0,0% | 0,0% | 0,0% | 0,0% | 0,0% |
| US5343174B1 | 2,0% | 5,1% | 0,0% | 0,0% | 0,0% | 1,2% | 0,0% | 100,0% | 0,0% | 0,6% | 0,0% | 0,0% | 0,0% | 0,0% | 0,0% | 1,0% |
| US5304761B1 | 0,0% | 0,0% | 0,0% | 0,0% | 0,0% | 0,0% | 0,0% | 0,0% | 100,0% | 0,0% | 0,0% | 0,0% | 0,0% | 0,0% | 0,0% | 0,0% |
| US5258733B1 | 0,6% | 0,5% | 1,1% | 0,0% | 0,0% | 1,1% | 0,0% | 0,6% | 0,0% | 100,0% | 0,0% | 0,0% | 0,0% | 0,0% | 0,0% | 3,7% |
| US5241289B1 | 0,0% | 0,0% | 0,0% | 0,0% | 0,0% | 0,0% | 0,0% | 0,0% | 0,0% | 0,0% | 100,0% | 0,0% | 0,0% | 0,0% | 0,0% | 0,0% |
| US5235303B1 | 0,0% | 0,0% | 0,0% | 0,0% | 0,0% | 0,0% | 0,0% | 0,0% | 0,0% | 0,0% | 0,0% | 100,0% | 0,0% | 0,0% | 0,0% | 0,0% |
| US5194840B1 | 0,0% | 0,0% | 0,0% | 0,0% | 0,0% | 0,0% | 0,0% | 0,0% | 0,0% | 0,0% | 0,0% | 0,0% | 100,0% | 0,0% | 0,0% | 0,0% |
| US5166651B1 | 0,0% | 0,0% | 0,0% | 0,0% | 0,0% | 0,0% | 0,0% | 0,0% | 0,0% | 0,0% | 0,0% | 0,0% | 0,0% | 100,0% | 0,0% | 0,0% |
| US5163175B1 | 0,0% | 5,6% | 0,0% | 0,0% | 0,0% | 0,0% | 0,0% | 0,0% | 0,0% | 0,0% | 0,0% | 0,0% | 0,0% | 0,0% | 100,0% | 0,0% |
| US5138122B1 | 1,1% | 0,8% | 0,0% | 1,9% | 0,0% | 0,8% | 0,0% | 1,0% | 0,0% | 3,7% | 0,0% | 0,0% | 0,0% | 0,0% | 0,0% | 100,0% |

Figure 4. Similarity matrix for the 85 patents of the ABB project: entire matrix (above) and close up on a reduced number of patents (below). The cells of the matrix can be colored according to one or more thresholds defined by the user (here 1% and 2% respectively) in order to highlight similar patents and clusters.

The resulting similarities have been compared with the outputs of the analysis manually performed by two operators as described above. Such a comparison has revealed a consistent coherence among the two set of results.

As an exemplary demonstration the following patents have revealed relevant matched features: US6,064,024, US5,763,847, US5,130,504, US4,424,428. Indeed all those inventions are characterized by the adoption of a permanent magnet aimed at the deviation and elongation of the electric arc (see also figure 2):

- US6,064,024: "[...] Thus the permanent magnet's strong field will always be oriented to enhance the potentially weak self magnetic field as described with respect to the embodiment in FIG. 1. Therefore the resultant Lorentz force acting on the arc will always be strong enough to drive the arc off the contact pads 30 and 32 and along stationary contact 17 even when the self magnetic field is weak (low current) [...]".
- US5,763,847: "[...] As the arc travels into the arc extinguishing chamber 34, it also interacts with the individual magnetic fields produced by permanent magnet 54 in each of the first type of splitter plates 40. [...]. The interaction of the arc current with this magnetic field around each plate causes the arc 77 to move in circles on the surface of the splitter plate casing 44. Thus the arc energy is not constricted to one spot on the casing surface as occurred in previous arc chambers, thus erosive effects of arcs impinging the splitter plates are reduced in the present design. [...]".
- US5,130,504: "[...] The permanent magnets 80-88 are polarized across the width thereof to establish a magnetic field B (FIGS. 10 and 11) directed front-to-rear through the respective arc chambers, the plates 54 and 90 forming a magnetic path around the outside of the switching apparatus and an air gap across the respective arc extinguishing chambers. [...]".
- US4,424,428: "[...] The magnetic field of magnet 38, which is present when the arc appears, leads to rotation of the arc along the annular tracks formed by contact surfaces 34, 36 and rapid extinction of the arc in a well known manner [...]".

A selection of the paragraphs containing the components and interactions contributing to the similarity score (in this case "permanent magnet" and related denominations like "interior magnet", figure 3) has been judged sufficient for a person skilled in the art to understand the role of the component and to assess the originality of the solution.

## 5. Discussion and conclusions

The technique proposed in this paper defines the similarity of two patents as the match in terms of functional structure of the inventions, instead of the traditional frequency of keywords co-occurrences. By doing so, patents are grouped into more appropriate conceptual classes and more intrinsically homogeneous clusters can be produced. As explained before, keywords co-occurrence analysis deals with the patents as a whole and considers only the frequency of co-citations. Thus, the result of grouping may be superficial or even spurious since those statistics would not reveal the internal structural relationships between patents.

Besides the proposed algorithm allows to find analogies between inventions described with totally different locutions, while general poorly informative elements (according to a ranking which depends on the specific project and not to a general terminology classification) are neglected.

An open issue is the definition of the rules to assign a proper value to the weights $\alpha$ (interactions), $\beta$ (components) and the threshold $\gamma$. According to the analyses performed so far, the components part of the formula (2) can lead to wrong estimations of the similarity when dealing with a patent having a reduced number of components: in these cases the similarity score is zero when the relevance score of the components is low, since there are no opportunities for matching other patents. Vice versa, if the relevance score of the components of an invention characterized by a reduced number of elements is high, the patent will result highly similar with many patents of the project. Besides, the similarity between patents with a reduced number of components is more suitably assessed by the interactions part of the formula (2). Inversely, in case of inventions with a high number of components described in the patent, also the components part of (2) significantly contributes to the similarity assessment.

A further emerging note is that the contribution of the interactions to the overall similarity score inversely depends on the value assigned to $\gamma$, i.e. the relevance/peculiarity threshold defining the number of components to be considered from each patent in order to perform the comparison. In other words, hierarchical and functional interactions between components provide relevant contributions for similarity assessment if a wider portion of the functional tree is considered for each patent under evaluation, while in a selection limited to the top-score elements from each patent the similarity is mostly evaluated in terms of components.

The authors are involved in a more extensive validation of the proposed algorithm with the aim of providing more detailed guidelines for the definition of the most suitable parameters $\alpha$, $\beta$ and $\gamma$ for a given set of patents.

# References

1. Fluck J., Zimmermann M., Kurapkat G., Hofmann M.: Information extraction technologies for the life science industry. Drug Discovery Today: Technologies, vol. 2, Issue 3, pp. 217-224 (2005).
2. Yoon B., Park Y.: A systematic approach for identifying technology opportunities: Keyword-based morphology analysis. Technological Forecasting and Social Change, vol. 72, Issue 2, pp. 145-160 (2005).
3. Fabry B., Ernst H, Langholz J., Köster M.: Patent portfolio analysis as a useful tool for identifying R&D and business opportunities—an empirical application in the nutrition and health industry. World Patent Information, vol. 28, Issue 3, pp. 215-225 (2006).
4. Bergmann I., Butzke D., Walter L., Fuerste J. P., Moherle M. G., Erdmann V. A.: Evaluating The Risk of Patent Infringement By Means of Semantic Patent Analysis: The Case of DNA-Chips, Proceedings of the R&D Management Conference, 4-6 July 2007, Bremen, Germany, ISBN: 0-9549916-9-9 (2007).
5. Daim T. U., Rueda G., Martin H., Gerdsri P.: Forecasting emerging technologies: Use of bibliometrics and patent analysis. Technological Forecasting and Social Change, vol. 73, Issue 8, pp. 981-1012 (2006).
6. Trappey A. J. C., Hsua F. C., Trappey C. V., Lin C.: Development of a patent document classification and search platform using a back-propagation network. Expert Systems with Applications, vol. 31, Issue 4, pp. 755-765 (2006).

7. Clough P.: Plagiarism in natural and programming languages: An overview of current tools and technologies. Internal Report CS-00-05, University of Sheffield (2000). Available at http://ir.shef.ac.uk/cloughie/papers/plagiarism2000.pdf. Last access 27 Apr 2008.
8. EVE Plagiarism Detection System. http://www.canexus.com. Last access 27 Apr 2008.
9. Turnitin. http://www.turnitin.com/static/home.html. Last access 27 Apr 2008.
10. Barrett R., Malcolm J., Lyon C.: Are we ready for large scale use of plagiarism detection tools? Proceedings of the 4th Annual LTSN-ICS Conference, NUI Galway, pp. 79-84 (2003).
11. Shivakumar N.: Detecting digital copyright violations on the internet. PhD thesis Stanford University (1999). Available at http://infolab.stanford.edu/~shiva/thesis.html, Last access 27 Apr 2008.
12. Lopresti D.: A comparison of text-based methods for detecting duplication in document image databases. Proceedings of Document Recognition and Retrieval VII (IS and T SPIE Electronic Imaging) San Jose (USA), pp. 210–221, January (2000).
13. Schleimer A. A. S., Wilkerson D. S., Aiken A.: Winnowing: local algorithms for document fingerprinting. Proceedings of the 2003 ACM SIGMOD International Conference on Management of data. ACM 1-58113-634-X/03/06. (2003). Available at http://theory.stanford.edu/~aiken/publications/papers/sigmod03.pdf. Last access 27 Apr 2008.
14. Heintze N.: Scalable document fingerprinting. In Proceedings of the 1996 USENIX Workshop on Electronic Commerce, pp. 191-200 (1996). Available at http://citeseer.ist.psu.edu/348631.html. Last access 27 Apr 2008.
15. Koala Document Fingerprinting (KDF). http://www-2.cs.cmu.edu/afs/cs/user/nch/www/koala-info.html. Last access 27 Apr 2008.
16. Mandreoli P. F., Martoglia R.: Un metodo per il riconoscimento di duplicati in collezioni di documenti. Proceedings of the Eleventh Italian Symposium on Advanced Database Systems, SEBD. (2003).
17. Zini M., Fabbri M., Moneglia M., Panunzi A.: Plagiarism Detection Through Multilevel Text Comparison. In Proceedings of the Second International Conference on Automated Production of Cross Media Content for Multi-Channel Distribution table of contents, pp. 181-185, ISBN: 0-7695-2625-X (2006).
18. Levenshtein V.: Binary codes capable of correcting deletions, insertions and reversals. Soviet Physics-Report, SEBD(10):707–710 (1966).
19. Cascini G.: System and Method for performing functional analyses making use of a plurality of inputs. Patent Application 02425149.8, European Patent Office, 14.3.2002, International Publication Number WO 03/077154 A2 (18 September 2003).
20. Cascini G., Russo D., Zini M.: Computer-Aided Patent Analysis: finding invention peculiarities. Proceedings of the 2nd IFIP Working Conference on Computer Aided Innovation, Brighton (MI), USA, 8-9 October, 2007, in Trends in Computer-Aided Innovation, Springer, pp. 167-178, ISBN 978-0-387-75455-0 (2007).
21. Cascini G., Neri F.: Natural Language Processing for patents analysis and classification. Proceedings of the TRIZ Future 4th World Conference, 3-5 November 2004, Florence, Firenze University Press, ISBN 88-8453-221-3 (2004).
22. Cascini G., Agili A., Zini M.: Building a patents small-world network as a tool for Computer-Aided Innovation. Proceedings of the 1st IFIP Working Conference on Computer Aided Innovation, Ulm, Germany, November 14-15 (2005).
23. Cascini G., Russo D.: Computer-Aided analysis of patents and search for TRIZ contradictions. International Journal of Product Development, Special Issue: Creativity and Innovation Employing TRIZ, vol. 4(1-2) (2007).
24. Yoon B., Park Y.: A text-mining-based patent network: Analytical tool for high-technology trend. The Journal of High Technology Management Research, vol. 15, Issue 1, pp. 37-50 (2004).
25. Khomenko N., De Guio R., Lelait L., Kaikov I.: A Framework for OTSM-TRIZ Based Computer Support to be used in Complex Problem Management. International Journal of Computer Application in Technology (IJCAT), vol. 30 Issue 1-2 (2007).

# Representing and selecting problems through contradictions clouds

**Denis Cavallucci[1], François Rousselot[2], and Cécilia Zanni[3]**

[1,2&3] Design Engineering Laboratory (LGeCo), National Instituted of Applied Sciences (INSA) Strasbourg. FRANCE, {denis.cavallucci, francois.rousselot, cecilia.zanni}@insa-strasbourg.fr

**Abstract:** Within the scope of Computer Aided Innovation, it is commonly agreed that problem formulation remains in need of robust improvement. Prior to this, means of conducting and representing problems are needed, so as the way a software implementation would help designers, for instance, in decision making. Our approach presents the originality of including the use of a contradiction formalism associated to the notions of problem network, parameter network and their interactions. Several other research outcomes have clearly presented interesting results in the direction of problem network constitution and defined its role within problem formulation and inventive design but have not yet clarified the way these networks are linked together. In this article, we present the notion of contradiction clouds and its manipulation in order to fulfil the objective of assisting decisions in a more advanced way than an intuitive decision method. These proposed rules of representation are based on the assumption that contradictions need to be associated with means of characterization for a graphical representation to be relevant and a decision to be engaged. A test procedure of our proposals has been conducted in two industrial case studies; one in a steel maker company and a second in an automotive supplier.

**Keywords:** TRIZ, Contradictions clouds, Inventive Design, R&D decisions

## 1. Introduction

### 1.1. The place of invention in innovation

It is now acknowledged in scientific and industrial circles that there is a major difference between innovation and invention [1]. Many works have highlighted these differences but can be summarized in the fields of engineering as follows:

*Please use the following format when citing this chapter:*

Cavallucci, D., Rousselot, F. and Zanni, C., 2008, in IFIP International Federation for Information Processing, Volume 277; *Computer-Aided Innovation (CAI)*; Gaetano Cascini; (Boston: Springer), pp. 43–56.

The status of Innovation (associated to the object or more largely what man have built: artifacts) is acquired whenever a society adoption of this same artifact appears as new in a group of consumers having a certain legitimacy.

The question then arouses about the role of invention in this scheme. Invention, being the cognitive fruit of inventors materialized in an innovative technical solution associated with its resultant in the novel object, this statement is not obviously connected with the concept of innovation described above. It is thus interesting to investigate which new facts can be at the origin of invention and in which ways they can result in an impact on innovation.

In other words, an innovation can have nothing inventive in it, just like an invention may never result in an innovation. The only semantic parallel between these two terms lies in the novelty of the idea for one, of the society adoption for the other. Moreover, the temporal aspect of states (both invention and innovation) for the same object remains often timely distant. Sometimes, as it was the case for photography, one century occurs before an invention does acquire the state of innovation. This rhythm seems to accelerate as the decades our industries cross, moreover since the era of innovation became a reality. Therefore the rhythm of emergence of inventions is ever more solicited with the necessity for a company to ever be intensively proposing innovations.

This distant temporal aspect between invention and innovation can nevertheless inspire a reflection: "does the original presence of an invention support the emergence of an innovation?" or "is this presence guaranteeing a particular kind of innovation, such as for example provoking a broader success of a more durable notoriety?"

By observing innovations which have landmarked this century, a brief reply is undoubtedly in favor of this statement, innovations which landmarked this century have in their immense majority at their origin a relevant invention and of a high inventive value (within the meaning of Altshuller's levels of inventiveness). We thus question also on the objective methods which characterize the emergence of inventions, since they seem to be sources of innovations provoking successes for companies.

## 1.2.  Which fundamentals make a mode of design "inventively-driven?"

In this section, we will start by clarifying the confused relation between creativity, often perceived and considered from the angle of a process or a stage of this process, and an inventive behavior which results rather in a particular capacity to address problem solving having certain specificities.

Creativity, seeming more and more a recognized process of a more global activity of design, is at the heart of many reflections [2]. We can draw this statement just by observing the ever increasing contributions these last years in the fields of Design Sciences around creative phases which tries to explain that time has come to increase in their effectiveness [3]. Let us add to that the emergence of theoretical and practical contributions to characterize them, like those around TRIZ. They confirm the tendency that many researchers in design sciences are considering them. This new fact comes like a logical evolution from expert practice (in the sense of social sciences and in which little computerization is proven to be possible), towards an axiomatization as an inescapable precondition of a computerization.

But this statement can be argued since it is dissociating man from creative act by claiming that he might not be responsible of its control. However we undoubtedly know that this is not the case, the error comes according to us from the amalgam between creativity, creative process and human intrinsic aptitude [4]. If the process of implementation of the human creativity is observable, teachable, reproducible, the human actor at the heart of this process must develop particular aptitudes in problem solving [5].

## 1.3.    How a computer can support an inventive mode of design?

This title is shocking in itself by the fact it partially associates two words "computer and invention". However as we described above, we do not fully associate invention and creativity. There is thus no question of bringing forward the assumption that creativity is computable, but simply to assert inventive steps assistance to the assistance of formulation and resolution of a certain typology of problems: inventive problems.

In our Design approach, our starting point concerning creativity is thus neither to supplant it, nor doping its processes of emergence, but to address the capacity of a designer to solve problems related with the specific situation he is facing with.

Regarding computerization of certain tasks related to designers, our choice was logically turned towards those in which a computerization would prove to be beneficial. In a past contribution, we proposed to assist extraction and storing of multi-disciplinary knowledge [6]. Later, we proposed to handle this knowledge and advanced specific representations useful for decisions in R&D departments [7].

In short, among the essential functionalities that a computer can handle to assist a designer in logic of inventive design, we propose to treat the following ones:

- To assist expert questioning and to transpose his knowledge in components of inventive problems (reduced in our case to contradictions).

- To store this knowledge in templates allowing their re-uses, their dynamic iterations.

- To assist link constitution of these components to provoke all the possible interpretation based upon the provided representation.

## 1.4.  Zooming on the formulation of inventive challenges

The characteristic for a problem to be declared "inventive" was already clarified by Altschuller in TRIZ theory (1). Here, we will only use the ontology of a contradiction posed according to the fundamentals of the theory. The challenging aspect is observed when an unsolved situation possesses outcomes potentially carrying both substantial benefits for the company but also some risks.

Let us remind that a contradiction within the meaning of TRIZ (see also figure 1) can be modeled as follows:

An Active Parameter (APx) having two states of values diametrically opposed (Va and Vā) influencing respectively two evaluating parameters (EPn and EPm). The state of contradiction is obtained since the opposite state (Va → EPm and Vā → EPn) is also true.

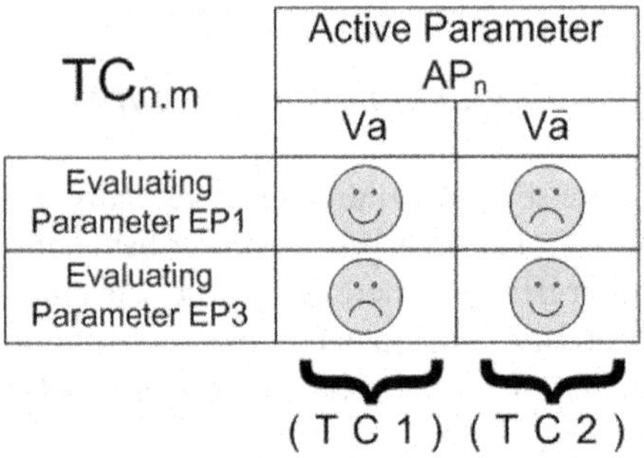

| $TC_{n.m}$ | Active Parameter $AP_n$ | |
|---|---|---|
| | Va | Vā |
| Evaluating Parameter EP1 | 🙂 | 🙁 |
| Evaluating Parameter EP3 | 🙁 | 🙂 |

( T C 1 ) ( T C 2 )

Figure 1 Schematic illustration on a contradiction

In TRIZ, we can associate an expressed physical contradiction to an inventive challenge when the two values of its AP are diametrically opposed and that the impossibility of placing AP at the same time in Va state AND in Vā state is ever more critical. Another element in the challenging value of a contradiction is the consequences of its solving; when above its own pair of EPs, its solving is diffused among many other EPs pairs (or other contradictions).

But such contradictions, when facing high challenges, are not easy to locate in the dense quantity of contradictions at the origin of complex problems. Our objective through the coming section is to propose a possible representation of multiple contradictions such as it emphasizes a reduced amount of contradictions at the heart of great challenges.

## 2. Supporting the selection of inventive challenges

### 2.1. On the acquisition of contradictions

Firstly, we will consider the acquisition of contradictions and the way this fundamental stage of inventive problems solving can be conducted. The synthesis of a contradiction passes by specific processes allowing the emergence of parameters related with the studied system. Among these processes, let us note three principal stages:

- Description of a first set of parameters by the comprehension of past-present evolution dynamics of a given system. This process is primarily supported by multi-screen analysis [8].

- Description of a second set of parameters by studying the positioning of the system through laws of engineering systems evolution. Here the need is to confront the studied system with each law and analyze its evolution by characterizing it in terms of parameters [9].

- The first two processes having highlighted a group of contradictions, it is then appropriate to differentiate the Active Parameters from the Evaluating ones. Then, respectfully to the ontology of a contradiction, to associate APs and the EPs by means of their respective Values (Va and Vā). The incompleteness of these associations (according the described contradiction pattern) forces to identify the missing components. This constitutes also another mean of parameter's emergence.

The outcome of this last stage is that a more or less important set of contradictions will be disclosed. But the use of methods and tools extracted from TRIZ can be considered only on the basis of one of them. In the case of complex problems, it's a large amount of contradictions which will be synthesized; problems to insulate the contradiction to be engaged in a tool or a method of TRIZ for resolution still remain.

### 2.2. On the concept of contradictions cloud

Our past reports led us to understand that contradictions in complex situations are numerous and connected to multiple problems [10]. Thus, these contradictions, to be differentiated, must be associated to particular characteristics leading, when associated to values, to a graphical representation.

Our observations of these characteristics led us to highlight three elements of contradiction characterization.

**First differentiation: Importance**

The contradictions components (an Active Parameter a pair of Evaluating Parameters) do not have the same importance; Evaluating Parameters are more characterizing the essentials of the problem than others. Thus, it is possible to associate a qualitative value to each Evaluating Parameters which compose a group of contradictions. This evaluation has only the aim to place them on a relative scale of importance. The essence to be preserved among parameters relationship is the scale amplitude to be simply established around a certain amount of divisions out of a scale allowing this differentiation.

Then, the role of the Active Parameter within a contradiction is not of the same order as the one provided by Evaluating Parameters. Very often, the active parameter represents the element on which it is necessary to act in a contradiction. We propose that the element which will allow differentiating a set of active parameters between them articulates around the potential impact that this APx (setted at Va AND V\={a}) will have on the problems to which it is related. In other terms an APx is going to atrophy or dope the importance of a pair of EP since we observed in Apx an evident capacity to influent EP's importance. The given coefficient ($\alpha$) will then allow the addition of both EP's (EPn+ EPm) to be reduced when facing a weak impact or to be multiplied when facing a strong impact. For this multiplying coefficient, we agreed on a range from 0,5 to 2.

Thus, the first criterion of differentiation between TCs will be following form:

$$X = \alpha APx \, (Coef. \, EPn + Coef. \, EPm)$$

*Where:*
*X: the association of an AP and its pair of opposite EP's*
$\alpha$*: the multiplying coefficient applied to the concerned AP*
*Coef. EPn and Coef. EPm: the two values of relative importance for each EP simply added.*

**Second differentiation: Universality**

In our observations of the typology of a set of contradictions, we noted that EPs are qualifying the objectives sometimes hidden in inventive challenges. Some of these EPs seem to appear in a recurring way in a large amount of contradictions. This observation led us to build the assumption that a simple measurement of the universality of a contradiction could be established. This measurement would aim at specifying that a contradiction having EP recurrently present in a large amount of other contradictions represents the universality of this same contradiction. The universality criterion Y thus takes the following form:

$$Y = Q \, EPn + Q \, EPm$$

*Where:*
*Y is the universality of a contradiction;*
*Q EPn, m: corresponds to the quantity of occurrence the EP has in a set of*
*TC's.*

### Third differentiation: Amplitude

In the structure of a contradiction, an AP is associated with a pair of EPs. But in a more general way, the same AP is often associated with a variable quantity of EPs. As a result, some AP involve the opposition of only one pair of EPs whereas others have an impact on a large amount of EPs and involve the opposition of a consequent series of pairs of EPs. Our proposal is thus to establish a third criterion of differentiation Z related to contradictions which would specify their amplitude by the sum of EPs pairs each AP is attached to within a contradiction group. This criterion would take the following form:

$$Z = \sum C \ [EPn;EPm] \in APx$$

*Where:*
*Z is the criterion of amplitude;*
*C represents any couple EPn; EPm*

We thus have 3 criteria X, Y and Z to differentiate contradictions. While placing criteria X and Y according to a system of axis, we obtain a cloud of dots. By associating each point of this cloud criterion Z, we obtain (as represented on figure 2) a group of dots with variable diameters.

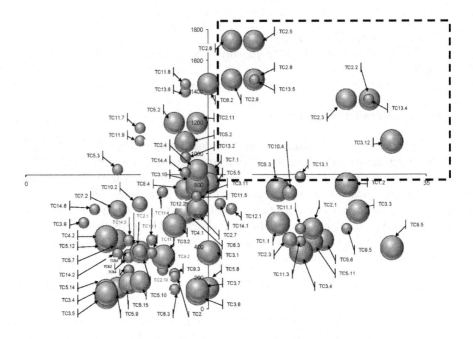

Figure 2 Cloud of contradictions with highligted top right corner

In such a representation, the zone of points in top right of the graph is of a particular importance. In order to highlight an even reduced amount of contradictions, a first method consists in isolating the set of contradictions of the top right quarter (figure 2).

But in the cases of complex situations, where contradictions are numerous, this pruning can not be enough. In such cases, we propose to highlight the top right front of points of this quarter cloud (figure 3).

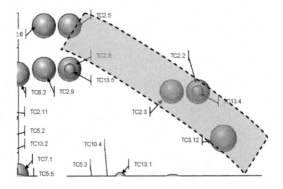

Figure 3 Dot's front zone of the top left quarter

Let us return now to the objective of such a representation. We have an important set of contradictions representative of a set of expressed problems in a given situation. Our main objective is to put the designer in front of his inventive challenges, those impacting most consequently on the set of problems of its initial situation. The reduced dots on the upper right front thus represent a reduced amount of variants to address an inventive way complex problem. But assuming that the result of the analysis of such a graph is a set of decisions which will initiate a set of R&D activities, we are facing with a situation where it will be necessary to express the potential resources of R&D actions. If for example a company has the capacity to address several R&D axes in parallel, several choices on the upper left front face could be made. If the R&D efforts must be reduced, a single choice (or a reduced amount of dots) will have to be selected.

## 2.3. On the computerization of the process

In a past contribution [11], we had already proposed a data-processing method for revealing contradictions materialized in a computer module. In order to associate this module the results of the analysis expressed in the preceding paragraph, we conceived a graphic extension of this module featuring the cloud of dots and the highlighting of its upper left front (figure 4).

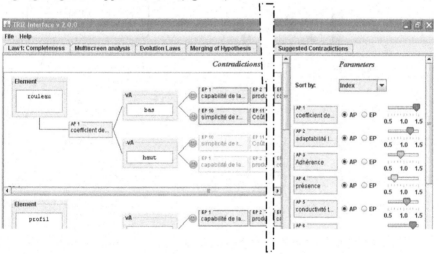

Figure 4 TRIZ acquisition screen capture – "Parameters & Contradictions" menu.

## 2.4. Results of experimentation of the new TRIZ acquisition module in two industrial cases

In the phase related to expert knowledge formalization of the industrialists we met, we tried out our module in two different industrial situations.

The first case was treated at a large automotive supplier, manufacturer of windshield wipers, the second in a steel industry in continuous annealing processing. The two cases treated summarized with their essential question was expressed to us the following way:

- Case 1: How to provoke the evolution of the windshield wiper from its present generation to its future?

- Case 2: How to decrease the amount of production stops in the manufacture of flat carbon steel sheets in continuous annealing processes?

Following the contradictions synthesis process in our two cases, we obtain the following results (figure 5):

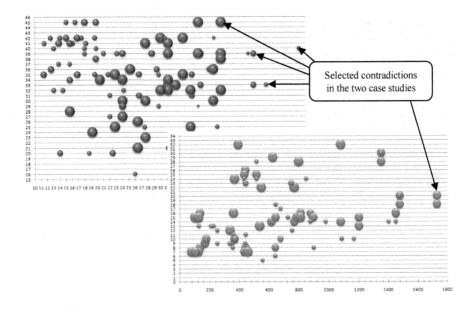

Figure 5a&b Graphical results (Dots clouds) of the two case studies

## 2.5.    Analyzes of the R&D decisions following the interpretation of the graphic data

In Case 1, the R&D decider agreed to engage the resolution of the TC3.12. This contradiction is placed on the left higher corner (see figure 5a). The current status of this case study is that several Solution Concepts have been disclosed out of the problem solving process and two of them are currently under patent applications. Another partial result is that an R&D activity has been launched and consists in building a specific machine for measuring accurately the impact between several critical Evaluating Parameters since some of our assumptions during the meetings have found unprecise answers. In order to move further regarding this issue, it has been decided to engage a relation with a subcontractor to build the manufacturing means to perform these tesings and procesely characeraize the relation between these EPs.

In Case 2, the study group in agreement with the person in charge of the project, decided to engage the resolution of following contradictions: TC6.1 – TC10.3 – TC2.8 – TC1.7 placed within and above the highlighted zone (see figure 5b). After the solvinf part of our activities, eleven solution concepts have been disclosed and classifyed in six different categories. Three categories have been placed in R&D activities priorities while one category has been sent to a subcontractor for calculations and characterization of the solution. The current status is that calucations came back with positive results, confirming what we felt during the sessions. The next step is to engage the realization of a prototype on a testing site for validation of calulation results.

## 3.    Discussions

### 3.1.    On methodology related to the choice

By considering as a starting point contradiction, let us remind that it is possible to implement the methods and tools brought by TRIZ the following way (figure 6).

We are then facing with a set of techniques which can be implemented to converge towards Solution Concepts recognized as inventive if they indeed solve at least the initial contradiction. Our objective is definitely not to obtain a large amount of concepts, but to increase the effectiveness of the problem solving step, it is thus important to choose only a reduced amount of contradictions, but to choose those which will increase the potential, when associated to their synthesized concepts, to significantly impact on the problem network we started with.

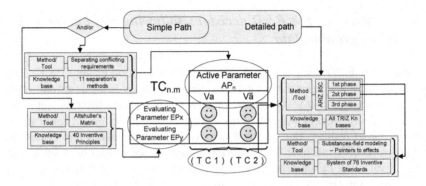

Figure 6 Addressing a contradiction with tools and methods brought from TRIZ

Another advantage of such a computerization is that it makes interactive and dynamics the graphic model established and the strategy of choice that the designer may start with is eased. Thus, if the set of contradictions (cloud of dots) on the graph is directly related to its values X, Y and Z, the designer can, for instance, decide to modify the parameter Y and to allocate a different ratio of importance to EPs since a particular strategy justifies it. It was the case in our study 1 where two parallel objectives were to be proposed to the decision makers. The first consisted in adopting a design of windshield wiper aiming at reducing the production cost without making compromise compared to the performances produced. In the same time, the R&D of this company wished to compete with another equipment supplier on several markets (with car constructors) by offering a new product whose performances would be increased and would allow him to be placed over its direct competitors by the originality and the effectiveness of its solution. These two approaches required engaging the resolution of different contradictions. They were re-stated ahead by a quasi-instantaneous rebuilding of the cloud thanks to computerization. The draback of such a freedom is that parameters value may be adapted until an expected result is reached. It is therefore important not to engage a value modification based on an individual designer's desire but until a majority of team members commonly agreed on a modification based on quantitative physical realities (not on personal wishes).

In the case of flat steels, four contradictions were chosen by the group of study, some of them not being located on the upper left front. This choice can be explained by the decision of the group to address a wider ways of resolution of the set of problems settled at the beginning. The strategy was here to isolate a reduced amount of contradictions but resulting from different APs. Indeed, to address two or several contradictions from the same AP often invites us to concentrate during the solving phases on the same operational zone. The resultant is that the solution concepts sometimes emerge in a recurring way from one contradiction to the other. On the other hand, when the AP at the origin of a contradiction is different, we have a new angle of observation of the problem and the concepts which emerge give solutions of another nature. The objective of the second company being to eliminate a large amount of problems from the starting network, we concentrate our R&D efforts in a larger set of directions so as to eliminate a maximum of problems as a result of this new strategy.

## 3.2.  On the universality of the process

Another remark to be formulated relates to the fact these two companies present a significant organizational structure, and problems of a very different nature were expressed. The first one expressed a problem of product evolution, whereas the second expressed a set of problems involved in a manufacturing process. We thus observe that our procedure, associated the notion of the generic management of complex problems, is not significantly influenced by the nature of the addressed situation. The limits of such an assertion are related to the fact that the two cases presented an identical corpus of knowledge from the fields of mechanical engineering. However, it is already an emerging universality and our further work will aim to test it in distant fields than traditional engineering disciplines.

## 3.3.  On the positioning of the process regarding TRIZ body of knowledge

From our investigations of TRIZ body of knowledge and the synthesis we made in the past, we remarked only rare contributions evoking the concept of management of multiple contradictions [12]. In spite of the fact that Altshuller himself evoked these problems, the convergence towards a relevant contradiction was only rarely addressed. In the software proposals where partial TRIZ elements can be found, some attempts at listing problems were made, but they do not rely on the axiomatic expression of a contradiction as recommended by one of the fundamental axioms of TRIZ. Some other work are currently expressed through the research around OTSM-TRIZ [13] but up to now a pragmatic way to support, operate and compute these problems is still not published in international peer reviewed journal or conference.

## 4.  Conclusions and further works

It has been observed, through two industrial studies, that the process at the origin of this article contributes to the formalization of inventive practices in R&D. Not only because it implements a pragmatic way to operate the fundamental of TRIZ, but also by the fact that such a computerization is likely to facilitate the adoption of new practices in companies. It remains however many axes in which further research is necessary. Among those, the formalization of organizational procedures to be integrated and adapted to companies typologies, customized to initiate an evolution of their design practices. Another one is the adaptation of Artificial intelligence techniques to automatically capture in texts, necessary knowledge to the gathering of contradictions in specific fields [14]. Our approach therefore has perspectives to evolve, compared to its first data-processing presented versions. We also note that it appears legitimate in the long term, to observe its output interfaced with the traditional CAD tools [15]. But there is still a consequent a gap to be filled prior to this. The one which separates an emitted inventive concept in a theoretical form and the necessary whole set of elements provoking its morphological characterization.

# References

1.  Coates J.F.: Technological Forecasting and Social Change, 64(2-3), pp. 121-32 (1996).
2.  Chen Z.: Knowledge-Based Systems, 12(7), pp. 333-39 (1996).
3.  Forgionne G., Newman J.: Decision Support Systems, 42(4), pp. 2126-36 (1996).
4.  Bink M.L., Marsh, R.L.: Review of General Psychology, 4(1), pp. 59-78 (1996).
5.  Treffinger D.J., Selby E.C., Isaksen S.G.: Understanding individual problem-solving style: A key to learning and applying creative problem solving, Learning and Individual Differences, in Press (2007).
6.  Cavallucci D., Rousselot F.: Structuring knowledge use in Inventive Design, 2nd IFIP Working Conference on Computer Aided Innovation. Michigan, Springer, USA (2007).
7.  Cavallucci D., Eltzer T.: Improving the Relevance of R&D's Problem Solving Activities in Inventive Design Context, 16th International Conference on Engineering Design, ICED'07, Ecole Centrale Paris, Paris, France (2007).
8.  Altshuller G.S.: Creativity as an axact science. The Theory of the Solution of Inventive Problems, Gordon and Breach Science Publishers (1984).
9.  Salamatov Y.P.: System of the Laws of Technical Systems Evolution Chance to adventure, vol. 5, pp. 7-174, Karelia Publishing House, Petrozavodsk, (1991).
10. Cavallucci D., Khomenko N., Morel 15th International CIRP Design Seminar, p. 10, Shanghai, China (2005).
11. Zanni C., Rousselot F.: Towards the Formalization of Innovating Design: The TRIZ example, KES2006- 10th International Conference on Knowledge-Based & Intelligent Information & Engineering Systems, Bournemouth, UK (2006).
12. Pinyayev A.: Transition from the administrative contradiction to the technical one in the analysis of inventive problems (1990).
13. Khomenko N., Ashtiani M.: Classical TRIZ and OTSM as a scientific theoretical background for non-typical problem solving instruments, 7th ETRIA TRIZ Future Conference, Frankfurt, Germany (2007).
14. Tseng Y.-H., Lin C.J. Lin Y.I.: Information Processing & Management, 43(5), pp. 1216-47 (1996).
15. Cavallucci D. Leon N.: Towards "inventiveness-oriented" CAI tools, WCC 2004 (IFIP 18th World Computer Congress), pp. 441-52, Kluwer Academic Publishers, Toulouse, France (2004).

# How an ontology can infer knowledge to be used in product conceptual design

**David Cebrian-Tarrason** [1] **and Rosario Vidal** [2]

[1] Engineering Design Group (GID) - Department of Mechanical Engineering and Construction. Universitat Jaume I, Spain, dcebrian@uji.es
[2] Engineering Design Group (GID) - Department of Mechanical Engineering and Construction. Universitat Jaume I, Spain, vidal@emc.uji.es

**Abstract:** In the past years, great advances have been made in the development of ontologies applied to the field of engineering design, essentially in functional and structural models. OntoFaBeS is an ontology whose objective is to formalize the knowledge about a product in order to infer different structures of that product from functional requirements set by the user. Hence, an effective tool capable of assisting the designer in the rational design phase is created. OntoFaBeS does not only provide the product redesign, but also allows for the evaluation of the different design alternatives created. OntoFaBeS can also capture the knowledge obtained from queries. This knowledge may be represented later in a CAE system. In order to illustrate the operation of OntoFaBeS, a mechanical pencil is used as an application example. This allows for a thorough assessment of the ontology design, wherein a query proves the ontology's ability to infer knowledge.

**Keywords:** Ontology, conceptual design, FBS, OntoFaBeS

## 1. Introduction

The end goal of Engineering Design is the conceptual creation of an object, product, system or process that meets functional requirements in order to fulfill the customer's needs in a workable, economical, ecological and manufacturable way. The development of technologies based on artificial intelligence and CAE (Computer Assisted Engineering) has facilitated access to information related to the structure and form of objects, although design know-how used in the conceptual design phase remains hidden due to its subjective nature and implicitness [1].

The development of KBE (Knowledge-Based Engineering) systems is aimed at improving this aspect [2, 3]. Nonetheless, the full use of these technologies is limited by the impossibility of fully reusing and sharing knowledge in KBE

*Please use the following format when citing this chapter:*

Cebrian-Tarrason, D. and Vidal, R., 2008, in IFIP International Federation for Information Processing, Volume 277; *Computer-Aided Innovation (CAI)*; Gaetano Cascini; (Boston: Springer), pp. 57–68.

systems, along with the lack of common knowledge from which to create a knowledge base and the limited success of methodologies for the extraction of knowledge [4, 5].

In the field of engineering design, more and more attention is being focused on the development of ontologies as a possible solution of the aforementioned deficiencies of KBE systems. This progress includes knowledge sharing and the development of a standard engineering language. One development of particular interest is to provide a structured basis for navigating, browsing and searching information through the hierarchical descriptions of the ontology [6, 7].

An ontology can be described as an explicit specification of a shared conceptualization, which can be taxonomically or axiomatically based [8]. Ontologies can be based around a single taxonomy or several taxonomies and their relationships [9]. Taxonomies consist of concepts and relationships that are organized hierarchically and whose concepts can be arranged as classes with subclasses [10, 11].

The structure of an ontology should be based on a taxonomy that allows for the modeling of a system based one certain functional descriptions [12]. In this way, a great diversity of methodologies for analysis of design process based on the FBS (Function-Behavior-Structure) framework have been modeled [13-16].

Notwithstanding, Suh [17] describes design as a zigzag between functional requirements and design parameters and Veyrat [18] questions whether design is actually a direct mapping between functions and structure. In order to resolve this question, we combine the concept of the OntoRFB (ontologically clean Functional Basis), Garbacz [12] based on DOLCE (Descriptive Ontology for Linguistic and Cognitive Engineering) [19] and the model B-FES (Behavior-driven Function-Environment-Structure) [20, 21] and create a new ontology with special emphasis on the importance of behavior as the link in the FBS framework.

The purpose of this paper is the design of an ontology for the formalization of knowledge about a product, in order to infer different structures of that product from functional requirements set by the user, with the objective that knowledge can be reused and shared between different applications.

The paper is organized as follows. The next section briefly overviews the different approaches to the FBS framework. On the basis of the ontology that is being proposed, ontologies for Engineering Design are discussed in detail in section 3. Section 4 broadly describes the FBS framework of OntoFaBeS and a skeletal plant of the structure of the OntoFaBeS ontology. In order to illustrate the function of OntoFaBeS, a mechanical pencil is used as an example in section 5. Section 6 discusses this work, followed by concluding remarks.

## 2. FBS framework

Though the terms function, behavior and structure had been used before, it wasn't until 1990 that they were clarified and used to define a framework to model and represent system functionality [13, 22]. In the FBS framework (Function-Behavior-Structure), function represents the functions that the system performs; structure represents the physical elements of the solution and behavior acts as the relationship between F and S. In design synthesis, behavior is derived from an intended functionality in order to reach a solution from it. When a solution is defined, its behavior is deduced from it to evaluate if the solution reaches the intended functionality. Then, behavior is related to the design physical state, which may be static or variable with time.

The FBS framework can also be used as a methodology for analyzing the design process, through the representation of the evolution of design state from the analysis of design protocols [23].

Roughly speaking, two approaches to FBS can be distinguished [24]. In the first, one relates functions to behaviors of an element, and then relates these behaviors to structural-physical descriptions of the elements. In the second approach, one models functions of objects in terms of inputs and outputs, and then relates these functions directly to structural-physical descriptions of objects (e.g. [25]).

The first approach was developed by Gero [22], who proposed a Function-Behavior-Structure model of designing, and by Umeda et al. [13], who proposed a Function-Behavior-State model of designing. The second approach is known as the Functional Modeling approach which considers behavior as the mathematical representation of the states of a device [14, 26-28].

We will focus on the first approach since it considers behavior as a key concept that suggests a clear ontological ordering: technical objects have their physical structure. This structure, in interaction with a physical environment, gives way to the objects' behaviors; and these behaviors then determine in some way the objects' functions [15].

Several investigations have been developed with respect to this approach. Mizoguchi et al. [1] use the FBRL (Function and Behavior Representation Language) model based in the work of Sasajima et al. [29] and expresses behavior as a conceptualization of the change of attribute values in the spatio-temporal space over time. Also, they consider that function is a teleological interpretation of behavior under a given goal.

The possibilities of search, exploration, combination and selection systems based on FBS representation have increased thanks to the B-FES model proposed by Tor et al. [21, 30, 31]. This model is an extension and a refinement of the dual-step function environment-behavior-structure (FEBS) modeling framework by

Deng et al. [32]. This model has been chosen by the authors because it maintains a clear ordering, which permits the establishment of direct relationships between function, behavior and design. However, structure is only considered on a superficial level.

After reviewing the above research efforts, it is evident that there is no integrated approach to modeling and a lack of a stable conceptual framework [33]. This is occurs mainly with respect to the concept of behavior. For example, Vermaas [34] indicates that the Functional Modeling approach does not manage to achieve an efficient relationship between those structures whose behavior is necessary in order to link with the function area. In the same way, in these situations behavior is partially subjective because depends on the designer [15]. Borgo et al. [15] formalizes behavior in order to consider it as 'a relationship between the object and the event in which it participates'. This analysis is carried out within the framework of the DOLCE ontology [19].

## 3. Ontologies in Engineering Design

In this section, we briefly discuss ontologies in the domain of engineering design. Generally, ontologies can be categorized by the subject of the conceptualization [35], among others:

**Top-level ontologies or Upper-level ontologies** describe very general concepts (e.g. substance, tangible, intangible) and provide general notions under which all root terms in existing ontologies should be linked.

**Domain ontologies** are reusable in a given specific domain (engineering, manufacturing, design, etc). These ontologies provide vocabularies about concepts within a domain and their relationships, the activities taking place in that domain, and the theories and elementary principles governing that domain.

**Task ontologies** describe the vocabulary related to a generic task or activity (e.g. diagnosing, scheduling). They provide a systematic vocabulary of the terms used to solve problems associated with tasks that may or may no belong to the same domain.

**Application ontologies** are application-dependent. They contain all the definitions needed to model the knowledge required for a particular application. Application ontologies often extend and specialize the vocabulary of the domain and of task ontologies for a given application.

In the domain of engineering design, such ontologies can be categorized into task ontologies and domain ontologies. As one of the principal ontologies of the Semantic Web, DOLCE is an upper-level ontology related to the area of engineering design. Thus, the goal of DOLCE is to provide a common reference framework for ontologies in order to facilitate sharing of information among them.

In its representation, DOLCE aims at capturing ontological categories underlying natural language and human common-sense [19]. Thus, OntoFaBeS uses DOLCE as a common upper-level ontology in order to alleviate the integration problem. This kind of action is a frequent approach in ontological engineering [7].

Based on an extensive study of different design theories, Garbacz [12] puts forward the OntoRFB, a taxonomy of artifact functions based on DOLCE and on RFB [36], analyzed from a perspective of philosophical logic. Table 1 illustrates the actions of OntoRFB taxonomy.

Table 1 Actions of OntoRFB taxonomy.

|  | Spatial Location | Topological conectedness | | Energy |
|---|---|---|---|---|
| Quale region | Locate | Connect | Branch | Energate |
| Achieve | Reach | Touch | Split | Switch |
| Accomplish | Channel | Attach | Disjoin | Load |
| Mantain | Moor | Join | Cleave | Conserve |
| Process | Move | Bind | Carve | Energize |

Gero, who improved his former study of FBS representation, establishes the basis for the computational modeling of process to support the design process based on the FBS representation [37]. He also developed the term "FBS Ontology" to refer to his model, although he did not develop a taxonomy, taking into account its own definition.

Engineering Design Integrated Taxonomy (EDIT) [8] consists of several taxonomies and their relations. As the integrated taxonomy is populated with instances, the relationships between concepts (or multiple concepts) are captured and the ontology emerges. Ahmed developed the EDIT ontology for the purpose of indexing, searching and retrieving design knowledge.

The DO (Design Ontology) is related to this work. Storga et al. [38] created the DO as a potential formal description of the shared engineering knowledge in design domain. Along these lines, Ahmed and DO created a comparison between both, where the DO is described as ontology conceived to describe design as a product. On the other hand, the EDIT was established design as an activity, incorporating the process as well as the product [8].

The majority of design ontologies that have been reviewed were mainly designed to facilitate knowledge sharing through well-defined ontological definitions. Applicability of ontologies for specific applications either remains unknown or they demonstrate their findings with very simple examples also known as "toy examples" [33]. That is, those consulted were not based on empirical research and therefore it is not possible to assess whether the ontology or taxonomy would be intuitive when used to index design knowledge [8]. The ontology developed by Kitamura et al. [39-41] is the only one that manages to develop a domain ontology and apply it to a practical example by means of the

SOFAST® program. However, the complexity of Kitamura's model makes its practical application difficult [41].

There exists a great diversity of languages for ontology representation, although the most frequently used is the OWL (Ontology Web Language). Nonetheless, the majority of ontologies developed in this field do not make use of this standard language. OWL language allows for the use of logic, particularly in the form of predicate logic (also known as first-order logic), which allows for the inference of new knowledge by means of a query based on reasoning [12]. However, only the AsD ontology [42] makes use of this application to the area of manufacturing, and is also the only one to link the results of the ontology with a CAD program.

In conclusion, current ontologies in engineering design have certain failures. The lack of a diverse application of the concept of ontology within the FBS framework, the lack of practical examples on an industry level, the lack of homogeneity or the superficial application of the capacities of an ontology are all issues to consider. In the following section, by means of OntoFaBeS, we will propose an attempt to resolve these problems.

## 4. OntoFaBeS

In this section, we introduce OntoFaBeS, an ontology which formalizes the knowledge about a product in order to infer different structures of that product from functional requirements set by the user, with the objective that knowledge is reused and shared between different applications.

OntoFaBeS is a domain ontology partly based on the B-FES modeling framework [21, 30]. It has been adapted to facilitate its modeling as an ontology. OntoFaBeS acquires its formal framework from the primitive notions defined in the DOLCE ontology [19], developed using the Protégé tool [43] and written in OWL, the standard ontology language.

The characteristics of OntoFaBeS have been defined with respect to its framework, function layer, behavior layer, structure layer and knowledge inference.

**Framework**

First, the connections between function and behavior were established, and then the connections between behavior and structure (Figure 1). The objective was to create a simple distribution. In part, this allowed for the construction of the taxonomy, while also facilitating the creation of logical rules upon the creation of the ontology.

**Function Layer**

The definition of the concept function (F) was established as the inherent action of the design that is being processed. As a result, actions carried out by elements as independent units outside of the design environment were excluded (e.g. the action carried out by a screw in an object is not a function). In this ontology design, the possibility of defining functions with natural language was considered, as well as the option than an object could have more than one function.

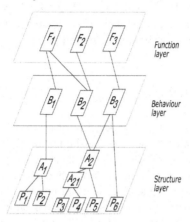

Figure 1 OntoFaBeS framework.

**Behavior Layer**

A new perspective was established, based on the definition made by Borgo [16], by considering the actions in Table 1 as behaviors. The behavior (B) is tied to an action with respect to an element. In the aforementioned taxonomy, the proposed classification of actions is always linked to an element constituent of part of the structure.

**Structure Layer**

A layer dedicated exclusively to structure was considered. It was organized in such a way that the elements of the structure phase could be linked with each other and with the behavior layer, taking into account the difference between parts (P) and assemblies (A). Since the proposed model could be made up of a large number of elements, the bases of modular design [44] were incorporated in order to optimize the assembly phase.

Thus, each part of an object, as part of a structure, has an implicit relationship with other parts or assemblies.

**Knowledge Inference**

Once the content is stored in the ontology, OntoFaBeS could capture the knowledge obtained from queries in order to directly relate the functions with the structure that would fulfill the requirements. This would allow the structures resulting from a java application to be represented later in a CAE system through an interface, after giving the program the necessary parameters to define the dimension of the parts. From the relationships created by the ontology, we can determine which elements could constitute the assemblies and their corresponding parts.

In this way, OntoFaBeS achieves an integrated approach to the FBS model due to its clarity, solid structure and simplicity. The use of a limited table of behaviors results in a detailed analysis of the knowledge that makes up the design. Also, it allows for the use of the logical bases of an ontology, by contemplating the possibility of inference. This creates great flexibility for considering different options, not contemplated or directly restricted.

## 5. Mechanical Pencil

A practical example has been considered in order to demonstrate the capacity of the use of an ontology as a base for translating the FBS scheme. It is the same example as previously employed by Gershenson [45]. It consists of a basic example, of which a detailed list of functions, behavior and structure is available.

A mechanical pencil is a metallic, wooden or plastic instrument that contains leads and is used for writing. It consists of a mechanism made up of four modules: Sleeve/Tip, Clutch/Teeth, Barrel and Cap. (Figure 2)

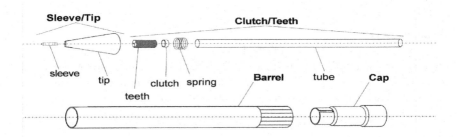

Figure 2 Mechanical Pencil.

The pencil is thus made up of the following elements: barrel, cap, clutch, sleeve, spring, tip, teeth and tube.

By establishing the FBS scheme for this example, we find that the function of the pencil is: write. According to the organization established by OntoRFB taxonomy [12], the behavior of the mechanical pencil with respect to the function write is to carve. We must also consider that the constituent elements are made up by the aforementioned four modules.

Each module of the example has the following behaviors:

- **Barrel Assembly:** *locate* (contains the leads within the pencil) and *touch* (allows for the pencil to be held)
- **Pencil mechanism (Clutch/Teeth Assembly):** *attach* (holds the lead) and *channel* (it channels the lead out of the pencil).

- o **Spring:** *move* (by offering resistance and allowing for the gradual advance of the pencil lead)
- o **Clutch:** *touch* (allows for the pencil to be held)
- o **Teeth:** *attach* (holds the lead)
- o **Tube:** *moor* (supports the lead so that it can be propelled by the spring)
- **Cap:** branch (allows the clutch to be propelled forward).
- **Pencil tip (Sleeve/Tip Assembly):** *attach* (holds the lead) and *reach* (the lead reaches the paper)
- **Pencil lead**[1]: carve (it erodes upon contact with the paper)

A behavior that describes the union of all the elements is *connect*, which establishes relationships between the elements that make up an assembly (e.g. cone *connects* spring). This lets us establish one of the essential logical rules established by the ontology, which will allow for the inference of knowledge.

These are the behaviors that allow the mechanical pencil to fulfill its function, to write. Nonetheless, these behaviors when linked to other elements can, in turn, lead to other functions. For example the *tube*, with different dimensions can be used in another design to conduct water, maintaining the same behavior but linking to completely different functions. These other functions can be fulfilled by other elements, which is how the inference of information is carried out by OntoFaBeS.

These are the behaviors that allow the mechanical pencil to fulfill its function, to write, since with the knowledge acquired by the ontology, it is concluded that the main part is the *pencil lead* and it must be connected to the next assemblies: *cone/tip*, *clutch/teeth*, *barrel* and *cap*.

Nonetheless, a behavior when is linked to other elements of a design can, in turn, link to completely different functions maintaining the same behavior. These other functions can be carried out with the help of other elements, which is how the inference of information is carried out by OntoFaBeS. For example the *tube*, with different dimensions can be used in another product design as a pipe. In that case, it would maintain the same behavior, *to moor*, but would be linking to the function *to channel water*. Thus, the product would also need a water pump in order to fulfill that function.

Finally, a query can be carried out from which the user can determine directly the indicated structure (Figure 3).

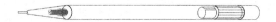

Figure 3 Mechanical Pencil inferred.

---

[1] The pencil lead has not been considered as a constituent of the pencil, since it is a consumable.

# 6. Conclusion

We have introduced OntoFaBeS as an intent to unify the existing criteria in the field of methodologies based on the FBS framework. This study illustrates the design of an ontology formally based on the B-FES [30] and whose formal framework is based on the upper ontology DOLCE [19], providing a novel approach that is centered on design behaviors.

This work opens up a new perspective in the field of design engineering methodologies. OntoFaBeS takes advantage of the formalization of knowledge in ontologies, that is, the evolution of knowledge based engineering [4, 45]. This results in a series of advantages that until now had not been dealt with in depth in the field of engineering design, such as the automatic inference of new knowledge.

It is interesting to note that OntoFaBeS deduces the knowledge necessary for the production of objects, based exclusively on the requirements established by the consumer. This also demonstrates that the great majority of ontologies existing in the field of engineering design are essentially taxonomies that give little importance to formal logic and the possible inference of new knowledge.

The results of this study are not surprising however, if we take into account that OntoFaBeS contemplates a novel focus on behavior within the FBS framework. Nonetheless, a great deal of knowledge is necessary on behalf of the designer in order to establish the relationships correctly. For this reason, the improvement of OntoFaBeS is under development. Also, a wider scope of actions is being considered, as well as a deeper analysis of the development of the functional layer.

The proposed example of a mechanical pencil demonstrates the importance of the appropriate definition of the three layers that constitute the FBS framework when it comes to constructing the ontology. This allows for the successful establishment of the information queries. This is especially in the behavior area, due to its role as the link between function and structure. It is important to note that the simplicity of the example was intentional, as the initial application of a new concept.

In future investigations, we intend to apply this model on an industrial level by means of its use on an existing design. Work is also being carried out to develop the ontology in order to apply it to areas outside of engineering design. At this time, OntoFaBeS is being adapted to encompass other aspects of the design phase, such as environmental aspects.

# References

1.Kitamura Y., Mizoguchi R.: Ontology-based systematization of functional knowledge. Journal of Engineering Design, 15/4, pp. 327-351 (2004).
2.Cebrian-Tarrason D., Muñoz C., Chulvi V., Vidal R.: Nuevo Enfoque En El Diseño Inteligente De Implantes Craneales Personalizados A Través De KBE. XI Congress International of Project Engineering, Lugo, Spain (2007).

3.Chulvi V., Sancho A., Cebrian-Tarrason D., Jiménez R., Muñoz C., Vidal R.: Knowledge-Based Engineering in cranioplasty implant design. Proceedings of the 16th International Conference on Engineering Design (ICED'07), Paris (2007).

4.Mizoguchi R.: Tutorial on ontological engineering. New Generation Computing, Part 1, pp. 365-384 (2003).

5.Baxter D., Gao J., Case K., Harding J., Young B.: An engineering design knowledge reuse methodology using process modeling. In: Research in engineering design, pp. 18, 37-48 (2007).

6.Ahmed S., Wallace K.: Reusing Design Knowledge. 14th CIRP Design Seminar, Cairo (2004).

7.Ahmed S., Kim S., Wallace K.: A methodology for creating ontologies for engineering design. Journal of computing and information science in engineering, 7/2, pp. 132-140 (2006).

8.Gruber T.R.: Toward Principles for the Design of Ontologies Used for Knowledge Sharing, K.A. Publishers. In Knowledge Systems Laboratory, Stanford University, Padova, Italy (1993).

9.Cottam H, Milton N., Shadbolt N.: The Use of Ontologies in a Decision Support System for Business Process Re-engineering, Information Technology and Knowledge Re-Engineering. Journal of the Austrian Computing Society, Vienna, Budapest (1998).

10.Gilchrist A.: Thesauri, taxonomies and ontologies - an etymological note. Journal of Documentation. 59/1, pp. 7-18.

11.Antoniou G., Harmelen F.: A semantic web primer, The MIT Press, Cambridge, Massachusetts (2003).

12.Garbacz P.: Towards a standard taxonomy of artifact functions. Applied Ontology, 1/3, pp. 221-236.

13.Umeda Y., Takeda H.: Function behavior, and structure. Applications of Artificial Intelligence in Engineering, vol. V, pp. 177-194 (1990).

14.Wood K.L., Greer J.L.: Function-Based Synthesis. In Methods in Engineering Design, pp. 170-227 (2001).

15.Borgo S., Carrara M., Vermaas P.E., Garbacz P.: Behavior of a technical artifact: An ontological perspective in engineering. Frontiers in Artificial Intelligence and Applications. 150 (Formal Ontology in Information Systems), pp. 214-225 (2006).

16.Umeda Y., Takeda H.: Development of design methodology for upgradable products based on function-behavior-state modeling. Artificial Intelligence for Engineering Design. Analysis and Manufacturing (AI EDAM), vol. 19, pp. 161-182 (2005).

17.Suh N.P.: The principles of design, Oxford University Press, New York (1990).

18.Veyrat N., Blanco E., Trompette P.: When Shape Does Not Induce Function: Why Designers Must Not Lose The Big Picture. 16th International Conference on Engineering Design, Paris (2007).

19.Masolo C.: WonderWeb Deliverable D18. Laboratory For Applied Ontology - ISTC-CNR. (2003).

20.Zhang W.Y., Tor S.B., Britton G.A.: FuncDesigner a functional design software system. The International Journal of Advanced Manufacturing, vol. 22, pp. 295-305, (2006).

21.Zhang W.Y., Tor S.B., Britton G.A.: A graph and matrix representation scheme for functional design of mechanical products. The International Journal of Advanced Manufacturing Technology, vol. 25(3-4), pp. 221-232 (2005).

22.Gero J.: Design prototypes: A knowledge representation schema for design. AI magazine. Vol. 11(4), pp. 26-36 (1990).

23.Takeda H., Yoshioka M., Tomiyama M., Shimomura Y.: Analysis of design processes by function, behavior and structure. The Delft Protocols Workshop, conference proceedings (1994).

24.Camelo D.: Modelado y desarrollo de un modelo computacional de síntesis interactivo y multirrelacional para guiar la actividad de diseño en la fase conceptual. PhD Thesis. University Jaume I (2007).

25.Chandrasekaran B.: Representing function: Relating functional representation and functional modeling research streams. AIEDAM. vol. 19(2), pp. 65-74 (2005).

26.Pahl G., Beitz W.: Engineering design. In Design Council (1984).

27.Pahl G., Beitz W.: Engineering Design. A Systematic Approach. London, Springer (1996).

28.Szykman S., Racz J., Sriram R.: The representation of function in computer-based design. Design Engineering Technical Conferences, ASME, Las Vegas, Nevada (1999).
29.Sasajima M., Kitamura Y., Ikeda M., Mizoguchi R.: FBRL: A Function and Behavior Representation Language. Proc. of IJCAI-95. pp. 1830-1836 (1995).
30.Tor S.B., Zhang W.Y., Britton G.A.: Guiding functional design of mechanical products through rule-based causal behavioural reasoning. International Journal of Production Research. vol. 40(3), pp. 667-682 (2002).
31.Tor S.B., Britton G.A, Zhang W.Y.: A knowledge-based blackboard framework for stamping process planning in progressive die design. The International Journal of Advanced Manufacturing Technology, vol. 26, pp. 774-783 (2005).
32.Deng Y.M.: A computerized design environment for functional modeling of mechanical products. Fifth ACM symposium on Solid modeling and applications. ACM Press, Ann Arbor, Michigan (1999).
33.Vermaas P.E., Dorst K.: On the conceptual framework of John Gero's FBS-model and the prescriptive aims of design methodology. Design Studies. vol. 28(2), pp.133-157 (2007).
34.Vermaas P.E.: The Functional Modelling Account of Stone and Wood: Some Critical Remarks. Proceedings of the 16th International Conference on Engineering Design, Paris (2007).
35.Gómez-Pérez A., Fernández-López M., Corcho O.: Ontological Engineering with examples from the areas of Knowledge Management, e-Commerce and the Semantic Web. Springer (2004).
36.Hirtz J., Stone R.B., McAdams D.A., Szykman S., Wood K.L.: A functional basis for engineering design: Reconciling and evolving previous efforts. Research in Engineering Design, vol. 13, pp. 65-82 (2002).
37.Gero J.S. and Kannengiesser U.: The situated function-behavior-structure framework. Design Studies, vol. 25(4), pp. 373-391 2004.
38.Štorga M., Andreasen M.M., Marjanović D.: Towards a formal design model based on a genetic design model system. Proceedings of the 15th International Conference on Engineering Design ICED 05. Melbourne, Australia (2005).
39.Kitamura Y., Mizoguchi R.: An ontology-based annotation framework for representing the functionality of engineering devices. In ASME 2006, Pennsylvania, USA (2006).
40.Kitamura Y. Mizoguchi R., Ontology-based description of functional design knowledge and its use in a functional way server. Expert Systems with Applications, vol. 24(2), pp. 153-166 (2003).
41.Ookubo M., Koji Y., Sasajima M., Kitamura Y., Mizoguchi R.: Towards Interoperability Between Functional Taxonomies Using An Ontology-Based Mapping, Proceedings of the 16th International Conference on Engineering Design, Paris (2007).
42.Kim, K.-Y., Manley, D.G., Yang, H.: Ontology-based assembly design and information sharing for collaborative product development. Computer-Aided Design, vol. 38(12) pp. 1233-1250 (2006).
43.Protégé 3.3.1., http://protégé.Stanford.edu. Stanford University. (2008).
44.Gershenson, J.K., Prasad, G.J., Allamneni, S.: Modular Product Design: A Life-Cycle View. Journal of Integrated Design & Process Science, vol. 3, pp.13-26 (1999).
45.Gero, J.S.: AI EDAM at 20: Artificial intelligence in designing,  Cambridge Univ Press (2007).

# Developing DA Applications in SMEs Industrial Context

**Giorgio Colombo[1], Dante Pugliese[1], and Caterina Rizzi[2]**

[1] Politecnico di Milano, Italy, giorgio.colombo@polimi.it
[2] Università Degli Studi di Bergamo, Italy, caterina.rizzi@unibg.it

**Abstract:** This paper discusses aspects related to the implementation of Design Automation applications within Small Medium Enterprises (SMEs) industrial context. It focuses the attention on some characteristics of the design process in SME context, and highlights issues of DA in relation to the characteristics previously evidenced. On this basis, it has been defined a methodology, named MEDEA (Methodology per Design Automation), to develop DA applications; it proposes a step by step roadmap and suggests methods and tools finalized to developers more skilled on products and design process than on IT technologies. Two industrial applications realized to evaluate the methodology are then presented. They are based on two different approaches: the first suitable to represent product structure and derived from Object Oriented programming and the second based on design process representation.

**Keywords:** Design Automation, Knowledge-based Engineering, SMEs, Knowledge representation, PDM/PLM

## 1. Introduction

In this paper we discuss aspects related to the implementation of Design Automation (DA) in industrial context, in particular within Small Medium Enterprises (SMEs) domain. This interest is justified by two considerations: first, we consider DA an important tool to effectively innovate and improve design procedures and, secondly, SMEs are the most interesting domain for this type of methodology, particularly in Europe where they constitute the main productive tissue.

DA can be defined as a set of methods, tools and applications that permit to automate the design process; it can be applied to all the phases of the process, from the conceptual to final one related to the production of technical documentation. However, in our opinion, it well fits the detailed design phase during which a technical solution is completely formalized. In particular, main

*Please use the following format when citing this chapter:*

Colombo, G., Pugliese, D. and Rizzi, C., 2008, in IFIP International Federation for Information Processing, Volume 277; *Computer-Aided Innovation (CAI)*; Gaetano Cascini; (Boston: Springer), pp. 69–82.

benefits from a DA application can be achieved when dealing with products and parts characterized by a well defined architecture and design process. Some examples of products falling within this category are heat exchangers, gears, machine tools and so on.

DA history matches with IT one; first applications were developed with general purpose programming languages and concerned specific aspects of design process such as kinematic analyses and synthesis. A remarkable improvement was gained when CAD techniques was developed. The integration between CAD models and programming languages permitted the development of automatic procedure to configure parts and simple products [1]. This approach was enhanced by the development of parametric CAD [2]; a lot of applications to configure parts and products have been developed by using parametric models and programmable tools such as spreadsheet. In SMEs this is actually one of more diffuse method to develop simple DA applications. The described DA evolution is "design oriented" and not focused on IT.

In fact, at the same time, a number of methods and tools derived from Artificial Intelligence appeared; in particular, Knowledge Based Engineering (KBE) tools based on Object-Oriented approach constitute the best approach to DA. They had a relevant impact within aeronautical and automotive companies [3] [4]. Side by side, researches on methods to acquire and formalize knowledge have been started. Knowledge formalization is a fundamental issue, and several efforts [5] have been carried out in this direction. KBE tools evolved from initial elementary implementation to the actual one characterized by programming language, powerful tools to define customized GUI and to integrate external programs (CAD systems, FE solvers, spreadsheet, data base, etc.).

Today KBE approach is the best solution to implement DA in industrial context; however its exploitation has not achieved relevant results, especially in SMEs. This is mainly due to resources and skills required to implement such a methodology.

In this paper we discuss the topics that, in our opinion, will permit a larger diffusion of DA in industrial context. We first introduce main issues related to the applications of DA concepts within SMEs domain, then a methodology, named MEDEA (MEthodology for DEsign Automation), specifically targeted to SMEs is presented as well as two case studies realized for its validation.

## 2. DA Issues within SMEs Industrial Context

In literature we can find various research works on DA methodologies [5-9] and applications [4] [10-11]. However most of them concerns big enterprises, such as automotive or aeronautical companies, characterized by a high number of skilled people and HW/SW tools, only few applications SMEs [7][11]. We adapted DA approaches to fulfill SMEs needs developing a targeted roadmap to implement KBE applications for such a context.

First, we carried out an analysis of the design processes in some SMEs to identify design situations and issues related to DA. The development of a new product is the result of two distinct sequences of activities: the first one dedicated to define and detail the product architecture and the second finalised to dimension system and parts, to choice components, to verify functional requirements. We identified two typical situations. The first one focuses on the definition of the product architecture; a family of press brakes for sheet metal bending is a typical example. The design process is centred on machine architecture and based on simple modifications of parts geometry; complex calculations are not required and some choices are based on company know-how.

In the second case the emphasis is on the design process. An example is the design of a shell-and-tube heat exchanger. The design process of such a machine starts from preliminary thermal dimensioning, continues with conceptual mechanical design and ends with detail one [12]. This articulated process requires dimensioning, standard verifications, iterations, tasks very time consuming, up to few dozen hours.

From this analysis we identify following requirements for a methodology applicable to SMEs context:

- capacity to structure product and process knowledge optimising company's design processes;
- maximize the reuse and sharing of company knowledge [13];
- integrate systems and documents within an application for product automatic configuration.

This means that a DA methodology has to deals with formalization and representation of product/process knowledge and product data management. Thus it necessary to identify and/or define proper methods and tools able to deal with above mentioned issues and affordable also by people with non specific skills on design automation, as typically happens within SMEs.

## 2.1 Product Knowledge Formalization

Several methods and tools are available in literature to represent knowledge necessary to develop a new product. They permit to formalize knowledge at different levels, capturing different aspects of the knowledge itself. In an approach based on CAD experience, the representation of product architecture is the first aspect to be considered. Gorti, S. R. et al. [14] Colombo, G. et al. [15-16] indicate Object – Oriented (O-O) approach as the most suitable and adopted technique to represent the product architecture, described usually as a tree. It approach permits to represent with a logic order the functional structure of the product and allows easily modifying, adding or deleting parts and subparts without having to heavily modify all the code. Moreover, each part or component can be considered independent each other; therefore, it is possible to consider them as small application, able to be applied to different levels of a tree structure of the same or other products, inheriting parents' characteristics.

To represent product knowledge, we propose to adopt UML Static Class Diagram (http://www.omg.org/uml). This type of diagrams represents the components and functional sub-assembly as O-O classes with associated properties and methods. It is possible to define relationships among properties of different classes, specifying the definition of the corresponding methods.

## 2.2   Process Knowledge Formalization

Typically, the development of a DA application requires a deep analysis of the design process, i.e., the acquisition of the knowledge the technical staff uses to design the considered product. This activity is particularly important for SMEs because the implementation of a DA application often requires a re-engineering activity to optimise the process itself and integrate company best practices with engineering knowledge. Business process modeling techniques, such as ARIS [17], IDEF (www.idef.com), UML (www.omg.org/uml) [18], can be used. There isn't a universal tool; the challenge is to find the right tool for the considered problem. We propose to adopt IDEF0 and IDEF 3 Process Flow (PF), even if more recent techniques, such as UML Eriksson-Penker Business Extension [18], have been developed.

Thanks to their graphic languages, IDEF0 and IDEF3 models can be easy understood and used also by people without a specific scientific background as sometimes happens within SMEs, thus facilitating the communication among work teams with different competences. This is particularly important to validate the model with process experts and to ensure that collected information has been correctly formalized in order to implement an adequate KBE application.

## 2.3   Knowledge Re-use and Sharing

This issue is particularly crucial in developing DA applications. Sainter [19] states that "the concept of project knowledge reuse and sharing is where the product knowledge can be shared within the same knowledge domain, but at different locations and allows the domain knowledge to be reused in new situations". Cheung [20] states that Knowledge Reuse is the adaptation of explicit knowledge (domain and/or strategic knowledge well formalized to be represented) of successful practices so as to generate new and useful ideas. From these definitions, we can ask ourselves what type of knowledge we can store to share and reuse. In a KBE application one can identify knowledge referred to a single part, to a product structure and to a design procedure.

The first type is referred to the elementary and structured "pills" of knowledge involved into product design; it concerns basic components that cannot be further subdivided. For example, the knowledge involved in the choice of a screw includes the rules for sizing the screw, the geometry to create it, the document to refer to, the procedure to configure the specific item (as M10 rather than M8X1.5). This pill is considered as undividable; the same approach can be extended to all the standard parts, some specific ones and sub-assemblies that can be used in different products or contexts. Number and types of the elements stored in the knowledge base depend on the KBE applications one intends to develop.

## 2.4 Integration between PDM/PLM and KBE applications

Another important aspect in the automation of the design process is the control on the definition of new parts; in fact, a KBE application must use standard or existing parts as much as possible. We think that the solution to this problem does not to rely on the definition of a local database for the specific KBE application but it should be based on the integration of the database managed by PLM/PDM system. We propose an approach that consists in defining specific coding of stored parts to make possible their automatic identification and selection. In particular, the code should represent a set of information on the specific component; i.e., the code should give information about geometry and other aspects such as assembly procedures, adaptability to a specific use, etc... A similar approach was used also in Group Technology to identify families of parts. We know that there are some problems to generalize this approach, but the present research wants to be only a first step in this direction.

## 3. MEDEA: A Roadmap for KBE Applications

On the basis of mentioned issues and our experience in this field we defined MEDEA methodology that proposes a step by step roadmap to develop KBE applications specifically targeted to SMEs. It is characterized by a reengineering activity of the design process and the use of tools more suitable to engineers than to IT experts. The possible process reengineering is related to the fact that often small enterprises have high competencies on strategic knowledge but not in domain one (standards, calculations and so on) and the development of DA application requires first integration in this direction.

At high level, the methodology is based on four main steps:

- *Specs definition*: identification of DA application specs and the criteria to make re-usable and sharable blocks of the product and process knowledge;
- *Knowledge acquisition*: collection of the knowledge related to the product architecture, the design process and the definition of the integration

strategies between the DA application and the data/document management system, such as a PDM (Product Data Management) system;

- *Knowledge formalization*: representation of product architecture (tree diagram and UML class diagram) and of the process model (IDEF0 and IDEF3 diagrams);
- *Integration with PDM/PLM system*: definition of the interactions among DA application, PDM system and end-users whose representation can be done using UML activity diagram;
- *Implementation of DA application* using a KBE system.

The choice of the KBE tools to implement the DA application depends on the considered domain. Depending on the KBE system, some activities of MEDEA cannot be carried out. In fact, some KBEs are based on process representation, others on product representation or even on a mixed product-process representation. In any case, the proposed methodology remains unchanged.

In collaboration with some Italian SMEs, MEDEA has been validated with various study cases: a shell-and-tube heat exchanger, a press brake for metal sheet, a family of industrial mixers, a spring coiling machine, and a gear box.

In the following we describe two applications: one for sheet metal brake press centered on product architecture and another one for gear box focused on process representation and integration with PDM system.

## 4. 1$^{st}$ Case Study: Sheet Metal Brake Press

This case study concerns the automation of the design process for a hydraulic press brake family characterised by a bending force up to 250 tons and bending length up to 5 meters. It has been carried out in collaboration COLGAR Spa, an Italian SME.

This is a typical example of product for which the designer selects a configuration on the basis of few parameters (e.g., bending force) and proceeds modifying parts sizes according to customers requirements.

In this case product knowledge has been acquired and formalised according to MEDEA. The product tree structure and UML static diagrams have been developed to describe relationships among parts and properties as well as design rules.

Figure 1 shows the tree structure where one can note the subdivision of the machine into three main functional sub-systems: bending group, frame and accessories & security. Figure 2 portrays a snapshot of the UML static class diagram representing the bending sub-system.

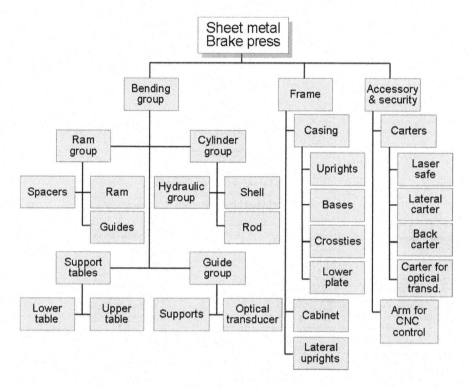

Figure 1 Tree structure of the press brake family.

The development of the DA application required the following tasks:
- definition of the press brake tree structure;
- definition of the properties of each part, sub-assemblies and complete assembly;
- rules representation;
- generation of parts and material databases;
- creation of the parametric geometric model of each part;
- automatic procedure definition;
- development of the graphical user interface.

Figure 3 shows a partial view of the tree structure implemented where each part, subassembly and assembly have been characterised by a set of parameters, geometrical, functional, and technological and so on.

All the parts, the sub-assemblies and the final assembly constituting the press brake were defined as well as their parameters; 3D parametric models of each part were modeled with a 3D CAD commercial system. The procedures that manage the complete dimensioning of the machine were represented by using the programming language of the development tool.

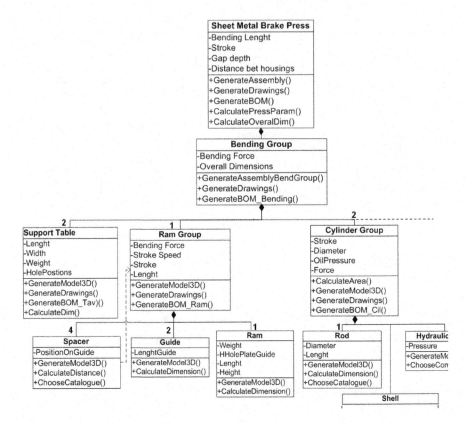

Figure 2 A partial view of the UML static class diagram for the bending group.

Figure 4 portrays the user interface to configure a brake press. The user choices a specific model (in this case PS75, with a maximum bending force of 750 kN) and, once introduced configuration parameters (bending force, bending length, distance between housing, gap depth, gap height and stroke), the application dimensions automatically all the parts and assemblies, generates 3D models, electronic BOM and 2D drawings. Figure 5 portrays the virtual prototype of a press brake produced by the application, and an example of a 2D drawing.

Summarizing, the results of the application are the correct dimensioning of parts and configuration of the entire product, the 3D CAD models and engineering drawings of each part, the EBOM (Electronic Bill of Materials) and finally cost estimation. In addition, with such an application the product development time, according to customers' requirements, has been dramatically reduced from some days to about 40 minutes.

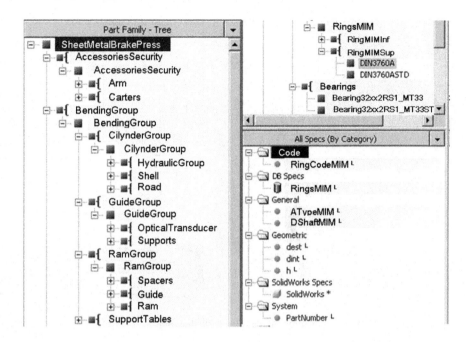

Figure 3 Tree structure implemented within DA application.

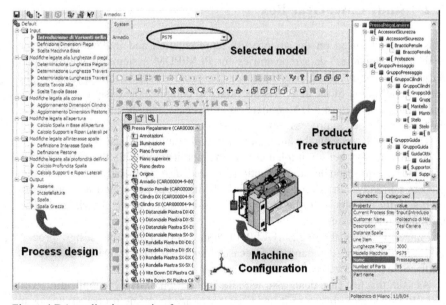

Figure 4 DA application user inteface.

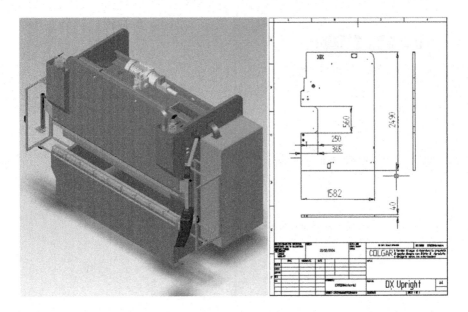

Figure 5 3D virtual model of the press and a related 2D drawings.

# 5. 2<sup>nd</sup> Study Case: Gear Box

This case is focused on design process representation and integration between KBE and companies' data repositories for PLM/PDM systems to improve part reuse process in mechanical companies. The process representation requires the software definition of the activities necessary to complete the design of a product, and the development of a DA application in this case, may be a direct mapping of the tasks evidenced in process formalization.

The test case concerns the automatic design of a family of gear box.

As previously, before implementing the application with the KBE kernel, knowledge acquisition and formalization are needed. A deep analysis of the design process currently carried out within the SME has been performed to identify for each activity the objects to be defined, the design tasks, tools, criteria and rules, information sources, etc..

Figure 6 shows the main IDEF0 diagram representing the design process followed within the company. It forecasts four main phases: Define number of shafts, Size gears, Size shafts and Size bearings.

As said, this test case deals also with the integration of the DA application with PLM/PDM system; therefore it has been necessary to define proper strategies to manage the interactions. We defined an approach based on the coding of the parts to solve this problem. The code should summarize functional information on the specific component. This method has some disadvantages due mainly to complexity and uniqueness of the code, but at the moment it seems the only reasonable approach. As an example, the following is the code used to define a specific gear (Figure 7).

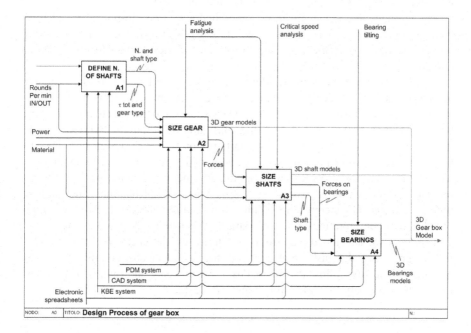

Figure 6 IDEF0 diagram representing the design process for a gear box.

ISRCMFAL50550

Figure 7 Code for a gear box.

The first four letters specify the type of gear (ISCR, cylindrical with right teeth), the two subsequent letters the fit type (MF), the two final letters the body type (AL), and, then, the teeth number, modulus and pitch diameter.

In such a way, to identify already existing parts, the KBE application can query in an automatic way company's data repositories. Moreover, such an approach makes possible to reuse previously developed specific applications.

We used as development tool a KBE system process-based. In this case, the KBE kernel of the DA application is a "master" that pilots a lot of "slaves, each of them executing a specific task. "Slaves" can be a spreadsheet, a CAD system, a FE solver, a calculus tool, a PDM/PLM module and so on.

The implemented DA application comprehends several sub-processes, each of them performing a specific design task, e.g., size bearings. These sub-processes properly manage electronic spreadsheet containing all design rules for each system components.

Figure 8 portrays the main window of the user interface where the designer introduces the main design parameters (e.g., transmission power); then the application automatically generates the code associated to the selected type of gear box, and searches for an already existing configuration within the PDM system. If it does not exist, the design procedure starts performing each design step through the execution of corresponding sub-processes and spreadsheets. The application can also proposes a standard solution but the designer can decide to accept it or go on with the definition of a new gear box. Once completed the configuration process, the system generates the 3D model of the final product. Figure 9 portrays two different configurations: one with parallel axis and another with incident axis. The applications developed can also used to train new designers. The possibility to follow gradually the task sequence and the simultaneous control of design parameters and rules allow the junior designers to easily and rapidly acquire the knowledge necessary to work within considered context.

## 6. Conclusions

The paper discusses some aspects related to development of DA application within an industrial context. It focuses the attention of some DA fundamental issues related to the main characteristics of design processes carried out by SMEs.

A methodology, MEDEA, specifically targeted to SME domain, has been presented. It covers all the aspects related to development of a DA application and proposes tools to be utilized in contexts without high-level skills and IT resources. The validation has been performed considering various case studies and the direct involvement of companies' staff more skilled in engineering than in IT technologies. This permitted to verify the effectiveness and the applicability of DA approach in SMEs. Two test cases have been described. The first has been developed applying a more classical way, and using a KBE kernel derived from the traditional approach based on Object-Oriented programming. The latter presents a new approach: the KBE tool utilized permits a direct representation of the design process. In such an application, KBE kernel has been used only to represent all the activities of the design process; the execution of these activities is left to specific slaves, implemented with different tools (CAD, spreadsheet, etc.).

Finally, we can say that DA is a tool to innovate the design process and not the product itself. Only a superficial analysis may consider an application to automate the design process of a family of products as an obstacle to innovation; but it is the better way to choice, configure and dimension parts and thus a powerful tool to obtain new technical solutions.

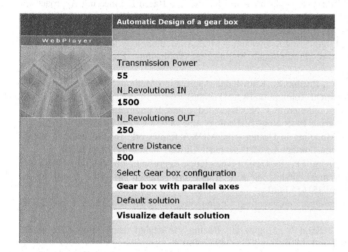

Figure 8 Application user interface.

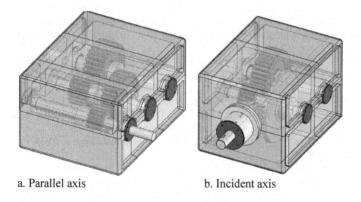

a. Parallel axis          b. Incident axis

Figure 9 Two gear box configurations.

# References

1  Choi J.C, Kim C.: A Compact and Practical CAD/CAM System for the Blanking or Piercing of Irregular Shaped-sheet Metal Products for Progressive Working. J. of Materials Processing Technology, n. 110, pp. 36-46 (2001).

2  Colombo G., Ferretti D., Cugini U.: How to Represent Design Rules in a Parametric Cad System. In: Proceedings International Symposium on Advanced Geometric Modelling for Engineering Applications, 8-9 November, Berlin, pp. 271-282 (1989).
3  La Rocca, G., Krakers L., van Tooren M.J.L.: Development of an ICAD generative model for blended wing body aircraft design. In: Proceedings 9th Symposium on multidisciplinary analysis and optimization, AIAA2002-5447 (2002).
4  Craig B., Chapman M.P.: The Application of a Knowledge Based Engineering Approach to the Rapid Design and Analysis of an Automotive Structure. Advances in Engineering Software, vol. 32, pp. 903-912, Elsevier (2001).
5  Stokes M.: Managing Engineering Knowledge – MOKA: Methodology for Knowledge Based Engineering Applications. Professional Engineering Publishing, London and Bury St Edmunds, UK (2001).
6  Pinfold M., Chapman C., Preston S.: Knowledge Application Methodology For Knowledge Based Product Development Automation (KAM) (2006).
7  Lovett P.J., Ingram A., Bancroft C.N.: Knowledge-based engineering for SMEs - a methodology. J. of Materials Processing Technology, pp. 384-389, Elsevier (2000).
8  Klein R.: Knowledge Modeling in Design - the MOKA framework. In: Proceedings of the International AI in Design Conference, JS Gero (ed), Kluwer, Worcester, MA (2000).
9  Forster J., Arana I., Fothergill P.: Re-Design Knowledge Representation with DEKLARE in: A domain model oriented, industrial KA framework applied to VT. Available at http://citeseer.ist.psu.edu/351655.html.
10 Harper A.P.: Knowledge-based engineering. Engineering Designer, vol. 25, n. 1, pp. 29-32 (1999).
11 Susca L., Mandorli F., Rizzi C., Cugini U.: Racing car design using knowledge aided engineering. AI EDAM, vol. 14, n. 3, pp. 235-249 (2000).
12 Shah R.K., Sekulic D.P.: Fundamentals of Heat Exchanger Design, John Wiley & Sons (2002).
13 Preston S., Chapman C., Pinfold M., Smith G.: Knowledge acquisition for knowledge-based engineering systems. Int. J. Information Technology and Management, vol. 4, n.1 (2005).
14 Gorti S.R., Gupta A., Kim G.J., Sriram R.D., Wong A.: An object-oriented representation for product and design processes. Computer-Aided Design, vol. 40 n. 7, Springer, pp. 489-501 (1998).
15 Colombo G., Cugini U., Pugliese D., Pulli M.: Levels of knowledge representation for Product Design. In: Proceeding International Conference on Product Lifecycle Management, Lyon, France, 11-13 July 2005 (2005).
16 Colombo G., Pugliese D.: The Role of Knowledge Management in Product Lifecycle. Innovation in Life Cycle Engineering and Sustainable Development, D. Brissaud, S. Tichkiewitch and P. Zwolinski (eds), Springer, pp. 397-406 (2006).
17 Sheer W., Abolhassan F., Jost W., Kirchmer M.: Business process excellence - ARIS in practice, Springer, Berlin (2002).
18 Eriksson H., Penker M.: Business modeling with UML. John Wiley and Sons (2000).
19 Sainter P., Oldham K., Larkin A., Murton A., Brimble R.: Product Knowledge Management within Knowledge Based Engineering Systems. In: Proceedings of ASME 2000 Design Engineering Technical Conference and Computers and Information in Engineering Conference, Baltimore, Maryland (2000).
20 Cheung P.K., Chau P.Y.K., Au, A.K.K.: Does Knowledge Reuse Make a Creative Person More Creative? In Proceeding The Ninth Pacific Asia Conference on Information Systems (PACIS-2005), Bangkok, Thailand (2005).

# Comparison of non solvable problem solving principles issued from CSP and TRIZ

**Sebastien Dubois[1], Ivana Rasovska[2], and Roland De Guio[3]**

INSA Graduate School of Science and Technology, 24 Boulevard de la Victoire, 67084 Strasbourg Cedex FRANCE, [1] sebastien.dubois@insa-strasbourg.fr, [2] ivana.rasovska@insa-strasbourg.fr, [3] roland.deguio@insa-strasbourg.fr

**Abstract:** Inventive problems from many domains are usually problems we are not able to solve. This problem insolvability is often due to the incomplete or unmatched representation model of the problem that does not correspond to the given problem. In this paper, we introduce two problem solving theories for the solutionless problems: Constraint Satisfaction Problem (CSP) and dialectical based methods and models (TRIZ). It is an exploratory analysis of both theories in order to compare grounding approach and tools of both theories. Their potential complementarities will be defined in further objective to improve problem solving strategy for the inventive problems by matching the CSP and TRIZ solving principles. We consider that it will contribute to better understanding of non-solvable problems, i.e. to improve representation models of the problems and to make the problem solving more accurately.

**Keywords:** Constraint Satisfaction Problem, Over-constrained systems, TRIZ

## 1. Introduction

Problem solving methods could be categorized in accordance with their resolution. One can recognize two kinds of problems: optimization ones, for which a solution can be found, at least theoretically, by adjustment of the value of problem parameters within the framework of a given model; and inventive problems, which requires some changes of the model of the problem in order to be solved. Among others, two different problem solving theories propose solving principles for such type of problems: constraint satisfaction problem (CSP) and dialectical based methods and models.

There are several reasons for choosing a CSP to represent and solve a problem. Firstly, set of constraints is a natural medium for people to express problems in

*Please use the following format when citing this chapter:*

Dubois, S., Rasovska, I. and De Guio, R., 2008, in IFIP International Federation for Information Processing, Volume 277; *Computer-Aided Innovation (CAI)*; Gaetano Cascini; (Boston: Springer), pp. 83–94.

many fields and is easily understood by users. Secondly, CSP algorithms are essentially very simple but can still find solution quickly. The constraint satisfaction involves finding values for problem variables subject to constraints on acceptable combinations of values [1]. Problems, where it is not possible to find valuation satisfying all the constraints, are called over-constrained. These over-constrained problems correspond to the solutionless optimization problems the solution of which requires changing the initial model of the problem. Typical CSP solving methods are designed for solving the optimisation problems; nevertheless several strategies for dealing with overconstrained problems are proposed.

TRIZ [2] is a theory designed for inventive problem resolution in technical domain, but several proposals have emerged to apply its axioms in other fields [3]. One among its main approaches for problem resolution is to state the problem in the shape of contradictions and use them for finding a contradiction free model within the framework of given objectives. An interesting point is that TRIZ propose principles for separating the contradictory properties of a situation, which leads to get satisfactory contradiction free model of problem.

We propose an exploratory analysis in order to compare grounding approach and tools of both theories and explore their mutual complementarities. In order to do so, we shall introduce concepts of representation model and solving principles will be presented; for CSP and dialectical approaches successively. Then similar points and differences of their model changing approaches will be defined and the building stones for a comparison of their solving principles will be established. A concrete example will be shown to illustrate this analysis. The evaluation of approaches for our purpose as well as ideas of their possible match will be discussed in the conclusion.

## 2. Constraint Satisfaction Problem

In this section the basic notions of CSP concerning the representation model and problem solving principles are introduced. Constraint satisfaction problems along with constraint networks have been studied in Artificial Intelligence starting from seventies. Constraint satisfaction has wide fields of applications, in areas ranging from temporal reasoning, scheduling problems, expert systems and robotics to machine vision.

### 2.1. Representation model

The basic notion of CSP theory is the constraint. It is a relation among several variables, each taking a value in a given domain. A constraint restricts the possible values that variables can take; it represents some partial information about the variables of interest. A **constraint satisfaction problem** model consists of:

- a set of variables $X=\{x_1,...,x_n\}$,
- for each variable $x_i$, a finite set $D_i$ of possible values (its domain),
- a set of constraints $C=\{c_1,...,c_k\}$ restricting the values that the variables can simultaneously take.

A **solution to a CSP** is an assignment of a value from its domain to each variable, in such a way that the constraints are satisfied all together. In our applications, variables can describe the physical system parameters while constraints may describe both relations between these parameters and given objectives. Over-constraints problems are problems the constraints of which cannot be satisfied all together.

## *2.2. CSP problem solving principles*

The traditional algorithms for constraint satisfaction are not able to solve over-constrained systems although the stochastic algorithms can maximize the number of satisfied constraints. Therefore, some alternative approaches have been proposed to solve over-constrained problems or generalize the notion of constraint respectively. We give a simple outline of these approaches:

- **Extending Constraint Satisfaction Problem** associates some valuation (usually a number) to each constraint and enables relaxing of constraints according to their preference level expressed by valuation. As the constraints in classical CSP are crisp these alternative approaches propose to enable non-crisp constraints. Examples of such method are fuzzy CSP proposing a preference level with each tuple of values between 0 and 1 [4], probabilistic CSP dealing with uncertainty in CSP [5] or weighted CSP taking into account for example the costs [6].
- **Partial Constraint Satisfaction Problem** is based on scheme of Freuder and Wallace [1] that allows the relaxation and optimization of problems via weakening the original CSP. Partial constraint satisfaction involves finding values for a subset of the variables that satisfy a subset of the constraints. The method "weakens" some of constraints by enlarging their domain in order to permit additional acceptable value combinations on a "similar" but different problem than initial given problem.
- **Constraint hierarchies** [7] describe the over-constrained systems of constraints by specifying constraints **with hierarchical preferences**. In many situations we can state required (hard) and preferential (soft) constraints. The required constraints must be hold but other constraints are merely preferences, it is tried to satisfy them as far as possible, but solutions that do no satisfy soft constraints may be generated. A constraint hierarchy consists of a set of constraints, each labelled as either required or preferred at some strength. An arbitrary number of different strength is allowed.

- **Alternative and generalized approaches** propose general frameworks to
  model features of various CSP problems. Among these approaches two approaches are the most popular. A compositional theory for reasoning about
  over-constrained systems is an extension to constraint hierarchies permitting to
  consider compositionality and incrementality in constraint logic programming
  [8]. This theory defines a scheme for composing together solutions to individual hierarchies and shows that hierarchy composition can be expressed very
  simply using multisets. The semiring-based constrained satisfaction is based on
  the observation that a semiring (that is, a domain plus two operations satisfying
  certain properties) is all what is needed to describe many constraint satisfaction
  schemes [9]. In fact, the domain of the semiring provides the levels of consis-
  tency (which can be interpreted as cost, or degrees of preference, or probabili-
  ties, or others), and two operations define a way to combine constraints together. Other way, the semiring specifies the values to be associated with each
  tuple of values of the constraint domain.

All these methods can be classified into two general principles:
- to state or evaluate preferences of the constraints or the combinations of constraints and to relax the "soft" ones (extending CSP, constraint hierarchies, alternative approaches)
- to relax the original CSP by modifying some constraints in such a way that the
  modified CSP has solutions.

For our purpose we will study these two general principles in their basic form:
constraint hierarchies and partial constraint satisfaction problem.

**Constraint hierarchies** specify hierarchical preferences of the constraints, hard
constraints are required and soft (preferential) constraints are satisfied as much as
possible. The solution of the problem is found by relaxing the soft constraints. In
constraint hierarchies [10], [7], each constraint is labelled by a preference express-
ing the strength of constraint – called **labelled constraint**. The labels can be expressed by names like required, strong, medium, weak and weakest. An arbitrary
number of different strengths is allowed. A **constraint hierarchy** H is a finite set
of labelled constraints. The set of constraints with the same label composes a
**hierarchy level** $H_j$. A valuation for the set of constraints is a function that maps
variables in the constraints to elements in the domain of variables over which the
constraints are defined. A **solution to the constraint hierarchy** is a set of valua-
tions for the variables in the hierarchy such that any valuation in the solution set
satisfies at least the required constraints.

There is a number of reasonable candidates for the predicate better, which is called
a **comparator**. The comparator formally describes the idea that satisfaction of a
stronger constraint is strictly preferred to satisfaction of an arbitrary number of
weaker constraints. A detailed summary of constrained hierarchies and the solving
algorithms can be found in [7]. In general, there are two types of special algorithms for solving constraint hierarchies: refining algorithms and local propaga-
tions.

For our purpose, we retain that this approach can only relax the soft constraints but change neither problem variables nor their domains. It is supposed that the problem is not well stated and so one can modify or in this case relax the constraints. This may be relevant in some domain applications such as planning or design where the constraints do not need to be a part of the described physical system. In this case the constraints make part of system objectives and do not describe relations in the physical system.

Contrary to the constraint hierarchies, **Partial constraint satisfaction problem** (PCSP) weakens both the constraints and the variables (their domains are enlarged) to permit additional acceptable value combinations. It involves finding values for a subset of the variables that satisfy a subset of the constraints [1]. The goal is to search a simpler problem (the representation model of the problem) we can solve. A problem space is partially ordered by the distance between the original problem and the new simpler one. A problem space is a partially ordered set of CSPs where order $\leq$ is defined the following way. Let $(sols(P)$ denotes the set of solutions to a CSP called $P$: $P1 \leq P2$ if $sols(P1)$ is a superset of $sols(P2)$. A solution to a PSCP is a problem P' from the problem space and its solution, where the distance between P and P' is less than N. If the distance between P and P' is minimal, then this solution is optimal.

Four ways to weaken a CSP [10] are possible: 1. enlarging the domain of a variable, 2. enlarging the domain of a constraint, 3. removing a variable and 4. removing a constraint. All previous cases can be considered in terms of enlarging the domain of a constraint only [1].

To solve the problem, partial constraint satisfaction problem weaken variables and constraint domains thus the representation model is enlarged. Nevertheless, PCSP does not permit to introduce a variable offering a new point of view (new dimension) to the problem and thus permitting to solve it more accurately.

# 3. Dialectical approaches

This section focus our attention on methods and models of TRIZ, a theory for inventive problem solving, based on dialectical thinking. One of the main characteristics of dialectical thinking is that it places all the emphasis on change [11]. Dialectics is looking for contradictions inside phenomenon as the main guide to what is going on and what is likely to happen. Basing evolution of systems on the elicitation, understanding and resolution of contradictions is also one of the main characteristics of TRIZ. TRIZ theory aims at understanding the way technical systems evolve and developing methods and tools for inventive technical problems solving. The principles of TRIZ have been widely applied in many domains. One of the benefits, which will be considered here, is the existence of models to represent problems and of principles to guide the change of model from a non-solvable one to a solvable one.

## 3.1. Representation models

One of the main ideas of TRIZ based theories is to identify inside systems the con-tradictions inherent to a problematic situation. In its original representation, con-tradictions, in TRIZ, are defined at three different levels:

- **Administrative contradiction**, which is the definition of a situation where an objective is given, but not satisfied.
- **Technical contradiction**, which is the expression of the opposition between two parameters of a system, when the improvement of one factor implies the deterioration of another factor.
- **Physical contradiction**, which objective is to reflect the impossible nature of the problem by identifying one parameter of the system that has to be in two different states.

Studies have been proposed to enlarge the scope of applicability of TRIZ princi-ples and methods to problems not relative to technical systems. Among these stud-ies OTSM-TRIZ proposed a description of the system of contradictions, which proposes a link between a physical contradiction and two technical contradictions. The system of contradictions is represented in bold in figure 1.

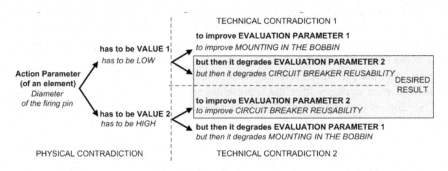

Figure 1 OTSM-TRIZ system of contradiction.

This system of contradictions is based on the existence of a physical contradic-tion and of two technical contradictions that justify the need of the two different states of the physical contradiction. The two technical contradictions are comple-mentary as they correspond to the increasing of the first parameter that implies the decreasing of the second; and of the increasing of the second parameter that im-plies the decreasing of the first. The two parameters of the technical contradictions are defined in [12] as taking part in describing the objective, they are called Evaluation Parameters, whereas the parameter of the physical contradiction is a mean to make the situation change, defined as Action Parameter.

## 3.2. TRIZ problem solving principles

As there exist different levels of problem formulation, there exist, in TRIZ different levels for problem resolution. In TRIZ one can recognize three empirical knowledge bases used to guide the model change.

- A set of 40 principles combined in a matrix is proposed to guide the model change for problems formulated as technical contradictions. For example, a principle is: segmentation (divide an object into independent parts; or divide an object into parts so that some of its part can be easily taken away; or increase the degree of object segmentation).
- A set of 11 principles is proposed to guide the model change for problems formulated as physical contradictions. For example, a principle is: separation of contradictory properties in time.
- A set of 76 rules is proposed to guide the model change for problems represented through the characterization of substances and fields interactions ("SFM" model in TRIZ terminology). For example, a rule is: If there is an object which is not easy to change as required, and the conditions do not contain any restrictions on the introduction of substances and fields, the problem is to be solved by synthesizing a SFM: the object is subjected to the action of a physical field which produces the necessary change in the object. The missing elements being introduced accordingly.

## 4. A comparison of CSP and TRIZ

This chapter will at first establish complementarities and differences between the previously defined models of problems' representation coming from CSP and from TRIZ based approaches. In a second part, the differences between the principles to solve problems and their possibilities to change the representation model of the problem will be discussed in regard of their potential complementarities to improve problem solving strategy for the inventive problems.

## 4.1. Comparison of representation model

If trying to build analogies between the two models of problem representation, of the CSP and of the system of contradiction, one can notice that problems in CSP are described by a set of variables and constraints on these variables. These constraints are of three kinds: required values for variables to satisfy the problem, domain of possible values for variables, and set of relations between the variables.

In TRIZ-based approaches, problems are modelled by two types of parameters (evaluation and action) and set of values. The evaluation parameters and their re-

quired values define the objective of resolution, whereas action parameters and
their values define means to act on the problem.

Parameters in contradictions and variables in CSP models can be matched. The
main difference between CSP and contradiction models is that, contrary to CSP,
contradiction model differentiates evaluation parameters and action parameters.
Evaluation parameters represent the desired domain for solutions and action parameters impact system and so represent the possible domain of variables. In CSP
the methods to solve problems could operate both on evaluation and action parameters.

Let us consider an electrical circuit breaker. When an overload occurs, the
overload creates a force (due to magnets and electrical field) which operates a
piece called firing pin. The firing pin opens the circuit by pressing the switch, located in the circuit breaker. In case of high overload, the firing pin, this is a plastic
stem, breaks without opening the switch. Components are presented on figure 2.

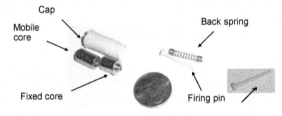

Figure 2 Components of electrical circuit breaker.

The problem has been studied and the main system parameters and their domain
have been defined as: A1: firing pin material (plastic – 1, metal – 0) ; A2: core internal diameter (high – 1, low – 0) ; A3: core external diameter (high – 1, low – 0);
A4: firing pin diameter (high – 1, low – 0) ; A5: spring straightness (high – 2,
medium – 1, low – 0) ; E1: circuit breaker disrepair (satisfied – 1, unsatisfied – 0);
E2: circuit breaker reusability (satisfied – 1, unsatisfied – 0) ; E3: spring core
mounting (satisfied – 1, unsatisfied – 0) ; E4: firing pin bobbin mounting (satisfied
– 1, unsatisfied – 0) ; E5: normal mode release (satisfied – 1, unsatisfied – 0) ; E6:
firing pin initial position return (satisfied – 1, unsatisfied – 0). The system behaviour was modelled by Design of Experiments and it is shown in table 1b.

The relations between system's parameters are described in the form of equations representing constraints in the table 1a. As example the following constraint:
"If the firing pin material is plastic then there is an irreversible degradation of the
circuit breaker" is defined as "(A1=1) => (E1=1)" in the table 1a. The objective is
to satisfy all the constraints, i.e. all evaluation parameters are equal to 1. In the table 1b we note that there is no such solution, so the problem is over-constrained.
The possible problem solving by constraint hierarchies and partial constraint satisfaction problem is shown in 4.2.

The analysis of the data by TRIZ approach leads to the identification of a set of
contradictions among which the most important has been identified by experts as

being the contradiction on the firing pin diameter, represented in italic in figure 1. This corresponds to the set of constraints in the CSP approach that could not be satisfied at the same time. So in general we are not able to solve the problem.

Since the comparison between the models is done, let tackle the comparison between the solving principles, this will be the object of the next part.

Table 1 a) Constraints for CSP model.    b) DoE for the circuit breaker example.

| Constraints |
|---|
| (A1=1) ➔ (E1=1) |
| (A1=0) ➔ (E1=0) |
| (A2=1) ◇ (A3=0) ◇ (A4=1) ➔ (E2=1) |
| (A2=0) ◇ (A4=0) ➔ (E2=0) |
| (A2>A4) ⇔ (E3=1) |
| (A3=1) ⇔ (E4=1) |
| (A5=0) ⇔ (E5=0) |
| (A5≠0) ⇔ (E6=1) |

| A1 | A2 | A3 | A4 | A5 | E1 | E2 | E3 | E4 | E5 | E6 |
|---|---|---|---|---|---|---|---|---|---|---|
| 1 | 1 | 0 | 0 | 1 | 1 | 0 | 1 | 1 | 1 | 1 |
| 0 | 1 | 1 | 1 | 1 | 0 | 1 | 0 | 0 | 1 | 1 |
| 1 | 0 | 1 | 0 | 0 | 1 | 0 | 1 | 0 | 0 | 0 |
| 1 | 1 | 0 | 0 | 0 | 1 | 1 | 1 | 1 | 0 | 0 |
| 1 | 0 | 1 | 0 | 1 | 1 | 0 | 1 | 0 | 1 | 1 |
| 0 | 1 | 0 | 1 | 2 | 0 | 1 | 0 | 1 | 1 | 1 |
| 1 | 0 | 1 | 1 | 0 | 1 | 0 | 1 | 0 | 0 | 0 |
| 1 | 0 | 0 | 0 | 1 | 1 | 0 | 0 | 1 | 1 | 1 |
| 0 | 1 | 0 | 0 | 2 | 0 | 1 | 0 | 1 | 1 | 1 |

## 4.2. Comparison of solving principles

The first element of comparison between CSP and TRIZ is the aim of each category of principles. A second element is the mechanism these principles use to transform the problem model into a solution model.

Two over-constrained solving methods issued from CSP (constraint hierarchies and PCSP) use relaxing of constraints while aiming and solving the problem. Constraint hierarchies will specify constraints with hierarchical preference and will relax soft ones. This could be done on constraints concerning the domains of both action and evaluation parameters and on constraints concerning the relations between variables. In our example, the evaluation parameters E2 and E4 described by related constraints are considered hard and E1, E3, E5 and E6 are considered soft without preferences between them. This statement of required and preferential constraints is done by experts. In this case, the equivalent solutions are coloured in grey in the table 4. The comparison of TRIZ solving principles with the constraint hierarchies leads to the conclusion that such a type of hierarchy is implicitly proposed in TRIZ. As the parameters in TRIZ are categorized into two kinds: evaluation and action ones, and as the evaluation parameters are parameters that have to be fitted to solve the problem, analogy presented in table 2 can be defined. To solve the problem in constraint hierarchies it is possible to relax action parameters as well as evaluation parameters and their constraints.

Table 2 Parallel in modelling between TRIZ and Constraint hierarchies.

| TRIZ | CSP |
|------|-----|
| Domains of Action Parameters | Soft constraints |
| Domains of Evaluation Parameters | Soft and hard constraints |

Generic principle of PCSP is the enlarging of the domain of a constraint; this principle could lead to two totally different actions. Either the enlarging of the domain will concern an action parameter; either it will concern an evaluation one. In our case, we can enlarge the domain of the evaluation parameters E5 and E6 and so the fourth line of the table 4 becomes a solution of the partial problem.

Relaxing a constraint when it concerns an evaluation parameter is something that is not admitted in TRIZ-based approaches, as it is considered changing the problem and not solving it. This is one of the main principles in CSP tools, to change the problem into a less constrained one, but then it cannot always be considered as solving the initial problem. If the problem "how to live ten days without water" is considered an over-constrained one, trying to solve the problem "how to live two days without water" is not solving the initial problem.

Relaxing a constraint when it concerns an action parameter is changing the representation of the system. This is something that can be considered in TRIZ-based approaches. Resolving the previously described example of breaking circuit with TRIZ methods leads to change the problem model. Bellow are given two methods for guiding the change of model and their possible interpretation.

1. *Separation in space: try to separate the opposite requirements in space.* The firing pin diameter is low in accordance with the bobbin diameter but high to avoid breaking. This can be done by enlarging the bobbin diameter, this means by locating the spring outside of the core.
2. *Elimination of harmful interaction by modification of existing substances. If there are a useful and harmful effects between two substances and it is not required that these substances be closely adjacent to one another, but it is forbidden or inconvenient to use foreign substance, the problem is solved by introducing a third substances (modification of the existing substances) between these two substances.* A part of the fixed core becomes movable and acts as the firing pin, thus the magnetic surface and the pin rigidity are increased. The pin has a high diameter from the fixed core to the mobile core and a low diameter but in a more resistant material from the mobile core.

The two presented rules to guide the change of model leads to the introduction in the initial model of problem representation of a new action parameter: spring location in the first case and fixed core mobility in the second one.

The table 3 summarizes the general comparison of two studied problem solving principles – TRIZ and CSP.

Table 3. Comparison of TRIZ and CSP models and methods for resolution.

| | TRIZ | CSP |
|---|---|---|
| Model of system | Action parameters<br>Link between physical and technical contradiction | Variables<br>Domains of variables<br>Constraints |
| Objective | Evaluation parameters + required values | Constraints |
| Methods to change model | Enlarge domain of action parameter<br>Introduce new action parameter | Enlarge domain of variable |
| Solved problem | Initial problem | New problem |

## 5. Conclusion and perspectives

An exploratory analysis of two different solving theories was proposed in order to compare grounding approach and tools of both theories. Now we will discuss some advantages and disadvantages of each theory according to their capacity to change the representation model of the problem for successful problem resolution.

The domain of CSP is quite well formalised by a fixed representation model. There exists a number of proved solving algorithms and quite a lot of automated CSP systems and informatics tools. On the contrary, CSP proposes only partial resolution of the problem by constraint relaxing. This means that CSP does not solve the initial problem but a new one which is sufficiently closed to the initial one. This approach does not permit to introduce a new variable. In consequence we cannot use any operator helping to pass from an actual representation model to a new one.

The TRIZ approach aims at solving the initial problem that means it allows the real change of the representation model. This approach distinguishes between action parameters and evaluation parameters and thus specifies the unchangeable objectives. Its solving principles are independent from the application domain. The big disadvantage is that there are neither formalised algorithms nor developed software tools to extract and analyse contradictions for the moment.

We consider that the match of CSP and TRIZ solving principles will contribute to better understanding of non-solvable problems. A new operator could be introduced in order to improve a CSP representation model, i.e. to pass from an old model that does not fit to a new one. Therefore the changed representation model of the problem will make the problem easier to solve by actual solving strategies. The possible strategy will be to search formal and computable CSP models which can use dialectical approaches, or conversely enrich computable CSP models by empirical data issued from dialectical approaches. The repetitive using of CSP solving strategies can help to characterize partial solutions or optimums according some criterion which is not possible in TRIZ approaches. On the contrary, CSP was not founded for inventive problems and so the model changing strategies are very basic and could be improved by TRIZ methods.

# References

1. Freuder E., Wallace R.: Partial Constraint Satisfaction, Artificial Intelligence, 58, pp. 21-70 (1992).
2. Altshuller G. S.: Creativity as an Exact Science, Gordon and Breach, New York (1988).
3. Khomenko N., De Guio R.: OTSM Network of Problems for representing and analysing problem situations with computer support, 2nd IFIP Working Conference on Computer Aided Innovation, Technical Center Brighton, Springer, USA (2007).
4. Ruttkay Zs.: Fuzzy Constraint Satisfaction in Proceedings of the 1st IEEE Conference on Evolutionary Computing, Orlando, pp. 542-547 (1994).
5. Fargier H., Lang J.: Uncertainty in constraint satisfaction problems: a probabilistic approach. In Proceedings of ECSQARU-93, pp. 97-104 (1993).
6. Schiex T., Fargier H., Verfaillie G.: Valued Constraint Satisfaction Problems: Hard and Easy Problems. In Proceedings of International Joint Conference on Artificial Intelligence, Montreal (1995).
7. Borning A., Freeman-Benson B., Wilson M.: Constraint hierarchies, LISP and symbolic computation. An International Journal, 5, pp. 223-270 (1992).
8. Jampel M.: A Compositional Theory of Constraint Hierarchies, pp. 189-206. Jampel, Freuder, Maher (Eds.), Over-Constrained Systems, Lecture Notes in Computer Science (1996).
9. Bistarelli S., Fargier H., Montanari U., Rossi F., Schiex T., Verfaillie G: Semiring-Based CSPs and Valued CSPs: Basic Properties and Comparison. Jampel, Freuder, Maher (Eds.), Over-Constrained Systems, Lecture Notes in Computer Science pp. 111-150 (1996).
10. Bartak R.: Modelling Soft Constraints: A Survey, Neural Network World, vol. 12(5), pp. 421-431 (2002).
11. Rowan J., Ordinary Ecstasy. The Dialectics of Humanistic Psychology, Brunner-Routledge (2001).
12. Eltzer T., De Guio, R.: Constraint based modelling as a mean to link dialectical thinking and corporate data. Application to the Design of Experiments, 2nd IFIP Working Conference on Computer Aided Innovation, Springer, Brighton, USA (2007).

# Engineering Optimisation by Means of Knowledge Sharing and Reuse

Olivier Kuhn[1,2,3], Harald Liese[1], and Josip Stjepandic[1]

[1] PROSTEP AG, 11 Dolivostraße Darmstadt, Germany
{Olivier.Kuhn,Harald.Liese,Josip.Stjepandicg}@PROSTEP.com
[2] LIRIS, University Lyon1, Bât Nautibus, 8 Bd Niels Bohr Villeurbanne, France
[3] LSIIT, University Louis Pasteur, Pôle API, Bd Sébastien Brant Illkirch, France

**Abstract:** Due to the increasing complexity of technical products and the decrease in product development time ("time to market") the urgent need for the optimization of cross-skill engineering collaboration demands short-term solutions. In this paper we will therefore introduce an approach to federate the established engineering tools and processes on the basis of commonly shared engineering models rather than to integrate or to harmonize them in a long-term and highly complex development process. The underlying methodology for this service oriented knowledge sharing concept will be based on a semantically enriched, formal notation for the definition of the necessary data mapping & linking between the different engineering models. Besides an introduction to this new collaboration approach this presentation will provide an overview of the state-of-the-art CA technology and artificial intelligence technologies capable to contribute to the conceptual design of a short-term solution and point out the individual shortcomings, that are currently addressed by an ongoing project at PROSTEP in collaboration with the Université Claude Bernard Lyon and the Université Louis Pasteur Strasbourg (France). The paper includes examples with the first implementation of free form deformation algorithms, artificial neuronal networks and functional DMU.

**Keywords:** Design Optimization, KBE, Conceptual Design, Multidisciplinary Simulation, Mechatronics

## 1. Introduction

The hard competition in todays markets obliges companies to reduce costs and time to market while pushing ahead with innovation. Customers demand high quality products at low prices. Therefore, the development process has to be optimized regarding not only the tools being used, but also the way of working.

*Please use the following format when citing this chapter:*

Kuhn, O., Liese, H. and Stjepandic, J., 2008, in IFIP International Federation for Information Processing, Volume 277; *Computer-Aided Innovation (CAI)*; Gaetano Cascini; (Boston: Springer), pp. 95–106.

The integration of analysis modules (workbenches) in most design systems, and therefore the emergence of simulation-driven design, has characterised the last decades.

One way to improve development process is collaborative engineering. Today several competence fields are involved in design phases and experts from these domains have to work together. This collaboration involves data exchanges, knowledge sharing and knowledge reuse. To tackle this problematic we are collaborating with LIRIS[1] laboratory in Lyon, where a team is specialised in collaborative systems and LSIIT[2] laboratory in Strasbourg where researches on data mining and evolutionnary algorithms are performed, in order to model and optimise the collaboration between experts in design phases.

Heterogeneity of data and tools is a big problem in collaboration. That can lead up to errors and is time consuming. A solution to prevent misunderstanding is to specify formally the domain where experts are working and its semantic. This can be done thanks to ontology. Ontologies are used to define concepts and relations in a domain, in our case a domain related to experts environment. They also allow reasoning among concepts to discover new relations that are not explicitly defined.

Modelling and specification of collaboration and of the domain can bring huge time benefits because information will be understandable and reachable to each participant and also reusable between experts and projects.

To push further the optimisation of collaborative work, we resort to artificial evolution. At several level in collaboration, things can be represented under graph from, for example exchanges between participants in collaborative design and for each level different objectives can be defined. A method to enhance current state of graphs is to use evolutionnary algorithms applied to graphs to get nearer from objectives.

The merge of semantically defined domain with ontology and evolutionnary algorithms is an interesting challenge which will certainly lead to an enhancement of cross-skill collaboration and thus reduce time to market and costs (see Fig. 1).

The most used approach is CAD centric. Generally, the basic CAD systems have been enhanced with Simulation modules (FEM, Multi Body Simulations etc), thereby enabling designers to perform first analyses before finishing the design models.

However, further simulation types are not yet implemented. According to most processes, CAD models are reviewed by senior designers and afterwards confirmed by the simulation department. Thus simulation engineers run analyses and make some change requests if necessary. After processing the change requests, designers have to improve the models and run further reviews, until the components are confirmed by the simulation department. Depending on some

---

[1]  http://liris.cnrs.fr/

[2]  http://lsiit.u-strasbg.fr/

factors, such as the complexity of the product to be developed, the size of the company as well as its internal organisation, many loops can be run between designers and simulation engineers.

This leads to a long product development time. Therefore, reducing the loops between these departments, through the use of analysis tools embedded in CAD tools, contributes to shortening the time to market.

These analysis tools may be used to perform first calculations and in certain cases some standard simulations, which might have been defined by the simulation department in advance.

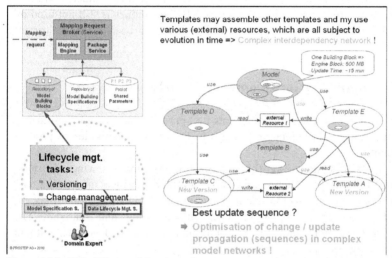

Figure 1 Model building and data mapping

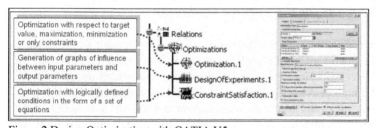

Figure 2 Design Optimization with CATIA V5

## 2. CAD Internal Analysis Tools

Examples of analysis and optimization tools embedded in design systems are the Product Engineering Optimizer workbench (Fig. 2) and the FEM-Analysis workbench of CATIA V5.

Additionally, some KBE features (Knowledge Based Engineering) can be used to perform other analyses such as automatic variation of design parameters.

Furthermore, simulation-driven design may rely on templates and processes, which might have been defined by the simulation department in advance. In these cases, designers run predefined processes in order to increase effectiveness.

However, the tools that are integrated in CAD systems are not appropriate to solve some specific problems, such as surface optimization, which plays an important role in disciplines such as aerodynamics.

In addition, these embedded tools generally have been developed in order to be run on a single machine. Therefore, it is difficult to perform some analysis without facing performance problems. This is especially the case when a designer attempts to generate a big number of variants and to evaluate them in a short time. Furthermore, the full potential of KBE techniques is still not used by these tools, although they can support designers for tasks such as variant evaluation.

## 3. Surface optimizer for Geometric Models

The optimization of technical components and products has gained significance in the last decades and belongs nowadays to the classical activities of product development.

Some application areas are the optimization of aircrafts wings in order to influence the lift, the volume optimization in the mechanical engineering and the area optimization in the automobile industry. Optimizations may be performed according to topology, form, dimensioning and material. The objective of form optimization is the deformation of a models area, without topology modification [1].

### 3.1 Requirements for the Surface Optimizer

Among other requirements at the beginning of the development of the Surface Optimizer, the quality of results and computation time were very important. In addition, its integration into the CAD environment with which designers were familiar, had a high priority. Given the fact that CAD models may be arbitrarily complex, it was necessary to use an optimization method that was independent, not only from the parameterization of the geometric model, but also from the CAD system. The concepts had to be implemented in CATIA V5.

### 3.2 Concept

The high complexity of CAD models runs hand in hand with a big number of optimization parameters. Therefore, the analysis and evaluation of the model to be optimized can be a tedious task, because the number of model parameters influences the computation time. Free-form deformation (FFD) is suitable to tackle these types of challenges, because instead of the CAD model, its surrounding space is deformed [2]. Consequently, the optimization refers to the parameters of the surrounding space.

However, free-form deformation is not an optimization method. Therefore, algorithms are needed to compute the search direction of the target value and the increment. After the evaluation of some optimization methods, the Quasi-Newton method was selected because of its integration characteristics and performance.

The objective of the optimization was the minimisation of the CAD model surface. The CAD model is then updated and visualized by users. For this purpose, special functions are used by free-form deformation to move the vertices of the grid surrounding the model [3].

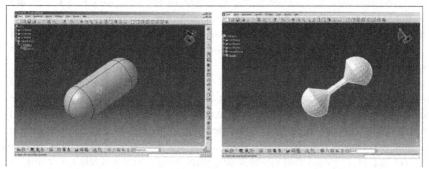

Figure 3 Generation of an object with minimal surface area according to constraints

## 3.3 Results and Integration into CATIA V5

The CATIA API (CAA) was used to integrate the surface optimizer into CATIA V5. Concerning the users interaction, the scenario consists of selecting a CAD model in the CATIA environment, fixing the areas that should be invariant during the optimization and launching the analysis. Fig. 3 illustrates an example of a simulation for which two areas (the ends) have been defined as invariant.

This solution differs from similar applications in that the optimization is not a pure mathematical variation of parameters. Instead, designers can define constraints with the interaction techniques they are used to. This is realised through the selection of areas of the model defined as invariant. Designers are therefore freed from the task of thinking about the mathematical foundations of the program before performing optimizations.

Apart from surface and volume optimization, a further application area is the packaging or enveloping of mechanical components. The principles of the optimizer may be applied to quickly derive appropriate envelopes from mechanical components or systems such as engines.

## 4. EvoCAT: Using Artificial Intelligence to Accelerate Conceptual Design

The phases of product design are planning, conceptualization, embodiment design (geometric modelling) and elaboration (detail design) [4]. Processes for the embodiment design as well as for the product elaboration phases are supported by diverse computer aided tools.However, product planning and conceptual design are still not efficiently supported.

Although diverse CAD systems have integrated optimization modules, designers still have difficulty influencing the results, especially from a design point of view.

The results that are delivered, for instance in the case of CATIA V5, are summarized in a table, whereby an end solution is presented to the user. Therefore designers have to analyse these values in order to evaluate different configurations. This task is very tedious when a large number of variants is available.

The challenge in this project consisted not only in generating variants, but also in evaluating these variants and selecting a small sample of them. This should be managed by designers. For this purpose, knowledge-based methods have been implemented in order to perform some decisions, but also in order to reduce the computation time.

EvoCAT is a system that enables designers to optimize models according to specific criteria. It makes use of evolutionary algorithms in order to support designers with optimizations in early stages of product development [5]. The capacity of evolutionary algorithms used in this case is the ability to choose an almost optimal variant from an arbitrary start population. Thus, these features of EvoCAT are suitable for generating and evaluating concepts. However, a productive use necessitated the involvement of further artificial intelligence methods.

The optimizer (EvoCAT) interacts with many CAD sessions (CATIA V5 in our case, but other systems may be used), which perform computations. Due to the large number of computations that are performed, the time that is necessary for completing optimizations is not satisfying without further adaption. Accordingly, neural networks have been implemented with the objective of taking over the job of the CAD system after a training phase. Practically, the neural network that has been implemented approximates the computations of the CAD system and enables, thereby, a reduction of the running time of EvoCAT.

### 4.1 Requirements

In fact, the aim of the main program consists in generating design variants and evaluating them in order to free designers from that task. This would be impossible to fulfil without computer support, in view of the large number of variants that are generated. Furthermore, the usability of the program is decisive.

A further requirement consists in enabling designers to use the optimization system without needing the help of a software specialist to integrate certain algorithms into the CAD system. Furthermore, designers have to be exempt from the task of importing computed variants into the CAD system. In fact, many optimizers deliver results outside of the CAD systems that contain the model. Therefore data inconsistencies may arise when switching from one system to another.

One of the well-known challenges of automatic variant generation is their evaluation and classification, because very large numbers of variants may be created. A solution had to be found, that enabled the classification of generated variants and therefore provided designers with information that facilitated decision-making. Accordingly, designers were to be exempt from checking many thousands of variants.

## 4.2 Concept

The main building blocks that are used for generating and evaluating variants are EvoCAT, the CAD system and an artificial neural network. In order to obtain a high level of performance, the calculations are performed in a distributed environment.

The technical approach of EvoCAT relies on using characteristics of evolutionary algorithms. The latter emulate the biological evolution by simulating phenomena such as reproduction, mutation, selection and survival of the fittest. Moreover, the approach makes use of probabilistic rules. These principles are applied in order to evaluate the variants generated by the CAD system in respect of criteria that have been defined by designer EvoCAT is made up of two main components, the server and the client. The server addresses the CAD system and the artificial neural network as well. Results are sent back to the client that enables visualization.

The geometric model is the basic element of the concept:
-    Input and visualization are taken over by the CAD system
-    The CAD system is used as a computation and simulation tool that generates variants
-    Data is available in diverse formats (CAD, CAE, export formats)

The third main component of the optimization system is the artificial neural network (ANN) that is involved in order to reduce computation time.

The ANN is trained during optimization and evaluated after each training session. Once the quality of the ANN has reached a satisfying level, it is involved in the calculation of target functions. In fact, the ANN takes the job of the CAD system by approximating its values; therefore EvoCAT obtains return values quicker than if the CAD system would have computed them. Doing so shortens the running time of EvoCAT and consequently the reaction time of the system. However, the quality of the results obtained remains decisive. Thus if the ANN delivers incorrect results, it is set once more in training mode. For this purpose, a monitoring approach has been realised.

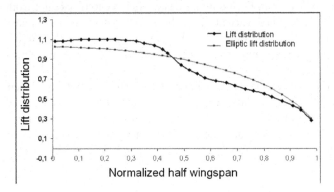

Figure 4 Lift distribution of a flying wing by extended flaps

## 4.3  Results and Integration into CATIA

EvoCAT has been applied for dimensioning and optimizing a flying wing. For this study, an additional module was involved for calculating aerodynamic coefficients.

The extended flaps increase the lift, however they change its distribution and therefore worsen the induced drag (Fig. 4). In fact, the elliptical curve is ideal for induced drag distribution.

The task of EvoCAT consisted in finding a wing form that provided an elliptical lift distribution even if the flaps were extended.

For optimization purposes, a so-called K-factor [6] had to be defined. It designated the ratio of the induced drag coefficient over the induced drag coefficient of an elliptic lift distribution. In addition, the flight stability was checked too. In so doing, it could be insured that the flying wing was not only theoretically dimensioned, but also could fly stably.

The flight stability factor and the K-factor were combined to determine a specific factor that was to be evaluated by EvoCAT.

As a result, an improved wing geometry that delivered best stability and lift distribution was expected. For test purposes, a student who was a non-expert in aerodynamics used EvoCAT, while an experienced aerodynamic engineer analysed the problem. Both test persons obtained the same results. However, the student was quicker.

The best variants that were computed by EvoCAT were visualized in CATIA V5 using design tables (Fig. 5). Real tests have confirmed the results obtained.

Figure 5 Carbon fibre reinforced flying wing with 2,6m wingspan

# 5. Functional DMU: Adjustment of Mechanical Components with Control Systems

Whereas simulation fields are traditionally quite disconnected from design (heterogeneous application landscape), one of the main choices for companies is to adopt a multi-disciplinary approach to attain a global optimization of their products. This is particularly appropriate for mechatronics, where mechanics, electronics and software are involved in the development of the final product.

During the design of a mechatronics product, it is very important to manage the interaction between the different disciplines, in order to develop suitable solutions.

According to an Aberdeen Groups benchmark report [7], the challenges for product development in the mechatronics domain rely on the link between disciplines.

That study illustrates that three of the top five challenges of mechatronics product development are related to a lack of integration in the development process.

## 5.1 Requirements

Different levels of coupling CAD software and behaviour simulation software have been proposed in the past, from the coupling of information in each component to the development of environments that integrate all the simulation domains [8, 9].

One of the main approaches currently used consists of extracting information from mechanical design data and inserting it into the simulation model. Traditionally, the transfer of information has been done manually, but automatic or semiautomatic approaches have been developed to map behaviour models onto mechanical models [10].

Although simulation tools enable the modelling of product behaviour, its simulationand analysis of its results, they are not focused on managing geometric information and its visualization in 3D environments. Therefore either the visualisation of the product is not possible with these approaches, or 3D models are reduced to simplified analogous models (Fig. 6). The perception of designers is consequently limited.

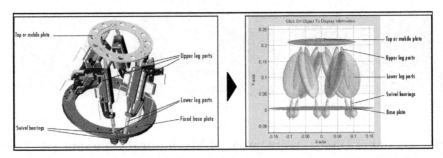

Figure 6 Simulation and visualization of a Stewart platform with SimMechanics [10]

Considering the arguments mentioned above, an interface that takes advantage of both CAD and control system design software was to be developed. In addition, the system had to enable simulation of the behaviour of a complex product from the early stages of the development.

To ensure the numeric coherence, it was important to synchronize the execution of both applications (CAD and behaviour simulation). Indeed, the values that are used for computation in the simulation tool must continually correspond with the positions and properties of the parts in the geometric model.

Furthermore, the realistic visualization of the simulation was mandatory. Modifications during multi-disciplinary simulation had to be considered immediately by the simulation loop in order to avoid data inconsistencies.

## 5.2 Concept

The CADSim Interface is independent of the software used for validation (CATIA and MATLAB). In practice, the CADSim Interface has been designed to be easily adaptable to other software. Therefore the tools that have been linked at this time can easily be replaced by a different CAD and simulation system.

Furthermore, the creation of a concept for coupling mechanical and behaviour models involves questions about the modelling of control system components and the communication of both models.

Starting from the observation that in the physical world, there are elements necessary to link the control system with the mechanical components, the key elements of the CADSim Interface are sensors and actuators. They are independent from both CAD and simulation-based applications, and they are linked with modules that manage the communication with CATIA V5, on one side, and with MATLAB on the other (Fig. 7).

## 5.3 Results and Integration into CATIA V5

The CADSim Interface has been developed in a project as an add-on for CATIA V5, and it uses some methods provided by MATLAB to realise the communication between both applications (COM approach), which are running simultaneously.

Changes performed on the models are immediately considered by the simulation loop.

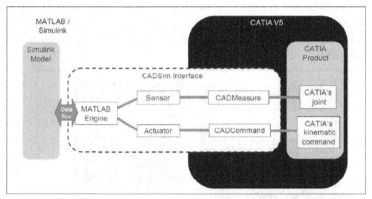

Figure 7 Concept of CADSim Interface

In order to run the simulation, an arbitrary CATIA model is to be loaded. After doing that, the user has to select the commands that should be considered as actuators and the components on which sensors values are to be measured. The CATIA specification tree is used for performing that selection.

In order to complete the configuration, the user indicates an arbitrary MATLAB model that should be loaded to run the simulation. The sensors and actuators of the geometric model are then mapped to corresponding objects of the selected MATLAB model.

The configuration file that contains this information is saved. Therefore the users are exempt from achieving configuration tasks as long as the same digital models are adjusted. Various tests have been performed with models of aircrafts and industry robots (Fig. 8).

Plots present the progression of current values and reference values during the simulation. Coupling that information with the realistic visualisation, designers and control system engineers can improve their digital models. In practice, control system engineers may define preliminary prototype models with minimal requirements (in fact features). Designers would already be able to adjust their CAD models to some preliminary behaviour models stored in a library during the first preliminary studies. That is the purpose of Functional DMU.

## 6. Summary

This paper has described projects of PROSTEP AG dealing with the reduction of product development time through accelerating the design process, stimulating the creativity of designers and synchronizing the development of partial product models.

An optimizer for surface minimization as well as EvoCAT for rapid generation and evaluation of design variants has been described. In addition, an interface that enables the coupling of mechanics and control systems for the development of mechatronics products has been presented. The applications are being steadily customized in order to satisfy the specific requirements of different customers.

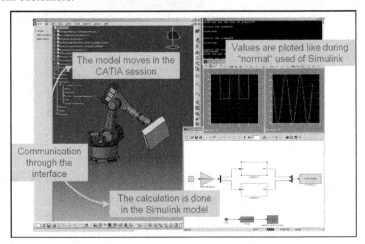

Figure 8 CAD model of industry robot being controlled by a MATLAB model

# References

1. Kemmler R.: Stabilitat und große Verschiebung in der Topologie und Formoptimierung, Dissertation, Institut für Baustatik der Universität Stuttgart (2004).
2. Sederberg T.W., Parry, S.R.: Free-Form Deformation of Solid Geometric Models. Proceedings of SIGGRAPH '86, Computer Graphics 20(1), pp. 51-159 (1986).
3. Hechler J.: Formoptimierung unter Nebenbedingungen durch Freiform-Deformation. Dissertation, Fachbereich Mathematik der Technischen Universitt Darmstadt (2006).
4. Pahl G., Beitz W., Feldhusen J., Grote K.H.: Konstruktionslehre - Grundlagen erfolgreicher Produktentwicklung, 6, Auflage, Springer (2005).
5. Slaby E.: Einsatz Evolutionrer Algorithmen zur Optimierung im frhen Konstruktionsprozess. Dissertation, Universitt der Bundeswehr Hamburg (2003).
6. Nickel K., Wohlfahrt M.: Schwanzlose Flugzeuge - Ihre Auslegung und ihre Eigenschaften, Birkhuser Verlag (2008).
7. Jackson K.C.: The Mechatronics System Design Benchmark Report - Coordinating Engineering Disciplines, Aberdeen Group report (August 2006).
8. Sinha R., Paredis C., Khosla P.: Integration of mechanical CAD and behavioral modeling. Proceedings of the IEEE/ACM Workshop on Behavioral Modeling and Simulation (2000).
9. N.N.: SimEnterprise-Extending Simulation to the Entreprise. MSC White Paper (2006).
10. N.N.: SimMechanics 2 - Users Guide (2007).

# Innovation in Information Systems applied to the Shoes Retail Business

**Vasco F. Teles[1] and Francisco J. Restivo[2]**

[1] University of Porto, Faculty of Engineering, Portugal, vascoft@hotmail.com
[2] University of Porto, Faculty of Engineering, Portugal, fjr@fe.up.pt

**Abstract:** Innovation is undoubtedly an essential part of the business process. Innovation management is as important as quality management and customer relationship management for the company success, independently of the business area.

Computer-Aided Innovation is emerging as a strategic domain of research and application to support enterprises throughout the overall innovation process. CAI systems should begin at the creative stage of identifying business opportunities and customer demands, then continue helping in developing phases and, further on, providing help up to the point of turning those inventions into successful innovations in the market.

In retail business, the way the offer is presented to customers is as important as product quality, and it is this combined service that is the main purpose for innovative solutions. Shoe retail business is a significant example where combining creative possibilities with technology-based applications makes it possible to introduce innovation in this branch of activity, particularly in the Portuguese business structure, characterized by the prominence of large shopping malls where the service itself gains an increased meaning.

**Keywords:** Innovation, information systems, shoe retail, creativity, CAI

## 1. Introduction

Retail business has been for long time an ideal field to implement new and innovative solutions, as costumers are very demanding, competition is strong and the business is mature, though constantly evolving.

In this business, innovation has to be very consistent throughout its stages: requirements have to be clear, problem-solving has to be creative, the project has to be very well planned, testing has to be exhaustive and implementation has to be reliable, because normally the store operation isn't interrupted. Since retail has a very large costumer and transaction base, computer-aided innovation acquires

Please use the following format when citing this chapter:

Teles, V. F. and Restivo, F. J., 2008, in IFIP International Federation for Information Processing, Volume 277; *Computer-Aided Innovation (CAI)*; Gaetano Cascini; (Boston: Springer), pp. 107–118.

greater importance in supporting considerably more complex operations, giving the possibility to offer new services to the costumer and implement new concepts in stores, usually in such traditional businesses.

This paper aims to evidence the importance of computer-aided innovation within the retail sector, detailing the above mentioned concepts, when new concepts are installed, new services are offered to the client and to shop assistants and how does all this integrates in companies' information systems. For this we will analyze a project in a retail business, which will implement the concept of costumer self service in shoe stores and providing the shop assistants the necessary tools to an efficient work, all integrated in the company main information systems.

In the next section, there is an insight of the business itself: the reason why it came to light, the market competition, the retail environment in Portugal, its investments in specialized retail, leading to the need to innovate and think ahead, in order to obtain competitive advantage and costumer attention, as supported by Yadav et al. "Detection, development, and deployment require the awareness of external opportunities and the anticipation of future events." [1]

In the following section, the needs and requirements of this business concept are detailed. Requirements are a critical issue in the innovation process and attention must be focused on the output of this activity.

Then it is explained the importance of information systems when innovating to meet the business goals while requirements are checked to compliance of those.

In the final section, the benefits the solution can bring to the business are discussed, and how will they be measured, and the authors discuss what value this analysis can bring to computer-aided innovation, and what value CAI can bring to the retail costumer and the company itself.

## 2. The business idea

In our context, one may define business innovation as an idea or practice that is perceived as being new by the adopting unit [2].

Market competition is fierce and becoming tougher as profit margins get crushed each year. Competitors who have the most optimized processes – business, technological, etc. – throughout the whole value chain are the ones who survive, succeed and grow. This includes dealing with procurement, suppliers, logistics, distribution, and at the end of the chain, the consumer.

Portugal is no exception to this, as the concept of "traditional commerce" is disappearing, while new large shopping centres are built and occupied by stores belonging to large economical groups who have those processes very well driven in order to provide the best products to the costumer at the minimum cost. These investments changed consumer's habits radically in a short period, innovating in many ways: increasing the available choice the client, lowering the average price of goods, introducing convenience of time and location, among others. Investments were made to implement large hypermarkets where the costumer is able to find almost everything and specialized retail stores focused on particular sectors.

But why a new shoe store business at this moment? The project we study in this paper is under development to a major retail player in the country, which owns a very large number of stores varying from food to consumer electronics, apparel, clothing, etc. Since several years, shoes have been being sold in company's stores, consistently growing their sales volume, resulting from a well-planned strategy that consists namely of controlling the whole product development process "in house" to self brands as well as selling other suppliers brands. As a result and along with this growth, administration and marketing professionals came to the conclusion that it was possible to open independent shoe stores in order to explore that market, as the whole business process was already integrated in the company.

Although it may seem that the market reached a saturation status, it is always possible to find new ways of doing business, even traditional ones, and achieving good results in a local or global market. In order to do so, innovation is mandatory: thinking ahead to foresee consumers' trends and expectations and implement them before rivals do so is vital to gain advantage, consumer attention and loyalty.

To support this innovation, and specifically in our case-study, information systems technology is used to create instruments which will provide services to the costumers that distinguish these stores from others, as well as tools to help the employees to better assist the clients, and thus providing the company fundamental data to compete, evolve and obtain its profit. Like this one, "some firms and industries are making giant productivity strides through IT and some are achieving new revenue streams and competitive advantages." [3]

## 3. Requirements

Requirements are critical in any project, and even more so in an innovative one as this. Care must be set on business needs, requirements and expectations in order to build accurate technical specifications and provide the correct output.

The business team provided four main requirements for the new stores which we had to follow in order to comply with the main target.

To begin with, the new stores would have be innovative and differentiate themselves from competition, building a new concept of shoe store. This was the key business asset for setting the new stores, so as to find their space in market, capturing costumer and media attention. In such a traditional business, implementing a new chain of stores is a risk namely because of market conditions, so a different kind of store would have to be developed, profiting from the constant search customers do to what is new, as well as those who do not identify themselves with conventional stores, thus trying to gain their loyalty offering good products, fair prices and a new pleasant shopping experience.

This leads us to another requirement, as in order to provide new and pleasant shopping experience, the customer would have to be autonomous in the store, from the moment he or she enters to the moment the payment is made. As Shaw and Alexander referring to Humphrey and Bowlby, "The development of self-service techniques (…) represents pivotal retail innovations of the twentieth century that transformed the process of selling and the act of shopping." [4] [5] [6] Meanwhile he or she would have been able to browse the store looking for a product, searching for styles, brands, colours, sizes, locating and trying them. This requirement was set thinking of many factors of today's culture, namely lack of time, independence, eccentricity. With this concept, the costumer wouldn't have to wait in line to ask information to store assistants, saving precious time and energy.

In order to keep store operation costs low, few staff will be available in store, thus the project would have to provide efficient tools to costumer, to the staff and to the company itself. The few staff present in store will be able to perform their tasks in a rapid, efficient and effective way, while assisting clients and operating the store. All these include orders, payments, item location and inventories, among others. These tools will have to be direct, reliable and usable.

The last requirement was that the store would have to be kept in order, as the staff would have to be focused in customer care and operation itself, rather than frequently resetting items in their original places. If a costumer picks up an item and has to carry it more than a very short distance to search information about it, the most probable consequence is that the product will be left somewhere else other than its original location. Consequently, in these new stores, the costumer will have no need of carrying items around and will only need to look up, press a button, stretch an arm or walk few meters, so as to obtain information.

As a baseline of all these, we had in mind what Gammal refers regarding technological innovation as to market success is concerned "Rather than technological failure, the pivotal reason is a lack of true customer relevance - either in the product itself or the way in which it is described and marketed." [7]

## 4. Methodology

### 4.1 Creativity process

As the requirements were set and integrated into the project team, the main question arose, as what kind of devices where going to be necessary to comply with not only business needs and requirements, but also its expectations and constraints. Thus for the moment it was the stage where it was needed to open-mindedly come up with ideas. In that sense, a creativity session with people from different backgrounds and competencies in the company was scheduled where it was expected to collect valuable contributions in order to arrive to a solution, as supported by King "the consensus assessment of a 'crowd' — a group of people, each having limited knowledge of a subject — can be far superior to expert assessments and even superior to the assessments of each and every individual member of the 'crowd.'" [8] The project team naturally had some ideas, but would like to face them with other ones, in order to assess their quality and feasibility.

To this session, it was vital group collaboration, as working together toward a common goal [2] when being apart from current tasks for at least a short period of time, as Yadav et al. sustain when citing Hambrick et al. "that creativity requires some amount of available time and cognitive resources, extremely high levels of job demands may squeeze out novelty and fresh thinking". [1] [9]

The session employed the Synectics process for creative problem solving [10]. This process consists firstly in setting a title for the task, summarizing the problem-solving objective. Starting this title with "How to..." lead to the question "How to implement self service to costumers in shoe stores?".

Afterwards, it is necessary to perform a task analysis alongside with the solution client – the business management, in this case – answering to questions such as: "Why is this a problem or an opportunity?", "What is its brief history?", "What is your power to implement the solution?", "What have you already tried or thought of?", "What is your dream solution?", "What outcome do you want from this meeting?". After this, the problem solving team starts proposing ideas, where exist some basic rules for this section of the work, like suspending judgment in order to open the mind and let others also do it, so every idea is valid; one ought to ponder of what does this problem and the other ideas make one think of, in order to refine ideas and come up with new ones; these should be headlined with "How to..." or "I wish...", as these forms can be particularly useful as they direct resources' attention to where their thoughts would be most valuable. These forms are commonly known as springboards.

A technique called "Excursions" is often used where ideas go round in a closed circle and with that it is possible to obtain fresh ones. It requires the main problem to be set aside and participants to think beyond current constraints. For this, each of the participants is given a specific subject under a theme, like sports or famous people, and tries to associate the subject to the problem, thus generating new ideas. E.g., in a shoe store, Pavarotti would have asked out loud "Where are my Pradas?", and this metaphor originated the idea "Natural language interface to search items in store".

After these idea-creation stages, it is time for the client and the group to select and organize the results. This is completed via a matrix that represents novelty and feasibility in xx and yy axes, respectively, and the ideas are selected based in intrigue and attraction factors, and placed into the matrix according to its less or more novelty and feasibility.

By the end of this process, we have a matrix of possible solutions, as depicted in figure 1, from where the client selects one or several ideas to develop, where only the most relevant solutions are mentioned and the circle size represents an approximate relation between value and complexity.

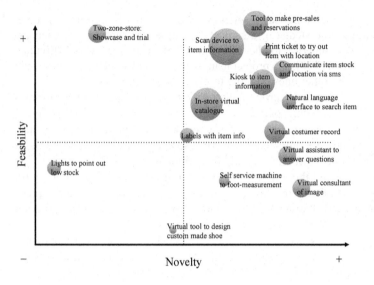

Figure 1 Matrix with relevant ideas resulting from the creativity session

The development is done firstly around the client paraphrases that springboard ideas ("How to…" or "I wish…") decoding any potential metaphors from each idea by asking the author to refine it in other words. After clarified, the idea is constructively evaluated, as the client lists pluses and major concerns about it. This is done once again in the form of "How to…". To overcome those concerns ordered by importance, the client and the group generate ideas, starting with "What you do is…". Finally the client modifies the original idea using the selected modifications, stating it as a possible problem solution. Naturally, this last process can be repeated if necessary, until the client has a comfortable solution.

In the process, creativity only becomes innovation if implemented, so an action macro-plan is set, stating what action is performed by whom and when.

We now briefly analyze some of the more relevant ideas located in the top right quadrant of figure 1, i.e., those which are more novel and more feasible:

- Point of information using barcode scanning devices – this was the se-lected idea to implement in a short term, complying with business de-mands. It will use company-based systems in order to provide the expected information and some application developments were needed;

- Interactive kiosk – similar solution to the previous one but with more in-formation, such as virtual catalogue, which would lead to a deeper invest-ment in development, as the whole interface had to be bought/developed as well as the hardware. It is in stand by to a near future;

- Item tags with product information – alike electronic price tags, but with larger displays, thus possibly showing product information as well as stock. It implied a store structure different than the projected, therefore only its concept was worked;

- Interface in natural language – this was one of the most breakthrough yet feasible ideas. It could be applied in a kiosk and provide the information without the device barrier. It was placed in stand by to some time in future.

Some other final ideas were generated, but these are the most significant and transmit the focus on the problem solving. In the end the idea which will to be implemented led from creativity towards innovation to the business, and fulfilled its balance between needs, requirements, expectations and constraints. These solutions meant to be ambidextrous when balancing between technical and organizational flexibility in response to external conditions and internal needs [1].

To finish with, as supported by Goel and Singh citing Prather et al., this whole process of "creativity and innovation involves the translation of our unique gifts, talents and vision into an external reality that is new and useful. Creativity refers to all activities that involve the generation of ideas. Innovation refers to the implementation of viable business ideas generated as a result of the organization's creativity-supporting culture and structure." [11] [12]

## 4.2  Technology

In this section, we briefly review the business needs, requirements and expectations previously presented, namely the new stores would have be innovative and differentiate themselves from competition, building a new concept of shoe store; the customer would have to be autonomous in the store while few staff would be available; and finally the store would have to be kept in order. So cross-analyzing all these and the solutions resulting from the creativity session, two of them have been considered as feasible in a short to medium term. Some of the others can be applied in the long run, and others still were just good creativity exercises, as often occurs in such processes.

We have seen that, as King supports, "there is also a growing awareness that IT can play an important role in the integration of entrepreneurship and strategy that is necessary if firms are to be quick at identifying opportunities and pursuing them to their advantage" which became clear in this creativity session [3].

Consequently, two of problem solving solutions are: the electronic point of information via barcode scanning and the interactive kiosk. Having this in mind, the solution procurement was started in the market to all its components: hardware, software, kiosks, integrated solutions, and so on. This procurement was made by the team browsing the market and more specifically company's regular suppliers and a major international kiosk fair.

A large range of solutions which could fit in the requirements was found, namely kiosk hardware from a large number of suppliers where software had to be developed and implemented with possibly different types of integration and systems, thus giving vast possibilities to the desired solution, but delivery and development time could be a critical issue; others were integrated and modular kiosk solutions with their embedded applications already focused in a specific business, but only one was found dealing with shoe store business, where cost was an issue; some additional type of solutions were barcode scanning devices, some integrated with a screen, where software would have to be developed according to the cos- tumer's systems and requirements, giving the opportunity to apply the company's base solution to price checking and developing it further to comply to the informa- tion required to deliver at the store; finally some touch screens devices were ana- lyzed in order to integrate them with an interactive application built in-house to another business, which was possible to adapt and custom develop.

The team them filtered and structured all the information in possible configura- tions building a proposal which matched the business requirements previously stated, and constraints, such as investments, timings, risk, scalability, equipment and store look and feel. The scenarios were developed around the two main types of solutions: the barcode scanners and the interactive kiosks.

These scenarios evolved along several meetings with the business team and the final decision was taken by the business leader, with technical, design and man- agement inputs. In the end, the chosen solution was the technology already used in company's stores, which employs a bar code scanning device that will display product information, such as name, brand, price and available sizes on its screen, having received that information from company's both checkout and ERP system in real time using web services.

As usually, the decision was taken due to some critical factors described above where this solution was compared to the others presented, and the technology that prevailed was the one which could balance better most of the needs, requirements, expectations and constraints.

## 4.3 Competencies

The search for the right competencies is a key issue in every technology project, and this was no exception. This search was conducted during the final stage of the assessment, where the team already had an approximate idea of what different kind of decisions could face, thus focusing the search. Which competencies from the equipment supplier would be needed in order to install the appropriate soft- ware in those equipments? Which competencies would be needed from the soft- ware supplier in order to deploy and integrate it in the company's systems? Was the software going to be "off-the-shelf" or custom developed, and if so did the company have internal competencies to build and integrate it?

Alternatively, development could be outsourced, and then again what type of competencies was it needed the development supplier to have in order to create and implement the application the way it was required? Still, with several of these options, internal resources and competencies would have to be employed so as to integrate the solution, whatever it would be, with the company's infrastructure, checkout and ERP systems, among others. This was the common base from which we knew we had to leave in order to build the whole technical team.

## 5. Computer-aided innovation

Information systems are not a goal by themselves but are useful only when delivering important insight to what they were designed for: decision support, as different information is produced to the costumer, the store assistant and the company in its different profiles – operative, manager, administrator – and handled in diverse manner, by helping the client deciding which item to choose; to support the shop assistant when locating a product; to help operations team decide which items to order; to aid managers and administrators knowing exactly the business status and providing them information to innovate by building new concepts of doing their business, as they are aware they can rely on information systems to go that way.

The project team was very aware of the business goals when projecting possible solutions that resulted from the creativity session, in order to be innovative as required by the business and the store concept itself, but also to be assertive when using information systems as described above. The solution to implement is depicted in figure 2 in a simplified approach.

### 5.1 To the client

Having the previous concepts in mind, the self service system was designed to allow the client to be autonomous when obtaining information about the desired items. Normally, in a shoe store, the costumer has to ask an assistant to find out if the a size is available and other information, sometimes after waiting in a queue, or look around until finding out if there is the correct size or not.

According to the business needs, expectations, constraints and goals, the project will implement in each store several barcode scanning devices with built-in 14cm colour screen as these devices are well known to the majority of the costumers, being quite intuitive to operate. The costumer will use this wall-mounted barcode scanner to obtain information, and for that will approach the item barcode to the device laser beam and hears a short beep indicating the product was read and recognized. Some moments after, the information appears on screen.

### 5.2 To the store assistant

Another equally important component of the system as a whole is the one used by store assistants while in their diverse actions during the day. This will include not only customer care in its various types, as providing product information, locating products, suggesting other options to clients, but also current operation as shipment reception, product placement, price tagging, inventory and so on.

While supporting costumers, the assistant will be able to locate exactly where an item is placed, confirm prices, sizes and other product information. To perform this operation, the assistant will have a wireless PDA with barcode scanning capability, making it possible to the device to read the item barcode and interpret its EAN code. When interpreted, the information flows the same way as previously referred as for the wall-mounted barcode scanning device was concerned.

This application gives complete mobility to the assistant inside the store to help costumers and to perform routine operational tasks such as receiving product shipments in the background, checking them and confirming the reception, then setting received items inside the store and marking those locations to future reference while assisting costumers. All the information is based in the systems we have previously mentioned, and interface is done via web services once again.

## 5.3 To the company

To end with, store operations, management and company administration rely on various integrated information systems in order to perform their assignments as accurately as possible.

To the operations staff, the ERP is vital so as to analyze stocks, order correct product shipments, minimizing store stock but also out-of-stocks, analyze sales, budgets, margins, legal procedures and others. Alongside, management also rely on information systems, as they have to manage product range, making the right choices to provide the best saleable offer to the costumer and within each product have to negotiate margins, profits and costs, controlling along the way sales in stores so as to perform good results and aim to their sales and profit goals. On top, administration handles data in an aggregate way, therefore usually operates with data warehouse information system which combines data collected. With this system, the company is managed as a whole, even if divided by brands, and steered strategically thus making everyday decisions influencing its course.

The information system will always be a source to decision making, whether it is a costumer in a store checking product information, or the assistant who is locating a product using a portable device connect to the a remote system, or the operations team who supplies the store, its management which decides in which products to bet, or in the end administration who decides the strategy of the company, based in the information provided from all the information systems.

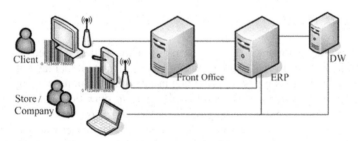

Figure 2 Simplified solution scheme

# 6. Results and conclusions

## 6.1 The goal

More than a requirement or a business expectation, it is a motivation that the solution is innovative and creates a new concept to shoe shopping in the country. Several analysis have been conducted in order to measure the attractiveness of self service devices in retail, and more specifically amongst this company businesses with quite extraordinary results, as costumers in the country adhere massively to these solutions, as for instance self checkouts in supermarkets.

Of course there is risk where high investment and image values are at stake, as there will be no smooth transition period to these brand new stores. To mitigate this risk, the solution itself and the information systems it integrates with have a very important role providing the client the expected information in a fast, efficient and reliable way. Along with the system, shop assistants also play a part in this equation, as they will need to interact with the client and the system simultaneously, forwarding the first to the latter when possible.

But the solution to be implemented is broader, comprising a powerful and useful tool to store assistants, giving them the possibility to perform their task in a rapid and efficient manner. Following a growing trend, each store will have a small number of employees, thus each one of them will have to do more work in less time. For this productivity issue, information systems are vital so as to provide the required information accurately on time. The based system is widely used in the company, thus having a low risk, but if it fails contingences can be activated.

This solution applies King's concept in which " when IT is focused on producing more flexible manufacturing capabilities, quicker order fulfilment, faster responses to customer inquiries and the like, it usually has direct impact on the bottom line and on 'intermediate outcomes' such as customer satisfaction and quality." [3]

In the end not all the benefits sum up to numbers, like investments, costs, profits, margins, items scanned, items received and so on, and although these are very important and the ones which will rate the project and the solution, there are other intangible gains like company image, costumer fidelity and pioneering that many times "pay" a project.

## 6.2 Conclusions

To conclude with, the authors expect this analysis can contribute to document what is being done when applying computer-aided innovation in the business world, namely in retail sector and shoe stores, to implement new shopping concepts which employ information systems.

The study case is an example of CAI application in order to satisfy specific business needs and requirements and meet the expectations created around the possible solutions, but also accounting the constraints that naturally emerge. As in all cases, the dream solution would not the one described and implemented but some other less realistic or even impossible for the time being. Thus it is important to point out that computer-aided innovation is built by real developments and implementations and even if it is possible to aim at higher objectives in the future, in many occasions it is preferable to take one step at a time, and implement consistent solutions that can offer some benefits or services to costumer or companies.

These latter are the ones investing large funding to compete in fierce markets and must think ahead of competitors in order to attract consumer attention and loyalty. Therefore, computer-aided innovation is vital to companies if it can provide them tools to compete in the market, bringing added-value to organizations' business. This added-value can be delivered to the company itself, helping it performing its tasks more efficiently and with more information, but also to the costumer, who is the ultimate user to this innovation.

In such a traditional and mature yet rapid and competitive market as retail business, computer-aided innovation makes the difference between those left behind and the ones who profit and grow by offering excellent services to their costumers.

# References

1.  Yadav M., Prabhu J, Chandy R.: Managing the future: CEO attention and innovation outcomes. Journal of Marketing, vol. 71, pp. 84-101 (2007).
2.  Tarafdar, M, Gordon, S.: Understanding the influence of information system competencies on process innovation: a resource-based view. Journal of Strategic Information Systems, vol. 16 (4), pp. 353-392 (2007).
3.  King W.: IT Strategy and innovation: the "IT deniers" versus a portfolio of IT roles. Information Systems Management, vol. 24: pp. 197-199 (2007).
4.  Shaw G., Alexander A.: British co-operative societies as retail innovators: interpreting the early stages of the self-service revolution. Business History, vol. 50 (1), pp. 62-78 (2008).
5.  Humphrey, K.: Shelf life: supermarkets and the changing cultures of consumption, Cambridge University Press (1998).
6.  Bowlby, R.: Carried away; the invention of modern shopping, Faber & Faber, New York (2001).
7.  Gammal, J.: Innovation that pays. Mass High Tech News 30 August (2004).
8.  King, W.: IT Strategy and innovation: recent innovations in knowledge management. Information Systems Management vol. 24, pp. 91-93 (2007).
9.  Hambrick, D., Finkelstein, S., Mooney, A.: Executive job demands: new insights for explaining strategic decisions and leader behaviours. Academy of Management Review vol. 30 (3): pp. 472-91 (2005).
10. Synectics Breakthrough Creativity. Synectics Limited (2007)
11. Goel, P., Singh, N.: Creativity and innovation in durable product development. Computers & Industrial Engineering, 35 (1), p. 5-8, Oct (1998).
12. Prather, C., Gundry, L.: Blueprints for innovation. AMA Membership Publication Division (1995).

# Virtual Product Development Models: Characterization of Global Geographic Issues

**Alyssa J. Walker[1] and Jordan J. Cox[2]**

[1] Brigham Young University, United States, alyssajanae@gmail.com
[2] Brigham Young University, United States, cox@byu.edu

**Abstract:** Because product development processes now take place within a geographically diverse international community, global geographic issues relating to both physical and human elements of geography must be considered to ensure optimal deployment through means of virtual product development. Virtual product development is a strategy that preplans the product development process through simulation. Generating all possible product development process designs and simulations through virtual product development makes it possible to determine the optimal deployment option. In order to optimize in deployment, it is necessary to score each configuration based on a series of metrics that measure issues relevant to and affecting deployment. This paper presents a method by which global geographic issues may be effectively characterized in order to accurately represent their role in and influence on the product development process prior to deployment.

**Keywords:** globalization, graph theory, network, autonomous agents

## 1. Introduction

Due to trends of increased globalization, the product development process is no longer localized or isolated. Execution of the product development process becomes increasingly complex as a result of its deployment within a geographically diverse international community.

The spatial variation across the globe of physical features, as well as human phenomena and distribution, impacts product development in ways that are often unexpected or overlooked, but that have potential to alter greatly the final outcome of any given process in terms of cost, time, quality, etc. Geographic diversity subsequently becomes an asset or liability, depending on the deployment strategy. How then does an international corporation accurately forecast what specific geographic issues will influence its deployment, and in what ways? A method for simulating and predicting possible outcomes and forecasting the impact of geographic issues for a given product development process prior to process execution is not only beneficial but essential to successful deployment.

*Please use the following format when citing this chapter:*

Walker, A. J. and Cox, J. J., 2008, in IFIP International Federation for Information Processing, Volume 277; *Computer-Aided Innovation (CAI)*; Gaetano Cascini; (Boston: Springer), pp. 119–131.

Virtual product development is a predictive modeling technique that explores the possible product development deployment options prior to actual deployment. It is based on the use of graph models that delineate processes, organizations, and other networks relating to product development. The methodology presented in this paper is an attempt to create models for predicting the impact of global geographic issues on potential product development deployments. We recognize the limitations in attempting to represent such complex and abstract issues in a model form. However, the consequences of failing to model are apparent in the ineffective deployments of transnational corporations that exhibit themselves in current business.

## 2. Literature Survey

The characterization and modeling of globalization's impacts on businesses and organizations involve a variety of techniques and methods. Examples of these methods are presented in this section.

The modeling of complex systems such as product development deployments in a global context is a challenging undertaking. Chittaro et al define the concept of a model as "a symbolic system designed to provide a representation of a physical system appropriate for a given purpose. So, a model is only a partial representation of reality and depends on subjective decisions of the model designer" [4]. In this modeling methodology, there are two primary parts to the model: the product development deployment representation and the secondary calculus used to evaluate the deployment. The product development deployment graphs are context-independent, and the secondary calculi provide the context-dependent knowledge.

Several different groups have focused on modeling geographic issues and their impact on product development. Raper and Livingstone discuss the role of representation in modeling physical and human geography [10]. Barnes, in "Retheorizing Economic Geography" indicates the need for both a quantitative and a cultural representation [1]. Bauer states that "indeed, in going about their business, geographers often borrow from the broad suite of alternative methodologies available in other disciplines" [2]. However, in this case, we borrow from geography to construct our models of virtual product development.

The literature provides many examples of case-specific models dealing with the issues of globalization. For example, Malnight presents an evolutionary perspective by outlining the history of the transition of a multinational corporation from decentralized toward a network-based structure [8].

Tratinsky and Jarvenpaa examined the influence of global versus local contexts on information technology distribution decisions [13]. Another example of trying to model geographic issues with respect to business organizations is the work done by Carpenter and Frederickson. They developed a model for studying the impacts of global geographic issues of top management team characteristics [3].

The issue of developing models of geographic phenomena in the midst of globalization continues to be a controversial one. In an editorial of the *Transactions of the Institute of British Geographers*, the comment is made, "we need to be more self-confident and forthright in highlighting the limitations and dangers of formal modeling approaches" [6]. The editorial also states, "a meeting of minds ought to be possible: a middle ground between what it calls the 'top-down' (model-building) perspective of the geographical economists and the 'bottom-up' (empirically grounded) perspective of economic geographers" [6].

Sheppard introduces the idea of scales and then indicates that the traditional hierarchy of territorial units (body, neighborhood, city, region, nation-state, supranational bloc, globe) often "splay" outward as they connect at higher scales. Additionally, Sheppard introduces networks as a way of representing the interconnections of the entities associated in globalization [11].

Subramaniam and Venkatraman recognize the need for determining product development capability [12]. Fulk and DeSanctis identify the need to represent product development in a model where issues such as communication technology can be explored [7]. Nault's approach to modeling transnational organizations incorporates the use of nodes, each of which are assigned specific quantities used in the application of a secondary calculus [9].

The work summarized in this literature survey clearly identifies the need for developing some form of a model for predicting the impact of global geographic issues on product development deployment. While it is also clear from the literature that models cannot completely represent global geographic issues, at the same time there are serious consequences for failing to model.

## 3. Incorporation of Global Geographic Issues into Virtual Product Development Models

Virtual product development (VPD) is a modeling technique used to explore before actual deployment all possible product development deployment options that are available to a company. VPD also provides a method for evaluating these options with respect to critical characteristics that have potential to impact the deployment such as time to execute, cost to execute, probability to achieve a level of quality in product offerings, etc.

Virtual product development is a modeling technique that employs graph or network models of both product development processes and the associated organizations that will execute them. Using these graphs, autonomous agents are created that represent the assignment of an actor to a given task. Agents are created for all tasks in the product development process. All possible assignments can be modeled, thus creating redundant agents. This means that there can be more than one agent who can execute a given task. All these agents are registered in a library.

Deployment options are then determined in an autonomous agent environment where graphs of agents are reconstructed using a deterministic mapping technique. A single deployment option is a graph of agents that satisfy all tasks of the original product development process. These graphs represent unique instantiations of the original process map with different combinations of the agents. Scoring of these instantiations is accomplished through secondary calculi imposed on the graphs of the important task and actor metrics thus allowing an overall time or cost-to-execute to be computed for the given instantiation.

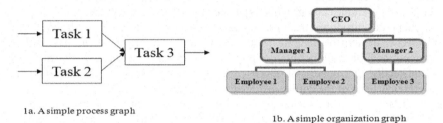

1a. A simple process graph

1b. A simple organization graph

Figure 1. Process and Organization graphs

In Figure 1a a simple example is shown of a process graph consisting of three tasks, two of which can be executed simultaneously (Task 1 and Task 2). Figure 1b shows an example of a simple organization graph with two levels of management and three employees who will actually execute the process tasks. Assume that the overall time to execute is a critical objective for the program that will launch this process.

| Tasks | Time to execute per Skill Level I | Time to execute per Skill Level II | Time to execute per Skill Level III | | Actors | Skill level for Task I | Skill Level for Task II | Skill Level for Task III | | Agents | Task-Actor Assignments |
|---|---|---|---|---|---|---|---|---|---|---|---|
| Task 1 | 20 | 10 | 5 | | | | | | | Agent 1 | Task 1 – Employee 1 |
| Task 2 | 50 | 20 | 10 | | Employee 1 | I | II | 0 | | Agent 2 | Task 1 – Employee 2 |
| Task 3 | 30 | 20 | 10 | | Employee 2 | II | III | 0 | | Agent 3 | Task 2 – Employee 2 |
| | | | | | Employee 3 | 0 | I | II | | Agent 4 | Task 2 – Employee 3 |
| | | | | | | | | | | Agent 5 | Task 3 – Employee 3 |

Figure 2. Enumeration of task and actor characteristics and Agent assignments

Figure 2 shows three tables, one listing each of the tasks with associated information about time to execute for three skill levels. These times to execute therefore represent the time required if an employee is qualified at a certain skill level. The second table shows each of the actors and their associated skill level for each of the tasks, and the third delineates agent assignments. These agents are created by assigning actors to tasks. Agent 1 is therefore defined as Task 1 being executed by Employee 1, Agent 2 is Task 1 executed by Employee 2 and so forth. Once all of the agent definitions are delineated, deployment options can be created.

Figure 3 shows three deployment options made from combinations of agents which complete all of the original process tasks. Each of these deployment options can now be scored using the secondary calculus. Notice that the times are dependent upon which employee is doing what task and at what skill level. Total time scores are then based upon whether Task 1 and 2 can be done simultaneously or must be done in series because they are done by the same actor.

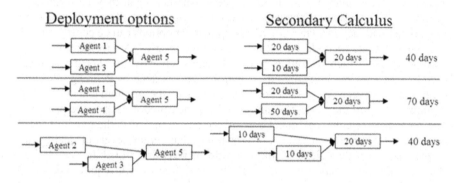

Figure 3. Deployment options and secondary calculus scores

With this in mind, notice that the time to execute for deployment option 1 is the sum of Task 1 and Task 3 since Task 2 can be executed simultaneously with Task 1. In the second deployment option, Actor 3 must execute both Task 2 and Task 3 and so the score is combined as 70 days. Finally, in deployment three, Employee 2 must complete Tasks 1 and 2 so the combined score is 40 days.

An in-depth discussion of virtual product development methods is deferred to other papers [5,14]. However, an overview of the techniques will be given. VPD is accomplished in several steps, each of which will be presented in the following paragraphs. The steps are as follows:

1. Identify desired product development program/project outcomes
2. Delineate process and organization models to the desired level of detail
3. Create agents by matching actors to tasks
4. Define secondary calculus to combine metrics
5. Generate possible deployment options through dynamic configuration
6. Score options

Step 1. Identify desired program/project outcomes. The first step in creating a VPD model is to select a product development process and identify desired program outcomes such as minimizing cost or time, maximizing quality, etc. There are usually one or two desired outcomes for any given program. For example, assume a company desires to launch a new product line by launching a product development process. The desired program outcomes might be profit margin, market window and quality level.

Step 2. Delineate process and organizational models to the desired level of detail. The next step is to create graph models of all the structural elements of a product development project. Structural elements include but are not limited to the process steps, all organizations that will contribute actors including sub-contracting organizations, facilities and resource networks.

Step 3. Create agents by matching actors to tasks. The VPD simulations are created using autonomous agents. A library of all possible agents is created by assigning all qualified actors to all the possible tasks they can execute within the graph models. For example, an engineer from the parent corporation may be assigned a stress analysis task in the process. Another agent may be formed by assigning a sub-contract engineer to do the same task. All tasks must be instantiated with actors so that complete deployment options can be configured.

Step 4. Define secondary calculus to combine metrics. A secondary calculus must be defined which determines how the program objectives will be measured at each task or actor through appropriate metrics. This is done by defining trackable metrics at the actor and task level which relate to the program outcomes. For example, many of the trackable metrics will be measured in cost to the program. The secondary calculus can then be as simple as a sum across the graph of these costs. If the metrics are measures of probability that certain levels of quality can be obtained, then the calculus will be a form of Bayesian probability or Markov chains accumulated across the graph. Each set of metrics will require a different calculus based upon the type of metric and overall impact.

Step 5. Generate possible deployment options through dynamic configuration. Using autonomous agent theory and dependency mapping theory, all possible deployment options are configured. This is done by finding agents whose output are the final deliverables of the process and then satisfying their inputs with other agents in the library until all dependencies are satisfied. This produces graphs of agents representing possible deployment options. Once these graphs are produced, they can be scored using the predefined secondary calcluli.

Step 6. Score options. The secondary calculi are accumulated across the separate graphs representing deployment options. Multiple scores are then registered for the different options. These scores can then be used to select the "best" possible option. Often these deployment options are only best with respect to some criteria such as time, cost, reliability, etc.

Virtual Product Development is a modeling framework and technique that provides companies the ability to explore all possible product development deployment options before actual deployment. It also allows them to evaluate these options with respect to optimality criteria such as time, cost and quality as well as criteria based upon the impact of global geographic issues such as language differences, different government regulations, etc.

## 3.1 Global Geographic Issues

As discussed in previous sections, the shift from local to global scale inevitably carries with it a host of issues and elements with considerable potential to influence the product development process. Globalization connotes a spatial distribution, and in the context of this paper global geographic issues are characterized as any phenomenon – social, political, environmental, or otherwise –

that influences a company's activities and varies on a global scale. The purpose of this paper is to provide a method for characterizing and incorporating these issues into VPD models, and not to identify all possible issues.

## 3.2 Method of Characterization

Once a VPD model has been developed for a given product development program, the impact of different global geographic issues on the program can be determined by expanding the existing secondary calculus. A five-step process is outlined below for converting a global issue into metrics that can be incorporated into the existing secondary calculus. For purposes of illustration, we will refer to the example used in Section 3.0 shown in Figure 1.

As shown in Figure 3, the first deployment option could be executed in forty days, the second in seventy, and the third in forty. The deployment options in reality represent different employees assigned to different sequences of tasks. For illustration of converting a global geographic issue into this secondary calculus, we choose international holidays as a global geographic issue which may affect the execution time of these deployment options. If the parent company wishes to hit a market window of March 15, 2008, they must determine when to launch the program.

Step 1. Identify the Global Geographic Issue. In this example, the global geographic issue of concern is international holidays and the impact they may have on the execution of a product development program. Obviously, this also involves the ethnic and religious backgrounds of the employees. Assume that Employee 1 is Chinese and is located in China, Employee 2 is Caucasian located in the United States, and Employee 3 is French located in France. Because the minimum time to execute the overall process is forty days, the program launch date needs to be in January, and execution will run through the February time frame. This means that at least two international holidays will occur during this program run: the Chinese New Year, which begins February 7 and will run through February 22; and Mardi Gras, which takes place February 3-5.

Step 2. Determine how Global Geographic Issue Affects Secondary Calculus Associated with the Program Objectives. Assuming that meeting the market window is a primary program objective, it is important to determine the program launch date. The actual calendar days required to execute a task must be calculated based upon time to execute the task plus the number of work days lost due to international holidays. Therefore, a new metric must be introduced into the agent secondary calculus.

Step 3. Assign Appropriate Metrics to Tasks, Actors, and Agents. Additional metrics are now required in characterizing each of the employees. Also, the agent metrics are expanded to include the number of days of impact due to international holidays for each of the tasks. In general, these metrics will be different for each type of global geographic issue and program objective.

| Agents | Task-Actor Assignments | Time for Task I | Time for Task II | Time for Task III | Holiday Impact |
|--------|------------------------|-----------------|------------------|-------------------|----------------|
| Agent 1 | Task1-Employee 1 | 20 | | | 15 days |
| Agent 2 | Task1-Employee 2 | 10 | | | 0 days |
| Agent 3 | Task2-Employee 2 | | 10 | | 0 days |
| Agent 4 | Task2-Employee 3 | | 30 | | 2 days |
| Agent 5 | Task3-Employee 3 | | | 20 | 2 days |

Figure 4. Additional metrics assigned to tasks, actors, and agents.

Step 4. Collect Data that Characterizes and Measures the Appropriate Metrics. In the case of the example, data for international holidays will include identifying all of the international holidays and their duration, as well as identifying those employees who potentially would be affected by them, either because of their location or because of their affiliation. Effective characterization of global geographic issues requires the establishment of a database of metrics that have been collected, normalized, and validated. Much like the role of a company's materials database, this global geographic issues database will provide the metrics necessary for a company's modeling of product development.

Step 5. Use Data to Generate Scores based on Secondary Calculus. Using the expanded metrics, a new score for each of the deployment options is generated. As shown in Figure 5, the updated score is given in the gray circles. Notice that Deployment Options 1 and 3 were previously indistinguishable in terms of time to execute, but now are significantly different due to the impact of the international holidays. It is now obvious that Deployment Option 3 would be the optimal choice and therefore would allow program launch to occur January 17 in order to meet the March 15 market window.

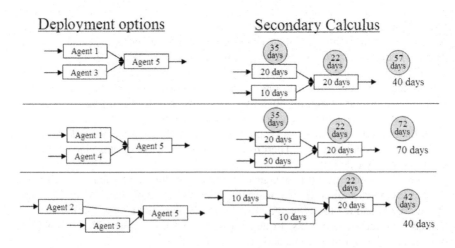

Figure 5. Updated process execution times based on international holidays.

## 3.3 Summary

Complexity in virtual product development models can come from complex processes, complex combinations of actors, or complex secondary calculi. Prediction of the actual impact of a global geographic issue on a product development program that has not yet been deployed is difficult without historical data. Consequently, companies will need to develop VPD case studies that can be correlated to actual impacts to improve the validity of VPD models.

## 4. Example

A specific example from the aerospace industry involving transnational product development programs will help to illustrate not only the method, but also introduce the types of global geographic issues and extent of their impact on current product development.

Located in the western United States is an aerospace corporation specializing primarily in the engineering and manufacturing of aircraft safety devices. A recent project requiring analysis and optimization involved this aerospace corporation and a design center located in India. The project involved a total of five actors from both organizations and provides an ideal test-bed for demonstrating the methods and techniques discussed in this paper, as well as insights into specific global geographic issues affecting product development programs.

The project involved the design of a frangible housing in which thicknesses needed to be specified for optimal performance with respect to stresses in the housing. The process involved eight steps requiring the calculation and modeling of stresses, in addition to the review of the resulting models. Progress was overseen through weekly teleconferences between both sites. Specifically, the process was composed of the tasks shown in Figure 6.

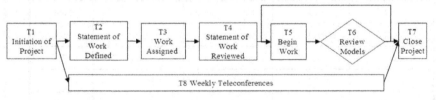

Figure 6. Sequencing of project tasks for aerospace safety project

The aerospace corporation in America made a strategic decision to acquire the design center in India in an attempt to reduce engineering costs. The decision to acquire was not necessarily based upon current need, but was motivated by the desire to establish a new company mode of operation in engineering. Consequently, direction from corporate management was given to find work that could be offloaded to the design center. This specific work project was selected because it could be completed in a relatively short amount of time and was not of critical importance to the overall program.

In this case, only two deployment options were of interest: deployment using actors from both the design center in India and the parent company in the U.S., and deployment using solely actors from the parent company. The purpose of the VPD models was to contrast the cost and time differences between the two deployments as a means of justifying the use of the design center in India. Figure 7 therefore provides a description of each of the possible agents to be used in the two deployments.

Using the agents defined in Figure 7, there were only two deployment options available, as shown in Figure 8. Figure 8a depicts the deployment using actors from both the parent company in the U.S. and the design center in India. Figure 8b represents the deployment option using actors only from the parent company.

The scoring of each deployment option involves the calculation of two different scores which represent the sum across the graph of the metrics in the circles above each task. Both deployment options could be executed in the same amount of time and the first deployment option was $625 less than the second. Based upon this information, the decision was made to execute using Deployment One. The project was deployed and it was discovered in the review of the work (Task 6) the wrong material properties had been used in the analysis, making the design irrelevant. The drawing had been misread due to errors in communication. Communication between engineers in the U.S. and India usually required at least a workday's cycle time due to time zone differences and limitations in direct communication.

| Agents | Task | Actors | Time to Execute | Cost |
|--------|------|--------|-----------------|------|
| Agent 1 | Task 1 | Actor 1 | ½ day | $500 |
| Agent 2 | Task 2 | Actor 2 | ½ day | $400 |
| Agent 3 | Task 3 | Actor 2 | ½ day | $400 |
| Agent 4 | Task 4 | Actor 4, Actor 5 | ½ day | $200 |
| Agent 5 | Task 5 | Actor 4, Actor 5 | 2 days | $800 |
| Agent 6 | Task 6 | Actor 2, Actor 3 | ½ day | $800 |
| Agent 7 | Task 7 | Actor 1, Actor 3 | ½ day | $700 |
| Agent 8 | Task 8 | Actor 1, Actor 3 | 1/8 day | $175 |
| Agent 9 | Task 4 | Actor 3 | ½ day | $400 |
| Agent 10 | Task 5 | Actor 3 | 2 days | $1600 |
| Agent 11 | Task 6 | Actor 2, Actor 3 | ½ day | $800 |
| Agent 12 | Task 7 | Actor 1 | ½ day | $500 |

Figure 7. Agent descriptions for VPD model

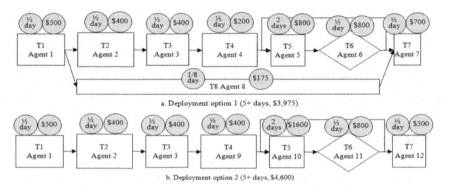

a. Deployment option 1 (5+ days, $3,975)

b. Deployment option 2 (5+ days, $4,600)

Figure 8. Two VPD predicted deployment options

A second iteration of Tasks 5 and 6 was then launched to correct the errors. At the end of the second iteration, it was discovered that the right properties had been used, but the analysis had focused on the wrong portion of the product. A third iteration was launched to correct this error and finally achieved correct results in the analysis. However, part of the statement of work was to optimize thicknesses throughout the product, and the optimization focused again on the wrong portions of the product. A fourth iteration was launched to correct the errors in the optimization.

The final result of this deployment (shown in Figure 9) varied greatly from the predicted deployment option of the VPD model shown in Figure 8a. Rather than requiring 5+ days as predicted, the process required 13+ days to execute. The associated costs were more than two times greater at $9,300, as opposed to the predicted $3,975. A post-mortem analysis determined that communication limitations, time differences, lack of contextual training, incomplete instructions, and diverse training of actors contributed to the results of the actual deployment. The analysis also determined that no one group was more culpable than any other for the errors made.

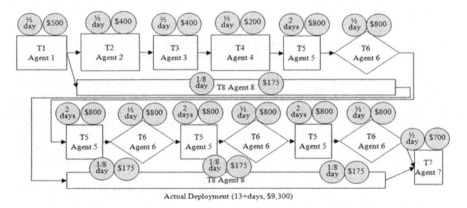

Actual Deployment (13+days, $9,300)

Figure 9. Actual deployment

The nature of these errors is such that they may be classified as global geographic issues. Enumeration of each of these with a secondary calculus is difficult. Often company officials, after having executed multiple projects, calculate a factor which represents the additional time needed to execute projects such as these due to the impact of these global geographic issues. The authors have seen factors ranging from as much as 75 percent longer to 400 percent longer.

## 5. Validation

As with any modeling technique, the value of the model is dependent upon the validity of the data used. In order to create these VPD models, there is need for data relating to the global geographic issues as well as historical case studies to provide meaningful statistical correlations. Since the virtual product development models are company-specific, the identification, collection, and validation must also be company-specific and impacts must be determined within a project-specific context.

## 6. Summary and Conclusions

Methods must be developed for leveraging global geographic issues rather than minimizing their negative impact. Virtual product development is a predictive modeling technique that explores the possible product development deployment options prior to actual deployment, generating scores for each through the use of a secondary calculus. These scores are inaccurate without the integration of global geographic issues and a quantified measure of their influence, requiring a method for the identification and characterization of such issues. That method, in addition to the need for validation and case studies, provides the focus of this paper.

## References

1. Barnes, T.: Retheorizing economic geography: from the quantitative revolution to the "cultural turn," Annals of the Association of American Geographers, 91(3), 2001, p.546-565.
2. Bauer, B.: On methodology in physical geography: current status, implications, and future prospects, Annals of the Association of American Geographers, 89(4), 1999, pp.677-778.
3. Carpenter, M-A.; Fredrickson, J-W.: Top management teams, global strategic posture, and the moderating role of uncertainty, The Academy of Management Journal, 44(3), 2001, 533-545.
4. Chittaro, L. et al: Functional and teleological knowledge in the multimodeling approach for reasoning about physical systems: a case study in diagnosis: Transactions on Systems, Man, and Cybernetics, 23(6), 1993, pp.1718-1749.
5. Daley, J.: Autonomic product development process automation, Master's Thesis, Brigham Young University, 2007.

6. Editorial: the 'new economic geography': challenge or irrelevance? Transactions of the Institute of British Geographers, 24, 1999, pp.387-391.
7. Fulk, J.; DeSanctis, G.: Electronic communication and changing organizational forms, Organization Science, 6(4), 1995, 337-349.
8. Malnight, T-W.: The transition from decentralized to network-based MNC structures: an evolutionary perspective, Journal of International Business Studies, 27(1), 1996, 43-65.
9. Nault, B-R.: Information technology and organization design: locating decisions and information, Management Science, 44(10), 1998, 1321-1335.
10. Raper, J.; Livingston, D.: Let's get real: spatio-temporal identity and geographic entities, Transactions of the Institute of British Geographers (24), 2001, 261-276.
11. Sheppard, E.: The spaces and times of globalization: place, scale, networks, and positionality: Economic Geography, pp.307-330.
12. Sheppard, E.: The spaces and times of globalization: place, scale, networks, and positionality: Economic Geography, pp.307-330.
13. Tractinsky, N.; Jarvenpaa, S-L.: Information systems design decisions in a global versus domestic context, MIS Quarterly, 19(4), 1995, 507-534.
14. Walker, A. J.; Cox, J. J.: Incorporating global characteristic data into virtual product development models, Journal of Computer-Aided Design and Application, 2008.

**IFIP WORLD COMPUTER CONGRESS 2008**

**COMPUTER-AIDED INNOVATION:**
**THEORY AND PRACTICE**

**Poster Presentations**

# DEPUIS project: Design of Environmentally-friendly Products Using Information Standards

**Anna Amato[1], Anna Moreno[2], and Norman Swindells[3]**

[1] ENEA, Italy, anna.amato@casaccia.enea.it
[2] ENEA, Italy, anna.moreno@casaccia.enea.it
[3] Ferroday Limited, UK, ns@ferroday.co.uk

**Abstract:** The design of environmentally friendly products requires data to assess the impact of the product on the environment throughout its life and the original design and manufacturing information that should accompany the product to manage the end-of-life process. Both of these requirements can be satisfied by the innovative combination of two groups of International Standards. The DEPUIS project provides e-learning systems to introduce the technology of data representation by standardised information models – product data technology – and shows how the information represented by data specified by these models can be used in Life Cycle Assessment to innovate life-cycle thinking in the design and manufacture of new products

**Keywords:** Life cycle assessment, product data technology, international standards, e-learning, innovative design

## 1. Introduction

DEPUIS (Design of Environmentally-friendly Products Using Information Standards) is a European funded project launched on the 1st September, 2006. The objective of DEPUIS is to support innovation in the environmentally-friendly design of new products and services through the use of standardised information models. The DEPUIS project is part of the Europe-INNOVA network [1] in the Sixth Framework Programme.

The project has two main actions:

- the provision of e-learning in product data technologies and the opportunities created by the ISO TC184/SC4 information standards and also by ISO 14048 and other ISO 14000 standards;

*Please use the following format when citing this chapter:*

Amato, A., Moreno, A. and Swindells, N., 2008, in IFIP International Federation for Information Processing, Volume 277; *Computer-Aided Innovation (CAI)*; Gaetano Cascini; (Boston: Springer), pp. 135–143.

- workshops to achieve interaction between users and developers of the standards to speed up the acceptance and dissemination of the new methods.

The outcomes from the workshops will be used to prepare policy recommendations to ISO and CEN in the areas of further standardization and innovation for reducing environmental impacts.

The main strategic objective of this project is to enable more companies, particularly SMEs, to use Life Cycle Thinking (LCT) on the environmental impact of their design of new products, in conformance with the Communication on Integrated Product Policy (IPP) [2] of the European Commission. Eco-innovation has to rely on the accessibility on environmental data during the whole life cycle of the product; therefore, standard product data models to integrate the necessary information about materials and processes are needed. [3] These standards and their technologies are important for the data representing the environmental information for sustainability because:

- data for making decisions about sustainability and the impact on the environment is generated in individual computer systems;

- this data has to be shared and exchanged between many different organizations with different systems and applications with many different methods of working;

- the data has to be conserved for longer than the lifetime of any computer system or software application;

- the data needs to be used and understood by unknown systems at unknown times in the future.

## 2. Life Cycle Assessment (LCA)

The environmental innovation of products is recognized as one of the principal instruments for the promotion and integration of competitiveness, innovation and sustainability that are key priorities for the European Union (COM(2004) 38 final) [4], (COM(2003) 302 final), (EC, 2004) [5].

The life-cycle of a product is often long and complicated. It covers several areas and phases involving many different actors such as designers, industry, marketing people, retailers and consumers. IPP attempts to stimulate each part of these individual phases to improve their environmental performance.

The term 'life cycle' refers to the notion that a fair, holistic assessment requires the assessment of raw material production, manufacture, distribution, use and disposal including all intervening transportation steps necessary or caused by the products existence. The sum of all those steps – or phases – is the life cycle of the product. The concept also can be used to optimize the environmental performance of a single product (ecodesign) or to optimize the environmental performance of a company.

Life Cycle Assessment (LCA) is an internationally standardised method (ISO, 2006) [6] for the evaluation of the environmental impact. It helps to avoid the "shifting of burdens" from one life cycle phase to another, among the various environmental implications, and to evaluate the options for improvement.

LCA is increasingly being used at the design stage of new products, where the need for changes can be more easily identified and the cost of making those changes is a minimum. Both retrospective assessment and LCA at the design stage need access to data and this will usually need to be collected from different sources and used in combination in an engineering computer system. However, different sources will have developed their data systems using different software and system platforms and each data system will therefore have a different internal representation for the data that it contains. The result is that data from different sources cannot be combined and used efficiently without a great deal of uncertainty, extra work and additional costs. The potential benefits of being able to use a combination of LCA data systems in the EU are therefore presently difficult to be achieved. In the field of LCA the agreement on the format of the data has been published as the international standard ISO 14048 (ISO, 2002) [7]. As the LCA is a method for assessing the environmental impact of a product through all of its life-cycle stages it requires a massive use of materials and processes data. On the other side, all the data are generated with electronic means by the users which hardly use any standard. The most important issues are therefore to achieve accessibility, comparability and quality assurance of data used in LCA of products and the integration of LCA in the design process.

## 3. Product data technology

The production and management of product information is every company's second business. Whereas most attention is paid to the management of the physical product throughout the lifetime, it is important to realize that the information that accompanies the product through its life is also important. It is well understood that the inputs and outputs of physical products have to managed by strict adherence to engineering specifications: otherwise there will be additional costs arising at a result of returns, rework, negotiations, etc. The same is true of product information. Inputs and outputs of technical information in the form of data associated with the product and its manufacturing processes have also to be managed by the equivalent of engineering specifications: otherwise costs will be incurred from the same causes as with the hardware.

International Standards for product data representation are the equivalent engineering specifications that provide a neutral mechanism for describing product data throughout the life cycle of a product and that are independent of any particular software system. The nature of this description makes it suitable for neutral file exchange between different computer systems but also as a basis for implementing and sharing product databases and long-term archiving. Just as with standards that are engineering specifications for hardware, these product data standards can be used as the basis for quality control and quality assurance of product data and so ensure its validity and reliability.

The standards for product data technology provide information models for particular application domains that are independent from proprietary software. The benefits are that each software system needs only to have one only conversion interface, between its own internal structure and the independent model, to be able to output data or to use the information that is specified in a received model.

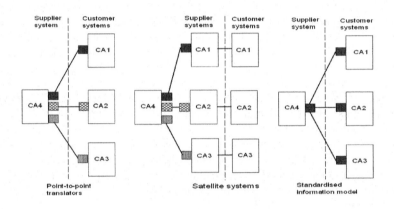

Figure 1 Alternative strategies for the communication between different computer software systems are shown in the figure above and illustrate the situation of a supplier with multiple customers (one-to-many and many-to-one)

Product data technology has been developed by the Sub-committee 4: Industrial data (SC4), of the ISO Technical Committee 184: Industrial automation systems and integration (TC184). ISO TC184/SC4 has developed the system of standards for the computerised representation of product and process data through the combined efforts of hundreds of engineers from the world's main industrialised nations and from most of the global industrial sectors.

The main standards of product data technology that are important for the whole life approach are:

- ISO 10303 Product data representation and exchange – the basis of the technology with generic information models and applications that satisfy particular industrial requirements (collectively known as STEP):

- ISO 13584 Parts libraries – information model for dictionaries of terms that can be referenced from ISO 10303 (collectively known as PLib);

- ISO 15926 Integration of life-cycle data for process plants including oil and gas production facilities – a reference data library that defines the terminology for products that are used in chemical process plant and off-shore oil and gas construction projects (collectively known as RDL).

## 3.1 ISO 10303 - Product data representation and exchange

ISO 10303 is a very large collection of standard documents that provide the base technology for methods for the representation of product data and specify many of its applications [8]. The collection of documents is divided into groups of numbered parts that fulfill related roles. Parts 40 to 60 are the Integrated Generic Resources that are the fundamental basis from which all applications of ISO 10303 are developed. Together these Parts constitute a single information model, although the division into separate documents has been made for ease of their development and maintenance.

Parts 200 and upwards are the Application protocols of ISO 10303 that are implemented in engineering software for industrial use. Each Application protocol is an extension of the single model in the Integrated Generic Resources that has been specialised for a particular industrial need. For the whole-life approach, a selection of probably the most relevant applications is:

- ISO 10303-203: Configuration of 3D designs of mechanical parts and assemblies;

- ISO 10303-210: Electronic assembly, interconnection and packaging design;

- ISO 10303-214: Core data for automobile design processes;

- ISO 10303-235: Engineering properties for product design and verification;

- ISO 10303-239: Product life cycle support.

## 3.2 ISO 13584 Parts Libraries

ISO 13584 specifies an information model for classifications of products, or processes, and their associated properties. The importance of this model is that it has proved to be also very valuable for the compilation of dictionaries of terms that can be accessed by reference from the application models of ISO 10303. The benefit is that the information models in the applications of ISO 10303 can be sufficiently abstract that they can be used in many different industrial situations but the terminology used in a particular domain can be defined in a dictionary that conforms to ISO 13584.

Applications of ISO 13584 are made easier by the availability of free software that implements the information model and provides a simple user-interface for the input of data. The software is called PLIB Editor and it is supplied by the University of Poitiers [9].

## *3.3 ISO 15926 Integration of life-cycle data for process plants including oil and gas production facilities*

ISO 15926 has been developed to overcome proprietary and system dependent data definitions that prohibit the effective exchange, sharing and integration of information, particularly, but not exclusively, in large construction projects. This international standard is based on an ontology and first order logic and has a generic concept model.

ISO 15926 is generic and defines a methodology for general handling of information data. It consists of several parts, Part 2 is the data model that defines the rules and the schema, and Part 4 contains the Reference Data Library (RDL). The RDL defines the semantic meaning of the terms used in a specific industry. An integrated information platform across disciplines can be established by extending the RDL of ISO 15926. Part 7 is implementation methods, which consists of templates and facades.

## 4. Application of product data technology standards to LCA data

The application of product data technology standards to the representation of life-cycle assessment data was successfully realised in the CASCADE Project of the European Commission [10]. The data fields defined in ISO 14048 were mapped onto the Reference Data Library of ISO 15926 and also onto the relevant data objects in ISO 10303-235: Engineering properties for product design and verification.

The CASCADE Project showed that there were no obstacles for the use in LCA of the representation of data for products, processes and their properties using the standards that have developed by ISO TC184/SC4. The unambiguous representations provided by these standards have advantages for computer-to-computer communication compared to other methods.

## 5. The DEPUIS Project

The EU Project DEPUIS – Design of Environmentally Friendly Products Using Information Standards has the objectives of enabling more companies to adopt the approach of the IPP and to enable more people to develop the awareness and knowledge to put this approach into practice. The method adopted to achieve these objectives is the creation of a web site that has two main sections:

a multi-media handbook on the standards for LCA and product data technology and which provides other useful information;
e-Learning courses to enable more SMEs and software developers to adopt IPP environmental tools such as Life Cycle Assessment and Eco-design with the aim of achieving and marketing environmentally-friendly products. The e-learning courses are free of charge.

The web site [11] is hosted by ENEA – the Italian national research organization for new technology, energy and the environment.

The aims of DEPUIS are also to provide basic knowledge for software developers to help them to produce software compatible with International Standards, and to provide feedback to the standards developers.

The multi-media handbook is a compilation of information from many sources that is also frequently updated. The main components are:

- Interested Parties registration

- Examples of application of PDT and LCA integrated approach

- Searchable data base for standards

- Searchable data base for good practices

- Searchable data base for courses

- Certification and training system

- FAQ

- Other useful stuff

The Handbook includes a self-evaluation questionnaire, as a tool to promote the awareness among SMEs on the need of a good product data management. It is composed of seven sections about the following issues:

- Interoperability

- Data archiving

- Environmental data management

- Materials data availability

- Knowledge of existing standards

- Training, qualification and certification

The self training learning courses allow anyone, anytime and anywhere, to gain the knowledge they need in order to participate in the workshops in a proactive manner. Workshops will suggest how to improve and how to implement what the Standards experts on PDT have developed and will be organized in the second half of the project when the multimedia handbook, the guidelines and the tutoring have been consolidated and the participants in the workshops should be more prepared in PDT and LCT. The courses are realized using a model set up by ENEA The methodology utilised by ENEA has been considered among the best 10 practices at international level by CEN ISS [12]. Each course is organized into a series of modules. The desired levels of attainment that have been identified for the each of the subjects in product data technology are one of:

- Awareness – familiarity with the scope and benefits of the technology;

- Knowledge – understanding of the principles and practice of the technology and the details of the scope of the standards;

- Skills – able to put the technology to use in engineering software.

The attainment of the Awareness level provides an introduction to everyone and would also be an appropriate level for managers and decision makers to reach. The attainment of the Knowledge level would be appropriate for design and project engineers, university academics and their students, IT managers, environmental consultants. The attainment of the Skills level would be appropriate for software engineers and their managers who implement the standards.


## 6. Conclusions

The DEPUIS Project has shown that there is a strong interaction between whole-life thinking and product data technology. The management of data throughout the life time of a product requires new methods that do not depend on the life-cycle of proprietary software and computer systems. Product data technology is available for this purpose now and new research is not needed in order to produce a solution to the problems of life-cycle data management.

There are now enough applications of product data standards to support:

- a supply chain of data both to and from accumulations of LCI data sets;

- support for the measurement of environmental data with an audit trail to provide validation;

- support for recording the changes in the life of a product as maintenance replaces components;

- detailed descriptions of complex product that will support end-of-life strategies.

The DEPUIS project has developed a distance learning system as well other useful tools in order to enable individuals and enterprises to learn about the estimation of the environmental impacts of their products and processes and to introduce product data technology based on the International Standards for specifying the technical data for products that these estimations require.

DEPUIS also promotes the use of the standards by raising awareness about the benefits of a consequent better management of the products from every point of view: reduction of time to market, reduction of mistakes, better maintenance services and, in the end, lower costs of production, which is a goal of every company.

# References

1. http://www.europe-innova.org/index.jsp
2  http://europa.eu.int/comm/environment/ipp/home.htm
3  Swindells, N, Moreno, A: Standards to support a sustainable world. A response from ISO TC184/SC4 to the Communiqué to ISO Committees on sustainability (2007)
4  COM (2004) 38 final, Commission of the European Communities, Stimulating Technologies for Sustainable Development: an Environmental Technologies Action Plan for the European Union, Communication from the Commission to the Council and the European Parliament, Brussels, 28 January.
5  COM (2003) 302 final, Commission of the European Communities, Integrated Product Policy. Building on Environmental Life-Cycle Thinking, Communication from the Commission to the Council and the European Parliament, Brussels, 18 June.
6  ISO 2006, ISO 14040:2006 Environmental management – Life cycle assessment – Principles and framework.
7  ISO 2002, ISO/TS 14048:2002 Environmental management – Life cycle assessment – Data documentation format.
8  http:://www.tc184-sc4.org/titles/STEPtitles.htm
9  http://www.plib.ensma.fr
10 http://www.pdt.enea.it
11 http://www.depuis.enea.it/
12 CEN 2007, Providing good practice for E-Learning quality approaches, CEN Workshop Agreement February 2007.

# PML, an Object Oriented Process Modeling Language

**Prof. Dr.-Ing. Reiner Anderl[1] and Dipl.-Ing. Jochen Raßler[2]**

[1] Prof. Dr.-Ing. Reiner Anderl, Germany, anderl@dik.tu-darmstadt.de
[2] Dipl.-Ing. Jochen Raßler, Germany, rassler@dik.tu-darmstadt.de

**Abstract:** Processes are very important for the success within many business fields. They define the proper application of methods, technologies, tools and company structures in order to reach business goals. Important processes to be defined are manufacturing processes or product development processes for example to guarantee the company's success. Over the last decades many process modeling languages have been developed to cover the needs of process modeling. Those modeling languages have several limitations, mainly they are still procedural and didn't follow the paradigm change to object oriented modeling and thus often lead to process models, which are difficult to maintain. In previous papers we have introduced PML, Process Modeling Language, and shown it's usage in process modeling. PML is derived from UML and hence fully object oriented and uses modern modeling techniques. It is based on process class diagrams that describe methods and resources for process modeling. In this paper the modeling language is described in more detail and new language elements will be introduced to develop the language to a generic usable process modeling language.

**Keywords:** process modeling language, PML, UML

## 1. Introduction

As the tendency of enterprises to collaborate growths steadily, industry faces new challenges managing business processes, product development processes, manufacturing processes and much more. Furthermore, discipline spanning product development processes are increasing, e.g. desired mechatronical products are in the need for knowledge from mechanical, electrical as well as software engineers. Humanists and economists also play a huge role in modern product development processes. Each individual discipline has its own, well-defined and specific processes, which typically are based on well-tried methodologies. These process descriptions are very powerful within the traditional discipline or the original enterprise, they were invented in. On the other side, they lack for flexibility, due to the reason that most existing process descriptions are

*Please use the following format when citing this chapter:*

Anderl, R. and Raßler, J., 2008, in IFIP International Federation for Information Processing, Volume 277; *Computer-Aided Innovation (CAI)*; Gaetano Cascini; (Boston: Springer), pp. 145–156.

based on a procedural approach. These are not powerful enough to meet requirements of describing cross collaboration. In particular OEMs challenge the integration of suppliers. Suppliers have different levels of access to the OEMs data base, data exchange is handled based on integration level. Furthermore the levels supplier get differ between suppliers and projects.

Taking everything into account, the need for a process modeling language that meets the above shown requirements is obvious. Not only must the different disciplines be supported, but also cross enterprise collaboration, as well as supplier integration. Still there is no proper description for this kind of flexible processes descriptions. To meet all these needs a new process modeling language is developed and demands the following requirements:

- Support of hierarchical structures.
- Support of flexible interpretation of a defined process without getting incompatible – support of generalization and specification.
- Robust process definition for flexible proceeding sequences of activities without losing process comparability – support of interchangeability of processes.
- Support of different integration scenarios and levels without changing process description at any time – support of flexibility of processes.
- Easy to learn and read – audience of those process definitions are very broad.

This paper summarizes the previous work done in defining a new process modeling language – PML – and introduces new aspects of the language. Although the development of PML isn't yet finished within the context of this publication, the process modeling language reaches a state, where it can be started to use in a productivity environment. A conclusion closes this paper.

## 2. Existing Process Modeling Languages

In this chapter some existing process modeling languages are covered. It is briefly described why they do not meet the requirements of modern process definitions. For an in depth analysis and further details we refer to [1].

IDEF0/SADT and Event Driven Process Chains (EPC) are procedural process modeling languages and support modeling processes with different levels of details. Both process modeling languages lack for transparency and clarity if they are applied to complex processes. Moreover, they are not very flexible regarding changes to the proceeding sequence of activities. [2, 3, 4, 5]

The Unified Modeling Language (UML) offers an all spanning modeling language. Regarding data and information model the language is object oriented. If UML is utilized to describe processes, UML reveals several disadvantages. UML is not an object oriented language for process modeling, because processes are still modeled procedural. Each activity is seen as an object. Relations between activities still base on logical states. Processes defined with UML are not very flexible regarding changes in the proceeding sequence of activities. [6, 7, 8, 9]

Business Process Modeling Notation (BPMN) representation of processes is quite similar to the UML activity diagram. It is a standardized graphical notation for drawing business processes in a workflow. Processes are defined as a sequence of activities in swim lanes. Again it is a state based connection between object oriented activities. Therefore the evaluation result upon BPMN is similar to the UML verdict. [10, 3]

The Integrated Enterprise Modeling as a refinement of SADT enables users to generate views on the complete enterprise, not only on its processes. Processes are still in a SADT kind of style. Due to its retaining on logical sequence of activities it has no real advantage in modeling flexible processes. It still lacks a powerful support of process flexibility. [11, 3]

The Process Specification Language (PSL) basically is an ontology for describing processes. As PSL's objective is to serve as an Interlingua for integrating several process-related applications without formal and graphical constructs, it is therefore not capable for process modeling. [12]

The Semantic Object Model (SOM) methodology allows flexible and robust process modeling, based on the division of an enterprise model into several model layers, each of them describing a business system from a specific point of view. Within the process model the activity objects are connected with events. In comparison, SOM is most progressive regarding the definition of relations, but its constructs are difficult to understand due to the complex, integrated approach. [3]

The modeling languages still describe relations on state based, proceeding sequences of activities. Taken together these results evoke the need for a new process modeling language facing the requirements of the paradigm change. [1]

## 3. Basic concepts of the Process Modeling Language

A new approach for a process modeling language has been introduced in [1], which uses object oriented techniques and hence meets all requirements. This approach uses the well known and widely used modeling language UML, that applies object oriented techniques to obtain modularization, reuse, flexibility and easy maintaining, among others, in the field of software and system modeling. Ongoing developments on the basis of UML, like SysML, prove the sustainability of the UML metamodel. Thus UML is a good starting point for the development of an object oriented process modeling language.

Fig 1 shows the definition of an UML class diagram including class name, attributes and methods.

Fig 1 UML class diagram

The class itself is time invariant as it is a generic description of the content of the context. But the instance of a class, an object, is time variant, because it holds characteristic values that can be checked to given times and can change over time. This means, the values can change, but the general structure of an object (number and kind of attributes) can not change.

Having a time variant object it can be derived by time regarding to [13]

$$\lim_{T \to T_0} \frac{Object(T) - Object(T_0)}{T - T_0} = \frac{dObject}{dT} = \dot{Object} \, . \tag{1}$$

Equation (1) shows that the content of an object, which means the attributes of an instance of a class, may change over time. Given a rule to change the attributes of an object one can express the change of the object's content as a process instance, which is shown in (2). Note that we use a discrete time $T$ instead of continuous time $t$ to implement "time steps". This is due to the result of the derivation as different process instances may need different time intervals to execute.

$$\dot{Object} = \text{Process instance} \tag{2}$$

As we have derived the object we now have to derive the object's content. Fig 1 uses the word attributes as defined in UML, in equation (3) we will derive the attributes, but using the word information to make the meaning clearer and more generic.

$$\lim_{T \to T_0} \frac{Information(T) - Information(T_0)}{T - T_0} = \frac{dInformation}{dT} = \dot{Information} \tag{3}$$

The derivation of information shows that the information may change over time. So the change of information, the change of attributes or data can be expressed as a method, which is shown in (4).

$$\dot{Information} = Method \tag{4}$$

The last field of a UML class diagram and thus in the object holds the methods, which act on the attributes. In the following we use the term operation for UML methods to differentiate between UML and our introduction. Operation and the just derived method are quite similar and are the same in several cases. In the following we derive the operation, which is shown in equation (5).

$$\lim_{T \to T_0} \frac{Operation(T) - Operation(T_0)}{T - T_0} = \frac{dOperation}{dT} = \dot{Operation} \tag{5}$$

The meaning of the derivation of an operation is quite complex. To express this mathematically we can use equations (3) to (5), which show, that dOperation/dT is the first derivation of an operation or the second derivation of information. This means dOperation/dT is the gradient of an operation or the curvature of information. The expression gradient of an operation seems quite handsome and opens the question: what does result in the change of an operation? Or, more exact, what does result in a change of the quality of the execution of a method?

Think also of the similarity of operation and method. This question directly leads to the answer to the problem, which is

$$\dot{Operation} = \text{Resource} \qquad (6)$$

Resources influence the execution of an operation. The use of more or less resources leads to faster or slower execution, influences the quality of the output, may lead to more innovation and so on.

Equations (1) through (6) have shown the derivation from a time variant object to a time variant process instance. Generalizing the process instance we get a process class, which again is time invariant. The diagram of a process is shown in Fig 2.

Fig 2 PML Process class diagram

UML uses assurances to guarantee the range for its attributes. We need assurances too, but not as static ranges. Deriving a static value by time normally leads to zero. But knowing that the integral of a delta impulse $\delta(t)$ is defined as 1 [14] and we derive the constant with this definition in mind, the derivation of the static assurance leads to the delta impulse, which can be interpreted as an event. This means, an assurance for the processes is an event, a constraint becoming true, a set of data becoming available, time is elapsed and so on.

We introduce the term PML, which stands for Process Modeling Language and can be seen as an extension to UML, as SysML is. Thus the known techniques of inheritance, association, and cardinalities can be used. Implementing those techniques processes can be modeled hierarchically with modularization, structure, exchangeability and reusability.

[1, 15] show the used way to derive PML. Starting from the time invariant UML class we have instantiated a time variant object. This is derived by time and leads to a process instance, or project, which is time variant, and finally generalized to a time invariant process. The class therefore describes the product in a generic way, while the real contents are stored in its instantiation. The same is true on process level. The PML process class describes the process in a generic way. It allows one to define all methods with assurances and resources needed for the process. The instantiation of a process is a project. This means, the instance of a process defines the current occurrence of resources, used data models etc.

Regarding to connections and dependencies between single process classes, PML features the well known UML-concepts of inheritance and associations. The concepts for inheritance of process classes follow the notation of standard UML classes through simple object-oriented means like generic super-processes, sub-processes, overwriting and inheritance of methods and resources. Structural and hierarchical modeling is supported by using the concepts of associations, aggregations, and compositions and the usage of cardinalities. [1, 15]

Now we want to illustrate the capability of PML means by a complex product development process and a manufacturing process. This example application stresses out the advantages of PML regarding flexibility of defined processes, reusability, clarity and understandability. In [15] we have introduced the product generation process of integral sheet metal parts with higher order bifurcations. Fig 3 illustrates the process model as an example for the strength of PML. For details of this algorithm driven development process we refer to [15, 16, 17].

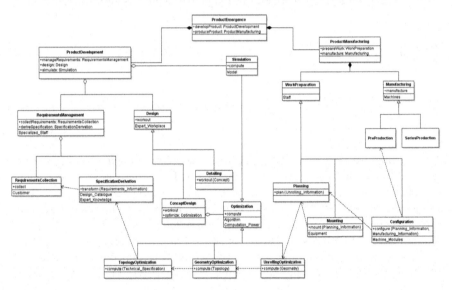

Fig 3a Process diagram for product emergence of integrated sheet metal products with higher order bifurcations

As the complete process model is expressed in PML, the generic process description remains at a level of utmost flexibility and is clearly structured. This enables all projects dealing with the product emergence of integral sheet metal products to be modeled with this generic process model by instantiating it. The model itself does not alter through instantiating it and remains unchanged. An instantiated process embodies exactly one project representing a specific integral sheet metal product.

UML supports instance diagrams, which basically are class diagrams with the instances built in to show the relations between instances and classes. The instance diagram additionally shows the actual object's occurrence and hence the used resources in our process models. As instance diagrams are not very handsome for complex models we will not use them here. Instead we use other diagrams to show the instances and – more interesting to processes – their timely and logical occurrences. These are the sequence diagram and the activity diagram respectively. As announced in [1] it is possible to derive sequence and activity diagrams with PML.

Fig 3 illustrates the activity diagram for the emergence of an integral sheet metal product. In the UML, an activity diagram represents the logical workflows of components in a system and shows the overall flow of control. This approach also fits for PML.

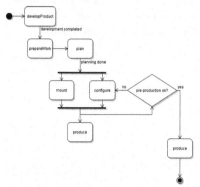

Fig 3b Activity diagram of manufacturing process

The general meaning of a PML activity diagram is the same as in UML. The black circle in the upper left corner shows the starting point, the black circle in the lower right corner shows the end point. Activities are modeled as rectangles with rounded corners, decisions are modeled as a rhombus. Straight horizontal lines are used to show the splitting of the process flow or the synchronization of processes. Note that in this example only a small extract of the above shown development and manufacturing process is illustrated.

Another way to show the instances is by using sequence diagrams. Fig 4 shows the appropriate sequence diagram for the manufacturing process. As in UML the sequence diagram shows the life time of objects with its construction and destruction events and signals.

Fig 4 shows the current instances with instance names and the corresponding classes they are instantiated of. *RollerTrailManufacturing* is active for the whole manufacturing process and activates different sub-processes as planning, mounting, configuring, and the series production. The pre-production is constructed and controlled by the configuration to allow iterations to optimize the machine configuration.

To show the real strength of PML Fig 5 details the manufacturing processes. *Manufacturing* consists of *SplittingProcess*, which has three sub-processes: *LinearFlowSplitting*, *LinearBendSplitting*, and *LinearBending*. To instantiate *Manufacturing* different *SplittingProcess*es are instatiated. But, using the concept of object orientation, not *SplittingProcess* but the sub-processes will be instantiated. The same is true for the resources in *Manufacturing*. Machines should hold the specialized machines, which are linear flow splitting machines, linear bend splitting machines, and linear bending machines. Thus having a generic process description, the product and its manufacturing process is dependent of the used machines, the splitting processes and their order in the manufacturing line.

The method names *manufacture* are used in the process classes *Manufacturing*, *SplittingProcess*, and its sub-processes. The *manufacture* method in the *SplittingProcess* and its sub-processes can just be implemented and used, but the *manufacture* method in *Manufacturing* has to be implemented on its own in the actual instance to specify the manufacturing process for the actual product.

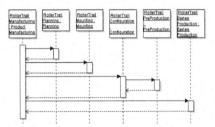

Fig 4 Sequence diagram of manufacturing process

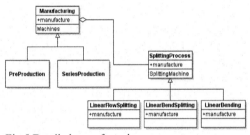

Fig 5 Detailed manufacturing processes

So the production depends on the resources and the order of the usage of the resources. Hence different products can be produced using the same generic process model.

## 4. Additional Aspects of PML

We have shown the derivation and usage of PML in the previous chapter. Now we want to integrate other UML concepts in the context of PML and, to be continuous, give a mathematical explanation of the concepts.

### Activity Diagram

In the previous chapter and in [15] we have used the activity Diagram, but without a mathematical description. As one can see in Fig 3 the concepts of activity diagrams use Boolean descriptions to model the activities. An activity gets started if the result of the previous activity gets true, e.g. has finished. Thus the model is based on Boolean states.

Decisions use one input and two outputs in their process flow. The input is again triggered by the result of an activity becoming true. The two outputs can be seen as the decision is true or false, expressed with variable $x$, the output is similar to $x$ or $\bar{x}$.

Synchronization lines can be expressed using the Boolean symbol *and* ($\wedge$) to model that all incoming events have to be true or with the Boolean symbol *OR* ($\vee$) to model that at least one of the inputs has to be true. Another possibility is the Boolean operator *XOR* ($\oplus$) to model that exactly one input has to be true and all other false.

Hence the activity diagram can be expressed mathematically using Boolean expressions. Discussing the Boolean expressions in the context of the timely derivation one can see that UML uses the activities of its classes in this diagram. The same is true for PML. The only difference is the used field of UML's or PML's class description, regarding to Fig 1 and Fig 2. UML methods are in the third field, PML methods are in the second, central field.

## Sequence Diagram

The sequence diagram lacks the mathematical description too. This is introduced in the available paragraph.

The sequence diagram uses objects, which are instances of process classes. This means the sequence diagram uses time variant objects and therefore is time dependent. This makes sense as the sequence diagram doesn't model a process but a given project.

Another important aspect of processes is that they do not necessarily converge. Think for example about product development. There may be a set of requirements for the new product that lead to a dead end development or a very expensive one that is stopped to save money for the company. Thus a process may diverge. Knowledge about the convergence of processes and the discrete time steps make it obvious to use z-transform [14] to describe sequence diagrams.

Using the example of the previous chapter shown in Fig 4 the sequence can be written as

$$y(z) = a(z) + a(z-1) + b(z-1) + a(z-2) + c(z-2) +$$
$$a(z-3) + d(z-3) + a(z-4) + d(z-4) + e(z-4) + \qquad (7)$$
$$a(z-5) + d(z-5) + a(z-6) + f(z-6) + a(z-7).$$

Equation (7) uses the letters $a$ to $f$ for the process instances and $y$ for the result to enhance the readability. Process instance $a$ is active for the life time of the example, starting all other process instances except of $e$ which is started from $d$.

## Interaction Diagrams

In the UML exist 4 types of interaction diagrams. These are the sequence diagram, the interaction overview diagram, the communication diagram, and the timing diagram [9]. The sequence diagram has just been described mathematically, all other interaction diagram types can be handled similar, but they show different aspects of interaction within the running time of a process instantiation. Thus we pass the in depth view to these interaction diagrams.

### State Machine Diagram
The state machine diagram in UML shows the actual state of time variant objects to given times $t_0$. The same is true in PML. The state machine diagram shows the actual state of a given process instance $P(T)$ at a given time $T_0$. This can be written as

$$StateMachineDiagram \mapsto P(T_0).\tag{8}$$

### Package Diagram
The package diagram is a structural diagram. It clusters processes and bears the capability to organize processes particularly for modularization and reuse.

Package diagrams can be described using the set theory. The membership operators *element of* ($\in$) and *subset of* ($\subseteq$) can be used to describe the relations of processes and packages to subordinate packages. The *union operator* ($\bigcup$) can be used to cluster processes and packages into a subordinate package. Fig 6 illustrates this concept.

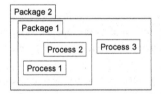

Fig 6 PML Package Diagram

### Use Case Diagram
Use case diagrams get a special meaning within the context of PML. In UML use case diagrams are mainly used to model the context of the system to be developed. Thus the use case diagram can be seen as a diagram to model requirements.

Although the use case diagram in PML can be used to model requirements for the processes to be developed, it gets its strength as a documentation tool for the processes or projects as instances of processes.

To make this more understandable, we introduce an example for quality management. The ISO 900x certification is approved on a certain process. This means a company describes a quality management process in a certain context and asks for approval. If the same company deploys products in a different context they need to describe the quality management process again and ask for approval once again. If the ISO 900x certification process is described in a generic way using PML it only needs approval once and can use this process for different projects in different contexts, using different parameters for instantiating the processes or specializing some process classes. Thus modified projects can be instantiated or enhanced without losing compatibility to the approved generic process.

To document the instantiation of processes use case diagrams can be used to describe reference instantiations and interactions of projects and sub projects without actual instantiation of a project.

## 5. Conclusion

The strength of the shown approach for process modeling is the complete object oriented view to processes and the differentiation and linkage of and between processes and projects. As in data modeling process modeling can now be done in a generic way. The introduced process description perfectly fits into PDM systems with the process class descriptions. Hence process management is now process modeling at running time. A process in a PDM system can be extended by more classes, that extent existing classes, or specialize them. The instances of those processes are used in projects, which define the parameters of the instances. The implemented technique of processes and projects within PDM systems is then similar to data models, where object orientation has been a standard since years. The object oriented approach of process modeling introduces a paradigm change not only to the view of process and project management, but also enables new possibilities for interoperability. Heavy use of modularization enables exchangeability and process reusability and hence strengthens the integration of third-party processes. This leads to more powerful cross-enterprise collaboration.

Another important point is the certification of processes. Depending on products or customers it is necessary to have certified processes. Think of ISO 9000 or certification for medical issues. With PML the process is only certified once but can lead to different instantiations – regardless to the project (in terms of same or different product).

Future work on PML will cover many important topics. Using PML to model more real world processes and using it for productivity projects will prove the usability of this new modeling language. Missing components will be added to complete PML. Also the formal description of PML, regarding to UML, has to be enhanced and will be covered in future work.

Most important concepts that are still missing are process and project management. Using PML process and project management get new meanings. Thus the meaning of process and project management has to be redefined in the context of PML and new management methods have to be developed.

To apply PML for productivity it may be very interesting to develop a model to map the PML process class diagrams into PDM (Product Data Management) systems and use the instantiation for actual projects within product development. UML tools have the capability to generate source code from the class diagrams. Future work will cover the possibilities to generate PDM descriptions from PML models to map processes into engineering tools.

This paper has shown the concepts of the new process modeling language PML. Deriving PML mathematically from UML led to a process model that supports object oriented process modeling capabilities. Thus the requirements for a modern process description language have been fulfilled, such as modularization, exchangeability, cross enterprise collaboration, easy maintenance, enhance ability and many more.

This paper has introduced and discussed many new diagram types that are known from UML. The usage of PML has been shown with a complex example that illustrates the strength of this process modeling language. Thus the basic work for the usage of PML in productivity has been done.

# References

1.  Anderl R., Raßler J., Malzacher J.: Proposal for an Object Oriented Process Modeling Language. Proceedings of the 4th International Conference on Interoperability for Enterprise Software and Applications (I-ESA), Berlin, Germany, March (2008).
2.  IEEE Std 1320.1-1998. IEEE Standard for Functional Modeling Language—Syntax and Semantics for IDEF0, IEEE, New York (1998).
3.  Bernius P., Mertins K., Schmidt G. (Eds): Handbook on Architectures of Information Systems, 2nd Edition. Springer Verlag Berlin, Heidelberg (2006).
4.  Scheer A.W.: ARIS – Business Process Frameworks, 2nd Edition, Berlin (1998).
5.  Scheer A.W.: ARIS – Business Process Modeling, 2nd Edition, Berlin (1999).
6.  OMG: Unified Modeling Language: Superstructure v2.1.1, of Feb 2007, www.omg.org, (2007).
7.  Eriksson H.E., Penker M.: Business modeling with UML: business patterns at work, John Wiley & Sons Inc, New York (2000).
8.  Burkhardt R.: UML – Unified Modeling Language: Objektorientierte Modellierung für die Praxis. Addison-Wesley-Longman, Bonn (1997).
9.  Booch G., Rumbaugh J., Jacobsen I.: Das UML Benutzerhandbuch, Addison-Wesley Verlag, München (2006).
10. OMG: Business Process Modeling Notation Specification, of Feb 2006, www.omg.org.
11. Spur G., Mertins K., Jochem R., Warnecke, H.J.: Integrierte Unternehmensmodellierung Beuth Verlag GmbH (1993).
12. International Standards Organization (ISO): ISO 18629 Series: Process Specification Language of 2004, www.iso.org, (2004).
13. Luh W.: Mathematik für Naturwissenschaftler, Bd.1, Differentialrechnung und Integralrechnung, Folgen und Reihen, Aula, Wiesbaden (1987).
14. Clausert H., Wiesemann, G.: Grundgebiete der Elektrotechnik 2. Wechselströme, Leitungen, Anwendungen der Laplace- und Z-Transformation, Oldenbourg, München (2000).
15. Anderl R., Raßler J., Rollmann T.: PML in Application – An Example of Integral Sheet Metal Design with Higher Order Bifurcations, Proceedings of the ASME 2008 International Design Engineering Technical Conferences & Computers and Information in Engineering Conference IDETC/CIE 2008, Brooklyn, New York, USA, August (2008).
16. Anderl R., Wu Z., Rollmann, T.: Eine integrierte Prozesskette in integralen Blechbauweisen, 5. Gemeinsamen Kolloquium Konstruktionstechnik, Dresden (2007).
17. Anderl R., Kormann M., Rollmann, T., Wu Z., Martin A., Ulbrich S., Günther U.: Ein Ansatz zur Algorithmen-getriebenen Konstruktion – Paradigmenwechsel in der Produktentstehung, 5-2007, Konstruktion, Springer VDI Verlag (2007).

# Innovative PLM-based approach for collaborative design between OEM and suppliers: Case study of aeronautic industry

**Farouk Belkadi[1], Nadège Troussier[1], Frederic Huet[1], Thierry Gidel[1], Eric Bonjour[2], and Benoît Eynard[1]**

[1] Université de Technologie de Compiègne, Centre Pierre Guillaumat
BP 60319, rue du Docteur Chweitzer, 60203 Compiègne Cedex, France
{fbelkadi; nadege.troussier; frederic.huet; thierry.gidel; benoit.eynard} @utc.fr

[2] Université de Franche Comté, Institut FEMTO-ST - UMR CNRS 6174 24, rue Alain Savary, 25000 Besançon, France, ebonjour@ens2m.fr

**Abstract:** To achieve different assembly operations on the aircraft structure, the aeronautic OEM needs to create and manage various fixture tools. To cope with these needs, the OEM begun to adopt the supplier integration into the tooling development process. This paper presents a conceptual PLM-based approach to support new business partnership of different suppliers. The new business partnership aims to improve the role of supplier in the different tasks of design, configuration and fabrication of the tooling. The use of the PLM concepts is proposed to enhance the collaboration between OEM and the equipment's suppliers. UML models are proposed to specify the structure of the PLM solution. These models describe the relation between the aircraft assembly project, and the tooling design process.

**Keywords:** Suppliers Integration, PLM, UML, Innovative Organisation

## 1. Introduction

The role of supplier in a successful assembly process of aircraft component is very important. Because of the specific aircraft structure, assembly department needs to constantly design new fixture tools used for new assembly operations. It obviously happens when the aeronautic OEM creates new aircraft model, and also when this OEM modifies the existing models to satisfy a particular customer requirement.

To deal with assembly tool costs and time to market optimization challenges, the collaboration between OEM and suppliers should rather go into strategic part-

*Please use the following format when citing this chapter:*

Belkadi, F., Troussier, N., Huet, F., Gidel, T., Bonjour, E. and Eynard, B., 2008, in IFIP International Federation for Information Processing, Volume 277; *Computer-Aided Innovation (CAI)*; Gaetano Cascini; (Boston: Springer), pp. 157–168.

nership, covering the whole tool's lifecycle. The purpose of our research is to develop a new business partnership that enables efficient collaboration between OEM and suppliers. This partnership would enhance the suppliers' role in the design process of assembly tools. The case study concerns the tooling design activities and manufacturing process in the aeronautic industry. The construction of this business partnership is obtained according the following perspectives:

- Definition of its mission and organization,
- Identification of new methodologies to optimize it's operating processes,
- Realization of a collaborative IT framework to support its activities.

The paper focuses on the last perspective and describes a conceptual framework to specify an innovative PLM-based approach. The originality of our approach comes from the high abstraction level of the proposed models based on the situation concept. These concepts are useful to describe different organization forms. It mainly provides specification of IT system that can gives innovation aided by enhancing the project organization in the context of extended enterprise and by favouring interoperability between heterogeneous information shared between OEM and supplier systems (for instance, between SAP system to capture Aircraft information at the OEM level and DELMIA system to identify the tooling behaviour in the assembly process, at the supplier level).

First, we present an overview of the context study and the interest of PLM approach to solve this problematic. Second, a literature review is presented concerning the use of PLM methodologies to support the OEM supplier partnership. Third, we develop our conceptual models of the IT structure. The specification of the PLM-based approach is defined according to a unified modelling that describes, at the same abstraction level, the product (assembly tools or equipment) data and process data. Fourth, the concept of project view is presented. Using the UML activity diagram, we detailed some functionalities of the future collaborative system to manage the equipment design project.

## 2. Context and aims of the study

Traditionally, in the aeronautic industry, the tooling supplier is a basic manufacturer of the assembly tools. The design and manufacture processes of these tools are considered as a sequential one. First the design department delivers the engineering documents of the different aircraft parts; the production engineering department specifies and designs the detailed assembly processes and needed tools to carry out the assembly operations. Then, the production engineering department sends the detailed specifications to the supplier for tools manufacturing.

Figure 1 shows this configuration. On the one hand, three departments are engaged in the global process of assembly tools purchasing: production service specifies the assembly needs, the equipment's R&D designs the tooling structure and the purchase service negotiates and sends the order to supplier. On the other hand, several suppliers located in different geographical locations are contracted

with to produce the various parts of the tool. After the completion of the tool, it is
sent directly to the production shop for use.

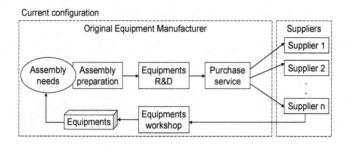

Figure 1 The current OEM-Supplier partnership.

During the manufacturing process of the assembly tool, some modifications
may occur on the initial configuration of aircraft components. These modifications
imply changes on the specification of the assembly process and thus of the assembly tool. The whole cycle of the assembly tool ordering is then repeated to cope
with the new specifications.

This approach proved its limits in the current context. The supplier is not integrated in the first stages of the tools specification and likewise, the OEM has not
access to the manufacture process of the tool. Thus, much iteration is occurred
before obtaining the final tool definition fulfilling the requirements of production
engineering department. Several problems have been observed during the preliminary study: Important time and costs of the assembly tools manufacturing (and
consequently for the assembly process of the aircraft parts, delivery date not respected); difficulty to manage the assembly tool range by the OEM (no-use of
standards, bad maintenance...); the OEM has to manage several product data interfaces with various partners.

In the future configuration, an innovative PLM-based approach is proposed to
support a new business partnership approach. PLM is used for the seamlessly integration of all the information specified throughout all phases of the equipment's
life cycle to everyone in the new organization (OEM and a new global supplier
network) at every managerial and technical level. Figure 2 shows the proposed
configuration of the new business partnership. In this configuration, design tasks',
configuration and fabrication of the assembly tool are performed collaboratively
with the new global supplier network. Suppliers are already informed by new
modifications of the assembly operations and design themselves the new tool.

This description shows important evolutions in the configuration of the development process that can be summarized by considering the shift from a linear and
sequential process to a much more "interactionnist" one [1]. This reconfiguration
should lead to significant improvement in cost and time saving in association with
a greater innovative potential [2], [3].

But, what is at stake in this study goes beyond the development process and the impact or the evolution has to be considered at the (inter)organizational level. We can both consider the renewal of the expected shared competences and new governance modalities for these new relationships [4], [5].

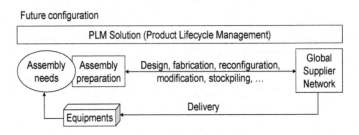

Figure 2 Future configuration of OEM-Supplier partnership.

First, in the traditional development process, the supplier's competences were exclusively manufacturing ones. In the new process, the expected incomes evolve towards innovation capacity, sub-system integration, proactive behavior during the process... This leads to consider the new role of the suppliers, not only as an efficient manufacturer, but more as a service supplier, collaborating in the definition and conception stages [6]. Thus, knowledge transfer and learning capacities are at the core of these new activities for these suppliers [7]. So, as we can see, this evolution will have to be encompassed in a wider evolution of the competences that is expected from the suppliers.

Second, to promote greater innovative potential, interactions between the different partners will have to be carefully managed, because of the change in the nature of their transactions. We can at least anticipate three significant modifications in their relationships. The advantage of the new process is a more important distribution of risk between the partners, previously only assumed by the OEM. In the new context, risk is distributed between all the involved actors. This collaborative organization implies that the partners reveal some of their competences, to combine and fertilize them. Thus, the management of core competences and the equilibrium between the individual interests of each actor and the collective objectives has to be questioned [8], [9]. And, to promote innovation, upstream monitoring and planning will necessarily have to be adapted, in order to facilitate the emergence of new opportunities, which were not anticipated at the beginning of the collaboration. This seems all the more important, that previous studies have shown that innovation through cooperation is linked to a sort of "plasticity" of the relationship, allowing to discover new opportunities and sources of learning [10].

These different preliminary elements shed light on the extended impact of this evolution in the development process, both in the vertical interactions (between OEM and suppliers) and in the horizontal ones (between suppliers). The innovation and collaboration objectives show that governance will have to rely on a new equilibrium between contractual prescriptions and trust based relationships [11].

Indeed, to promote innovation, contracts will necessarily remain uncomplete and could lead to strong inertia during the collaboration, while trust, both on competence and behavior, will bring more flexibility in front of novelty and knowledge mutualisation. This vertical and horizontal integration that necessitate risks and benefits sharing, implies developing common practices and methodologies. By sharing project management approach, problem solving methods or design methodology, the partners would in turn shared objectives and decision processes.

Even if this contribution is focused on the definition of a PLM platform, these different elements have to be mentioned. They necessarily won't be neutral for the definition and appropriation of this new support by the different partners.

PLM is used for the seamlessly integration of all the information specified throughout all phases of the equipment's life cycle to everyone in the new organization (OEM and a new global supplier network) at every managerial and technical level. The following section presents a literature review about PLM concept.

## 3. About Product Life Management

PLM is defined as a systematic concept for the integrated management of all product related information and processes through the entire lifecycle, from the initial idea to end-of-life [12]. In [13], PLM is considered as a strategic business approach that applies a consistent set of business solution in support of the collaborative creation, management, dissemination, and use of product information across the extended enterprise.

Such as in the automotive industry, the aeronautic industry is seen to adopt the supplier integration into the development process. The new management culture considers necessary the PLM approach to get these goals [14]. Tang [15] present a literature review of PLM approaches used in automotive industry to improve collaboration between OEM and suppliers. The lifecycle currently support the OEM supplier partnership can be grouped in collaborative environment with three main phases [16]:

- Designing the systems to be used in the OEM's product.
- Supply chain integration to produce and deliver the requested systems to OEM.
- Provide services for the components for both OEM and supplier systems.

The IT solution to support PLM results from the integration between enterprise resource planning (ERP), product data management (PDM) and other related systems, such as computer aided design (CAD) and costumer relationship management (CRM) [17]. A critical aspect of PLM systems is their product information modeling architecture. In the literature, several representations of the product data are presented [18], [19]. The unified representation of the product knowledge can favor semantic interoperability of CAD/CAE/CAM systems at the conceptual level [20]. UML is currently used to support product models [2]. STEP and XML are used to obtain interoperability at the implementation level [22]. Sudarsan [23] propose a product information-modeling framework that aimed at support PLM information needs and intended to capture product data, design rationale, assembly, tolerance information, the evolution of products and product families.

However, product model is not the unique element in a PLM data models. Nowak [24] present architecture of a collaborative aided design framework integrating Product, Process and Organization models for engineering performance improvement. Danesi [25] propose the P4LM methodology which allows the management of Projects, Products, Processes, and Proceeds in collaborative design and that aims to allow the integration of information coming from different partners which are involved in a PLM application. This framework allows a top-down approach by defining functions in an abstraction level according to four modules (Project, Product, Proceed and Process).

In aim to get best integration of suppliers in the automotive design and manufacturing processes, Trappey [26] develops and implements an information platform called advanced production quality planning (APQP) hub. The information hub mainly provides a collaborative environment that enhancing the visibility of the supply chain operations and contributes in collecting and delivering APQP documents among both the OEM and all supply chain. This information platform applies the concept of modularized assembly and consists of five major functions: Categorized part library, project based collaborative design, real-time information exchange, on-line confirmation of modularized products, and on-line negotiation and ordering. Each one of the obvious functions is implemented according to an interactive process.

Our work deals with the integration of Product, Process, and Organization dimensions of a design project. Several models are developed to support, at the conceptual level, this integration.

## 4. The Package model of the PLM approach

At the conceptual level, our approach is based on the concept of working situation proposed in [27]. According to this model, each process and activity in a collaborative design project is considered as an interactional entity that refers to links between various entities of the situation. These entities may bring together different physical elements such as human resources and material resources (product, drawings, documents, CAD tools, planning tools, etc). It may bring together, also, other interactional entities (activities, processes, communities).

The nature of the contribution made by each entity to the interactions is formalized in this approach using the concept of specific role that is a systemic extension of the role proposed in the organization theory [28]. Five kinds of specific roles are distinguished:

- The "actor" role concerns every entity who/which participates directly in the interaction and who/which is responsible for the end result.
- The "customer" role brings together all the entities that are going to be receiving the end result of the interaction.

- The "manager" role concerns every entity who/which regulates the functioning of an interaction.
- The "support" role includes every entity who/which give help in an interaction.
- The "object" role concerns every entity on whom/which the interaction acts.

Figure 3 describes the global package model structuring the PLM data. According to this model, the assembly tool (equipment) may be considered as a mediation artifact since it is simultaneously a support of the assembly aircraft project (that is performed in the OEM Assembly Workshop) and, the main object of the equipment project (that are realized by the new trade organization). Aircraft project plays the role of customer of the equipment project. The different needs of the equipment project are specified according to the different activities of the aircraft assembly process. Thus, Aircraft processes take also the role of customer in the equipment processes.

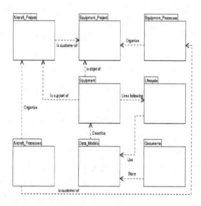

Figure 3 The package model structuring our PLM approach.

The processes packages (of aircraft and equipment) group various processes that organize the functioning of related projects. For example, design and fabrication processes are the principal processes of the equipment project, its play the role "actor". The process data concerns both the assembly process of aircraft parts and design process of the equipment. Saved information is used to recognize the activities evolution of each partner (new requirement of the OEM, new kind of assembly tools proposed by suppliers ...).

The data model package organizes, according to various sub-models, the equipment's information that are produced and manipulated during different stages of the whole equipment lifecycle. The detailed data are stored in different documents represented by "documents package". For example, the structural model contains information about the physical composition of the equipment. The detailed structure is stored in CAO documents.

## 5. The project view

We consider the concept of project as a form of operational interaction including a set of processes in order to obtain specific goals. The project structure consists of a systemic decomposition into different sub-projects regarding to the product complexity.

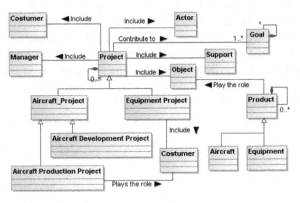

Figure 4 The project view.

Figure 4 shows the Meta model of the project structure, the project is considered as an interactional entity according to the situation concept (cf. section 2). Each project contributes to one or several goals. The class "goals" make dependence between the project view, the process view and the task view.

The project Meta model presents the contribution of different elements similarly at the organizational level (organization of different human resources and communities) and at the operational level (organization of different processes). The contribution of all project elements is presented by an instantiation of: {the class entity, the class role (replaced by a specific subclass) and interactional entity (in this case project)}. For instance, the Aircraft project is associated to the Equipment project by mean of the "Customer" class.

The main idea is that both the aircraft design project and equipment design project are described under the same main project reference. When a manufacturing order of an assembly tool is submitted, a new sub project for this need is created. All aircraft sub-project that are concerned by this equipment are related to the above project in the global situation framework. For this use case, three specific roles where to be considered:

- The aircraft R&D takes the role of actor in the aircraft design process and the indirect "customer" in the equipment design process (send the original needs through the production department). We note this entity "Aircraft_R&D".
- The production department takes the role of support in the aircraft design process; it performs different assembly operations. At the same time, it takes the

role of "customer" in the equipment design process (define the assembly procedure and assembly tool functions). We note this entity "Aircraft_Prod".

- The R&D service of the new business partnership takes the role actor of the
  equipment design process. We note this entity "Equipment_R&D".
- The manufacturing service of the new business partnership takes the role support of the equipment design process. This entity is noted "Equipment_Prod".

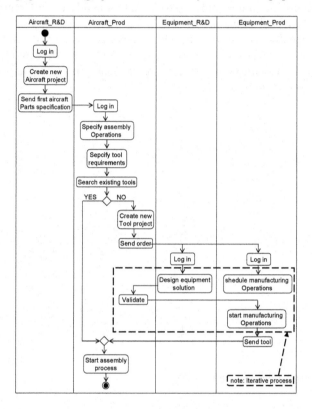

Figure 5 Scenario of creating new equipment project.

Several modeling tools are used to describe process achievement (IDEF, GRAI,
UML, etc.). UML formalism give more advantages since it gives possibility to
represent the static view (class diagram, object diagram) and the dynamic view
(activity diagram, state diagram, etc.) In our approach, we used the Activity diagram of UML formalism as it is shown in the previous figure (figure 5) to describe
the interaction process during the creation of a new project. At the beginning, Aircraft R&D creates a new project and sends initial specifications to the production
department. It defines the different operations of the assembly process and specifies the functions of the assembly tool to be realized. After, it searches in the fur-
niture warehouse a tool which satisfies these functions. If no tool is founded, pro-

duction department creates new equipment sub project and sends information to the supplier network (equipment R&D and manufacturing).

In fact, the real process is established in concurrent way. When, the equipment R&D starts the design process, manufacturing service is simultaneously schedules the manufacturing operations and researches the available technological solutions. Thanks to the collaborative system, the specification and manufacturing of the assembly tool is performed progressively and co-jointly by different partners according to the global scenario.

When a modification in the aircraft structure is occurred, the system informs the members of the business partnership and sends him the new requirement to consider in the specification of the related assembly tool. Figure 6 presents the interaction process for this case.

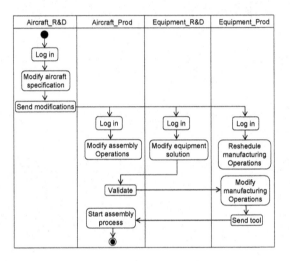

Figure 6 Scenario of modifying requirement.

## 6. Conclusions

In this paper, we have proposed a modeling framework to support, at the conceptual level, a new PLM approach to improve information sharing in collaborative design, and then to enhance the integration of supplier in the design and manufacturing processes. The final goals of the project is to reduce costs and time to market of the assembly tools, and consequently thus of the aircraft product.

The new business partnership implies to establish new collaboration strategy between OEM and supplier. Other benefits can be obtained from this framework by monitoring the evolution of collective work and facilitating its coordination.

The developed framework deals with the integration of Product, Process and Organization dimensions of a design project, and, in future works, the corresponding extension of CAD/CAM and PDM existing tools. The proposed Product model gives the structure of the product data base. It uses a generic semantic that can favor, in our sense, the conceptual interoperability between different product data coming from different partners.

Although our work is developed initially to resolve a particular problem in a special firm of the aeronautic industry, the use of a modeling framework based on the generic concepts of entities and interactions in the working situation may gives more interests.

In this contribution, one specific dimension has been developed, related to the PLM platform, to support the shift from a sequential to an interactionnist development process. Face to the complexity of such a change, success will not only rely on this support dimension. This PLM platform will have to be considered in a more global system/organisation, to take into account the entanglement of technology, market and usage dimensions. At an operational level, this integrated approach will enhance the chances of success and at a more analytic level, it will allow to precise the conditions of application and transposition in other contexts.

Further research work will be performed to improve and validate these different issues. A prototype is under development and is being tested thanks to our industrial case study.

# References

1.   Kline S.J., Rosenberg N.: An overview of innovation. In: Landau R., Rosenberg, N. (eds) The positive sum strategy. pp. 275-306 (1986).
2.   Nishiguchi T., Ikeda M.: Suppliers' innovation: undestated aspects of japanese industrial sourcing. In: Nishiguchi, (Ed.), Managing Product Development. pp. 206-232, Oxford University Press (1996).
3.   Chung S., Kim G.M.: Performance effect of partnership between manufacturers and suppliers for new product development: the supplier's standpoint. Research Policy, vol. 32, pp. 587-603 (2003).
4.   Foss N.J.: Theories of the firm: contractual and competence perspective. Journal of evolutionary economics, vol. 3, pp. 127-144 (1993).
5.   Ben Mahmoud-Jouni S., Calvi R.: Les coopérations interentreprises dans les projets de développement. In: Garel (ed.): Faire de la recherche en management de projet, Vuibert (2004).
6.   Calvi R.: Le rôle des services achats dans le développement des produits nouveaux: une approche organisationnelle. Revue Finance, Contrôle, Stratégie, vol. 3(2), pp. 31-55 (2000).
7.   Nooteboom, B.: Learning and innovation in organizations and economies, Oxford (2000).
8.   Hamel, G., Prahalad, C.K.: Strategy as Stretch and Leverage. Research-Technology Management, vol. 36(6), pp. 40-47 (1993).
9.   Ouchi, W.: Markets, bureaucracies, Administrative Science Quaterly, vol. 25(3), pp. 129-141 (1980).
10.  Huet, F.: Capacités d'innovation et coopération de PME: des effets auto-renforçants. Revue Internationale des PME, vol. 19(1), pp. 95-101 (2006).

11. Adler, P.S.: Market hierarchy and trust. The knowledge Economy and the future of capitalism. Organization Science. vol. 12( 2), pp. 215-234 (2001).
12. Saaksvuori, A., Immonen, A.: Product Lifecycle Management. Springer, Berlin (2004).
13. Jun, H., Kiritsis D., Xirouchaki, P.: Research issues on closed-loop PLM. Computer in Industry, vol. 57, pp. 855-868 (2007).
14. Gomes, J.O., Vallejos, R.V.: Applying a benchmarking method to organize the product lifecycle management for aeronautic suppliers. Product Lifecycle Management, vol. 3 (2007).
15. Tang, D., Qian, X.: Product lifecycle management for automotive development focusing on supplier integration. Computer in Industry, vol. 59, pp. 288-295 (2008).
16. Schilli, B., Dai, F.: Collaborative life cycle management between suppliers and OEM, Computers in Industry, vol. 57, pp. 725-731 (2006).
17. Schuh, G., Rozenfeld, H., Assmus, D., Zancul, E.: Process oriented framework to support PLM implementation. Computers in Industry, vol. 59, pp. 210-218 (2008).
18. Terzi, S., Cassina, J., Panetto, H.: Development of a metamodel to foster interoperability along the product lifecycle traceability. International conference on Interoperability of Enterprise Software and Applications. IFIP-ACM/SIGAPP INTEROP. Geneva, Switzerland (2005).
19. MOKA.: Managing engineering knowledge: methodology for knowledge based engineering applications, Wiley (2001).
20. Szykman, S., Fenvesa, S.J., Keirouzb, W., Shooter, B.: A foundation for interoperability in next-generation product development systems. Computer-Aided Design, vol. 33, pp. 545-559 (2001).
21. Eynard, B., Gallet, T., Nowak, P., Roucoules, L.: UML based specifications of PDM product structure and workflow. Computers in Industry, vol. 3, pp. 301-316 (2004).
22. Fenves, S.J., Foufou, S., Bock, C., Sudarsan, R., Bouillon N., Sriram R.D.: CPM2: A revised core product model for representing design information. National Institute of Standards and Technology, NISTIR7185, USA (2004).
23. Sudarsan, R., Fenves, S.J., Sriram, R.D., Wang, F.: A product information modeling framework for product lifecycle management. Computer-Aided Design, vol. 37, pp. 1399-1411 (2005).
24. Nowak, P., Rose, B., Saint-Marc, L., Callot, M., Eynard, B., Gzara L., Lombard, M.: Towards a design process model enabling the integration of product, process and organization. 5th International Conference on Integrated design and Manufacturing in Mechanical Engineering IDMME, University of Bath, UK (2004).
25. Danesi, F., Gardan, F., Gardan, Y., Reimeringer M.: P4LM: A methodology for product lifecycle management. Computers in Industry vol. 59, pp. 304-317 (2008).
26. Trappey, A.J., Hsio, D.: Applying collaborative design and modularized assembly for automotive ODM supply chain integration. Computers in Industry, vol. 59, pp. 277-287 (2008).
27. Belkadi, F., Bonjour, E., Dulmet, M.: Modelling Framework of a Traceability System to Improve Knowledge Sharing and Collaborative Design. CSCW in Design. Lecture Notes in Computer Science, vol. 3865 (2006).
28. Uschold, M., King, M., Moralee, S., Zorgios Y.: The Enterprise Ontology. The Knowledge Engineering Review, vol. 13, pp. 1-12 (1998).

# Development of the ALIS IP Ontology: Merging Legal and Technical Perspectives

**Claudia Cevenini[1], Giuseppe Contissa[2], Migle Laukyte[3], Régis Riveret[4], and Rossella Rubino[5]**

[1] CIRSFID, University of Bologna, Italy, claudia.cevenini@unibo.it
[2] CIRSFID, University of Bologna, Italy, giuseppe.contissa@unibo.it
[3] CIRSFID, University of Bologna, Italy, migle.laukyte@unibo.it
[4] CIRSFID, University of Bologna, Italy, regis.riveret@unibo.it
[5] CIRSFID, University of Bologna, Italy, rossella.rubino@unibo.it

**Abstract:** The paper is partly based on research done for the EU-funded (IST-2004-2.4.9) project ALIS (Automated Legal Intelligent System) on Intellectual Property Law. We describe the development process of the ALIS Intellectual Property ontology from both a legal and a technical perspective. We discuss the scope and the features of this IP ontology, the lessons learned, and the problems solved. This is done by comparing our ontology (the ALIS IP ontology) with the IPRonto ontology, which too is dedicated to IP. The paper also points out the benefits of both the ALIS system in general and the ALIS IP ontology in particular. Future development of ALIS will involve expanding its ontology to also include law and trademark law. Once these three legal ontologies are in place, they will be consolidated into a single ontology that will provide the framework for a general IP ontology.

**Keywords:** Intellectual property law, legal ontology, IPROnto, ALIS system

## 1. Introduction

It was as early as the end of the 20th century that computer scientists began to explore the possibility of using ontologies for the law [1, 2]. Yet, for all that experience, we cannot say that we have made much progress today: while the tools for building legal ontologies have definitely improved, law is usually conceptualized in the abstract, without entering into particular areas of law, such as labour law, insurance law, and intellectual property law. Today, there is only one ontology for intellectual property law (IP law): it is called IPROnto [3]. This was the ontology from which we took inspiration and with which we compared our own. In this paper we attempt to create another IP ontology, called the ALIS IP ontology, based on research done under the ALIS project. The paper is

Please use the following format when citing this chapter:

Cevenini, C., Contissa, G., Laukyte, M., Riveret, R. and Rubino, R., 2008, in IFIP International Federation for Information Processing, Volume 277; *Computer-Aided Innovation (CAI)*; Gaetano Cascini; (Boston: Springer), pp. 169–180.

organized as follows: Section 2 provides an overview of the ALIS project and the role an IP ontology plays in it. Section 3 discusses two perspectives that we adopted: the legal perspective (3.1) and the technical one (3.2). Section 4 presents the method used. Section 5 brings the ALIS IP ontology into comparison with IPROnto. Section 6 presents the lessons we learned and the problems we solved in the process of building our ontology. Section 7 presents our conclusions and an outlook for the future research.

## 2. ALIS and Its Ontology

ALIS—a project funded under the 6th Framework Program—stands for Automated Legal Intelligent System (IST-2004-2.4.9). The project is aimed at modeling a legal system for IP law and providing citizens and public as well as private organizations with fast and reliable access to the European IP law.

The problems the project is intended to solve are thus both legal and technical. There are four ways in which this is so. First, ALIS seeks to apply to IP law different kinds of research in artificial intelligence, ranging from knowledge representation and reasoning to game theory. Second, while most of the work involved in building such a system is in computer science, the people who will benefit from it will be in the first place will be the lawyers. Third, the legal problems connected with IP law are being solved using technological solutions, namely, the ALIS system. And fourth, IP law is at the same time an area of law designed to protect technological works of mind, providing for authors and creators a guarantee that their rights will be protected. (The ALIS system is no exception.)

The reason why we decided to make the ALIS system specific to IP law is that we believe IP rights to be a central concern in European society today, a concern owed to the progress of science and technology, and Internet technologies in particular. Indeed, there is a time lag between law and technology, with technology renewing on a monthly basis, or nearly so, and law taking years to catch up. The ALIS system will try to contribute toward bridging this gap.

The scientific community is working actively and organizing many conferences on legal ontologies and neighbouring technologies (witness LOAIT'05, LOAIT07, SW4Law07). These conferences have given birth to a number of publications aside from their proceedings, including *Law and the Semantic Web: Legal Ontologies, Methodologies, Legal Information Retrieval, and Applications* [4] and, recently, two special issues of the journal *Artificial Intelligence and Law* [5, 6].

The ALIS system requires at least two main ontologies: the IP ontology and the game-theory ontology. The IP ontology is useful for processing the legal documents crawled by ALIS system. This is done analyzing the contents of such documents and mapping these contents onto generic concepts.

Practical use of the ALIS system (as enabled by this ontology) brings benefits to both the private and the public sector. The copyright collection societies (public sector) can apply this system in e-governance, while companies and enterprises in e-commerce (private sector) can take advantage of the ALIS system for DRM management, for systems by which to manage IP contracts automatically, and finally for agent-based systems dedicated to IP products. Further, the ALIS system is important in labour relations (in both the private and the public sector), where the authorship of a creation (mainly software products) may provoke disputes, which institutions and organizations prefer to prevent.

## 3. Two Perspectives in Creating the ALIS IP Ontology

*Every ontology is an agreement, a social contract among people driven by a common purpose* [7]. The ALIS legal ontology is likewise an agreement—an agreement between lawyers and software engineers who have to work together in this initiative. This section examines the ontology-building process from these two perspectives of the lawyer and the software engineer.

### 3.1 *The Legal Perspective*

For the legal perspective we tried to follow French IP law strictly construed, without legal interpretation, without taking into account the way in which other laws come to bear, and without changing the legal terminology: the terms and concepts used in the ALIS IP ontology are the same as those used in French IP law. This ontology thus follows the letter of the French law and so takes from it its normative shape: this was made necessary by the aims the ALIS project is meant to achieve, especially the aim of making laws easier to draft. ALIS includes an isomorphic [14] representation of norms through a formalized set of rules. The same approach—strict adherence to the body of norms in question—was taken for the ALIS IP ontology, even though this ontology was built to achieve not so much isomorphism as *comprehensiveness* and *correctness* [1].

The concepts making up the ontology were selected by including, from the start, all the copyright terms that could be relevant to the same ontology: these include the fundamental legal terms of IP law, such as *author* and *work of mind*; the different types of works of mind recognized under the law (*collective, collaborative, single,* and *composite*); and other terms such as *moral right* and *economic right*.

This selection of concepts did, however, pose a few problems. One of these was list of works of mind. The law describes this as the list of all the works of mind protected by copyright, but it does not also define a work of mind, and so it leaves open the possibility of any further number of works making it into the list, so long as they enjoy copyright protection. This is therefore a cautious list: an incomplete list containing only such works as are encountered on a daily (or almost daily) basis, which means that it may take in combinations of such works, or works deriving from them, or any other outcome of human creativity. In other words, there is room for judicial interpretation on case-by-case basis.

But this way of framing the law and reasoning around it does not help toward building an ontology: from ontological point of view, whatever terms are not in the ontology do not exist in the law. The problem of works not mentioned in the list but which might enjoy copyright protection anyway might be solved in the future by updating the ontology with new concepts as necessary, on case-by-case basis. Otherwise the ontology could fall behind what the law deems a work of mind.

Every concept the lawyers chose to bring into the ontology was checked with software engineers to see whether the concept (a) falls under a rule and (b) is relevant within the overall conceptual map of copyright law. For instance, terms such as *contract for hire* and *service contract* do come under a rule—this being the rule that no contract made by the author of a work of mind can undermine the author's ability to enjoy his or her rights to that work—but they are nonetheless irrelevant to IP law, and for this reason we decided not to include them into the ALIS IP ontology.

In making a selection of terms for the ontology, we drew up a glossary explaining what each of these terms means. The meanings so ascribed in the glossary is broader than that which these terms have under French IP law, and this was done on purpose, the point being to include all the possible meanings of certain term that the user might be interested in.

## 3.2  The Technical Perspective

The technical perspective involves the three concepts of *author, work of mind,* and *intellectual-property rights*, a triplet of fundamental importance to French IP law. In what follows, we will describe these concepts separately and list related concepts in italics.

The first concept in the ALIS IP ontology is that of *work of mind*, which is a creative expression of intellectual work and may be of different types. French IP law defines the following types of works of mind: *abstract authorship, address, applied art work, architectural work, artistic writing, audiovisual work, book, choreographic work, cinematographic work, circus act, collection of miscellaneous works or data, dramatic musical work, dramatic work, drawing work, dumb-show work, engraving work, fashion work, feat, geographical map work, graphical work, illustration work, lecture, literary writing, lithography work, musical composition with words, musical composition without words, painting work, pamphlet, photographic work, photography analogous work, plan work, pleading, scientific writing, sculpture work, sermon, single work, sketch work, software work, three dimensional work, typographical work.*[1]

Furthermore, this list does not specify works of mind exhaustively, for these also get classified on the basis of the manner in which they are created, as *collective, composite,* or *single* works, or again as works executed *in collaboration.*

A work of mind is further defined by a *term of protection,* specifying the period during which there is an exclusive right to exploit the same work.

The second concept of the triplet is that of *author.* A work of mind is created by an *author,* who may be a *natural* or *legal* person, and who may also be anonymous or pseudonymous. Hence, a work of mind may itself be *anonymous* or *pseudonymous.*

The third main concept in the ontology is that of *intellectual property rights,* which every author is entitled to, and which may also be referred to as *incorporeal property rights.* French IP law distinguishes between moral and economic rights. *Moral rights* protect an author's personality and reputation. *Economic rights* enable the copyright owner to benefit economically from the work's exploitation, and they may be transferred to an *economic right holder (publisher, editor, producer)* either in part or in full.

French IP Law identifies nine types of moral rights as follows: *right of disclose under the name, right of disclose under to direction, right of divulge work, right of make a collection, right of reconsider assignment of exploitation, right of respect for authorship, right of respect for name, right of respect for work, right of withdraw assignment of exploitation.*

Economic rights are in turn divided in two groups of rights: *right of performance* and *right of reproduction.* The former is the right to communicate the work to the public by any process whatsoever (*perform dramas or lyrics, present or project or recite publicly, telediffuse or transmit also through satellite*). The latter is the right to fix a work into a physical medium by any process enabling it to be indirectly communicated to the public (*publication, cast, draw, engrave, execute, make photos, print, use graphic or mechanical process*).

All italicized concepts in this section are represented as OWL classes connected by datatype or object properties. Fig. 1 is a UML diagram showing the relationships between the main concepts of French IP law.

---

[1] The terms in this list, as well as in all further lists, appear in alphabetical order and are lifted *as such* from the English translation of the French IP law: for this reason, we have chosen not to change them even when they are nonstandard or seem to make little sense. The same applies to all italicized terms and expressions from here on out.

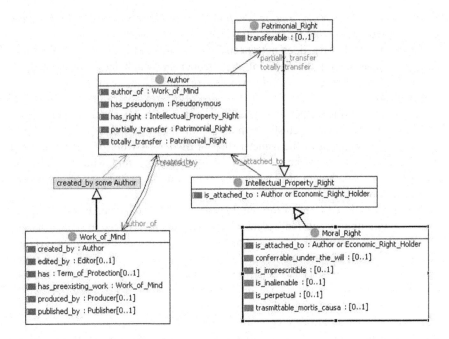

Figure 1 UML diagram laying out main IP concepts

The ALIS consortium, taking inspiration from IPROnto, created the model to illustrate the lifecycle of the ALIS IP ontology. This is called the OCATU Model [13].

The lifecycle of an IP case can be defined by the five stages making up the global process of the OCATU Model:

1) *organize* – team setup and creation preparation

2) *create* – source transformation

3) *assert* – assert the created copyrights (works of mind)

4) *transfer* – transfer rights

5) *use* – use the created copyrights (works of mind)

By combining all key data through different stages, we get a tree structure representing the key facts in a uniform language. Case after case, the tree's branches are enriched and yield a common database of copyright cases. Any new case can then be placed in the tree in the form of a unique path presenting key events.

When a particular IPR case is analyzed, not all the stages appear explicitly, but all are necessary to understand the case. The OCATU Model is designed to structure real cases, especially copyright cases, so as to facilitate the development of a game theory ontology.

The process starts from the creation of an object that may be subject to copyright and ends with the object's use. It forms a sequence in which no stage can begin until the previous one has been when completed. The final stage ("use") may generate another creation, in which case the five-stage process can be represented as a cycle.

If we want to generate a path from the "organize" stage to the "use" stage, we have to design a "solution tree," which includes all the actions a user may take or does take. Three kinds of paths can be distinguished depending on the point of view one takes: *action* paths, showing all the actions a user has taken; *status* paths, showing the entire status resulting from user's actions; and *complete* paths, which combine the two other paths.

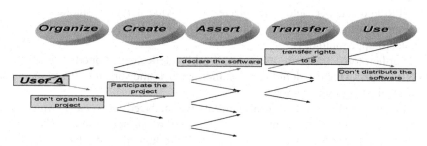

Figure 2 Status path of OCATU model

## 4. Method

In designing the ALIS IP ontology, we followed the main stages described in [10], which consist in determining the scope of the ontology; considering the reuse of its concepts; listing these terms; defining a taxonomy, properties, facets, and instances; and checking for anomalies. Moreover, we used the text of the French IP law to extract rules and model them in Prolog, and we also extracted definitions and formalized them in the OWL language.

Like any development process, so the process of developing an ontology is not linear: some of its stages will have to be iterated, and at any point it may be necessary to backtrack. Thus, for example, we have extended the ontology with new concepts from the legal rules expressed in the Prolog language.

The tool chosen for creating the ALIS ontology is Protegé. But we also used TopBrain Composer, which produces a very useful UML-like documentation but is not free.

The two ontologies developed for ALIS are used in the ALIS knowledge-base platform to support different tasks, including document annotation, game-theory reasoning, checking for legal compliance, and transcribing law into RuleML rules.

Completing these tasks makes it necessary to access the different concepts and properties defined in the ALIS ontologies, and it also requires tools that can reason about such concepts and properties for a number of purposes, such as to detect contradictions or infer new properties. The ALIS consortium decided to develop an ontology engine using the Pellet reasoner [12].

## 5. IPROnto and Comparison with the ALIS IP Ontology

This section describes the IPR Onto ontology, which we took as a benchmark in building ours, and which to date remains the de facto benchmark for all ontologies in IP law. The table below (Table 1) compares the ALIS IP ontology with IPROnto.

IPROnto's upper ontology, selected to provide a robust ontology basis for interoperability, is SUMO, a result of the SUO IEEE WG [8] attempt to establish a standard upper ontology.

Furthermore, IPROnto uses the World Intellectual Property Organization (WIPO) [9], which is defining a common legal framework for IPR, to complete the legal parts of the ontology.

Following are the main legal concepts we analyzed: *agreement*, which takes two dependent elements, namely, *IPRContract* and *IPRLicense*; *IntellectualPropertyRight*, associated with multimedia digital content for automatic e-commerce on the Internet (it includes *copyrights*, *sui generis rights* (applicable to databases) and *neighbouring rights* (which apply in particular to singers and performing artists); *copyrights*, which include *moral rights* and *exploitation rights* (or economic rights); and *LegalEntity*, which divides into two categories, namely, *CorporateLegalEntity* and *NaturalLegalEntity*. A work protected by copyright has a lifecycle that establishes a flow among the several IPROnto legal concepts. The lifecycle involves roles (*Creator, RightsHolder, ContentProvider, MediaDistributor*) as well as actions (*create, transfer, transform*).

We have chosen to not use IPROnto for two main reasons. The first one is that the aim of IPROnto is totally different from ALIS IPR Ontology. Indeed, while IPROnto Onto aims at facilitating the automation and interoperability of IPR frameworks, ALIS Ontology is devoted to ensure that the templates, which will serve as users interface, were consistent with the information required by the ALIS system.

The second reason is that the ALIS project limited the scope of its system to copyright and the ALIS consortium chosen, as reference, the French IPR Law. This was due to the fact that the system validation will be performed by a French partner. We have therefore analyzed just the legal concepts cited in this text.

Table 1 The ALIS IP Ontology and IPROnto compared

|  | ALIS IPR Ontology | IPROnto |
|---|---|---|
| Area | Intelligent legal systems | E-commerce in multimedia content |
| Purpose | 1) to better manage legal documents repositories; 2) to make the document-retrieval system more versatile; 3) to create a common layer between legal and game-theory concepts; 4) to create a general "shared" language enabling the modules and the Web services of the ALIS architecture to exchange information; thus, for example, the GUI module will be "ontology-based," connecting every user input to a particular norm; this norm might establish a certain obligation for the user, who in game theory also figures as a player, whose strategy will consequently take that obligation into account. | To facilitate the automation and interoperability of IPR frameworks, integrating both the Rights Expression Language and the Rights Data Dictionary. |
| Upper Ontology | LKIF-core, which embeds the concepts of Manifestation and Expression. | SUMO, which does not embed the concepts of Manifestation and Expression but rather describes them through a new, specifically designed sub-ontology. |
| WIPO? | No | Yes |
| Life Cycle | Yes (OCATU Model) | Yes |
| Granularity | Yes | No |

# 6. Lessons Learned and Problems Solved

First thing we learned is that the larger the domain an ontology seeks to cover, the more the ontology will be abstract. Abstractness is precisely the feature of IPROnto, whose domain is much larger than that covered by the ALIS IP ontology, which confines itself to a specific part of French IP law and describes it with highly accurate terms and concepts.

The abstractness of IPROnto may be owed to its direct use of two abstract legal sources, namely, the Berne Convention and the WIPO Copyright Treaty, both of which are sketched out in broad strokes and serve mainly as guidelines for the domestic law of other countries. The ALIS IP ontology also draws on these two sources but does so indirectly, meaning that the ontology's direct source is the French IP law, which is modelled on the WIPO IP sources and so (like any other national IP law) acts to concretize the WIPO ideas and guidelines.

The use of French IP law is also to account for other features that distinguish the ALIS IP ontology from IPRonto.

First, certain concepts mean the same but are expressed using different terms: IPRonto has *exploitation rights*, corresponding to *patrimonial rights* in the ALIS IP ontology. Another example is *creator* (IPROnto) and *author* (ALIS IP ontology). The division of economic rights is also different: while IPRonto sub-divides *exploitation rights* into *transformation rights, communication rights, distribution rights*, and *reproduction rights*, the ALIS IP ontology divides *patrimonial rights* into only two classes, that is, *rights of performance* and *rights of reproduction*.

Second, because the ALIS IP ontology has a more restricted domain, it does not yet have the concepts or the French equivalents of *SuiGenerisRights, NeighbouringRights, WithdrawalRight, ContentProvider*, and *MediaDistributors*. These concepts can be found only in IPRonto.

Third, even though the two ontologies share the concept of *Moral Right*, the ALIS IP ontology specifies it in greater detail, thus enables users (especially non-lawyers) to have a better grasp of its meaning even without looking up its definition.

Fourth, the ALIS IP ontology makes it is possible to specify which economic rights transfer to the right-holder and which remain with the author(s): this is especially evident in comparison with IPROnto, where such specification is impossible.

Fifth, the ALIS IP ontology specifies the concept of *Right Holder* through the constituent concepts of *Publisher, Editor, Producer*, and *Performer*.

And sixth, the ALIS IP ontology specifies the concept of *Work of Mind* using the list of works that the French IP law deems amenable to copyright protection in France. Also, works of mind are further specified by classifying them on the basis of the manner in which they are created, as *collective, composite*, or *single* work, or as works created *in collaboration*.

Another lesson we have learned is that focusing on a well-defined domain makes it possible to exclude terms from other domains, thus avoiding what happens in IPROnto, which takes in terms foreign to the IP domain, such as *Customer*. This concept was introduced into IPROnto because this ontology covers not only IP law but also addresses the domain of commerce. Embracing two domains will enlarge the ontology's field of application, to be sure, but it also makes it more difficult to understand and manage this ontology, especially if designed (at least on paper) to cover only one of the two fields of application from which it draws its concepts.

We also realized how much work is still left to be done: the ALIS IP ontology covers only the main chunk of the legislative part of French IP, and its concepts therefore not only fail to account for the whole of the legislative part but also leave out the regulatory part. This is the reason why the ontology is still without many concepts, such as that of *agreement*, that IPROnto does, by contrast, include.

The general concepts of the ALIS IP ontology come from LKIF-core [11]. The lesson learned here is that it is important to share the tools of the other European projects we have taken part in. Further, the LKIF-core ontology makes it possible to connect the ALIS IP ontology with business-intelligence tools, such as KnowledgeTools and RuleBurst, and so these tools can use the ALIS IP ontology.

We can now analyze the problems we set out to solve. The first problem is that the ALIS IP ontology is based on the English version of French IP law: we worked with the English version of French concepts, and this made it necessary to go back to the original at every turn to figure out what the translation meant or simply to make sure it was correct.

This problem connects to another we faced, which is that the French IP law quite often uses different words for the same concepts. So here, too, we had to study the text closely at many places to determine whether we were dealing with a single concept designated by two synonyms (which was most often the case) or whether the two words in question designated two different concepts (which did happen on a few occasions). This acted as a reminder of the problems involved in legal drafting and how important it is to produce a good text.

The last problem was that of deciding, for some of the concepts involved, whether they are better represented as classes or as properties. For example the concept of collaborative work should be represented as a class or as a property of a work of mind? We chose to represent the four ways of creating work of mind as separate classes so that these classes, in consequence, could have their properties.

## 7. Conclusions and Outlook

We have explained why the ALIS project needs an IP ontology and how this ontology was built proceeding from both a legal and a technical perspective. We have also compared this ontology to the only other existing IP ontology, called IPROnto. Further, we discussed the method used, the lessons learned, and the problems faced, for which we sought a solution.

The method used to create the ALIS IP ontology can be implied as a model for the construction of other legal ontologies that may be of direct interest to commerce. This holds in particular to the legal ontologies for business law, insurance law, labour law, and contract law.

We hope that in this effort to build an ontology we have done a service to other scholars with an interest in these issues.

We will continue in this effort. Apart from enriching the ALIS IP ontology with all of the concepts in French IP law, we will be expanding the ALIS ontology to also include patent and trademark law. Once these three legal ontologies are in place, we will consolidate them into a unique ontology making up the framework for a general IP ontology.

# References

1. Valente A.: Legal knowledge engineering. A modeling approach. IOS Press, Amsterdam (1995).
2. Visser P.R.S, Bech-Capon T.J.M.: The formal specification of a legal ontology. In: Van Kralingen et al. (eds.), Proceedings of JURIX 96 (pp. 15–24). Tilburg University Press, Tilburg (1996).
3. Delgado J., Gallego I., Llorente S., Garcia R.: Regulatory ontologies: An intellectual property right approach. In: On the move to meaningful internet systems, OTM Workshop, pp. 621–635, Springer, Berlin (2003).
4. Benjamins R., Casanovas P., Gangemi A., Breuker J. (eds.): Law and the semantic web: legal ontologies, methodologies, legal information retrieval, and applications. Lecture Notes in Computer Science, Springer, Berlin (2005).
5. Lehmann J., Biasiotti M.A., Francesconi E., Sagri M.T. (eds.): Legal knowledge extraction and searching & legal ontology applications. Special issue of Artificial Intelligence and Law, n. 7 (2007).
6. Breuker J., Tiscornia D., Winkels R., Gangemi A. (eds.): Ontologies for law. Special issue of Artificial Intelligence and Law, n. 4, December (2004).
7. Gruber T.: Every ontology is a treaty (2004). Available via SIGSEMIS bulletin http://tomgruber.org/writing/sigsemis-2004.pdf. Accessed 7 March 2008.
8. Standard Upper Ontology (SUO) IEEE Working Group. Available via https://suo.ieee.org. Accessed 3 March 2008.
9. World Intellectual Property Organization. Available via https://www.wipo.org. Accessed 7 March 2008.
10. Noy N.F., McGuinness D.L.: Ontology development 101: A guide to creating your first ontology. Stanford knowledge systems laboratory technical report KSL-01-05 and Stanford medical informatics technical report SMI-2001-0880 (2001).
11. Breuker J., Hoekstra R., Boer A., van den Berg K., Rubino R., Sartor G., Palmirani M., Wyner A., Bench-Capon T.: OWL ontology of basic legal concepts (LKIF-Core). Deliverable 1.4, Estrella (2007). Available via http://www.estrellaproject.org/lkif-core/. Accessed 14 March 2008.
12. Pellet Reasoner. Available via http://pellet.owldl.com/. Accessed 14 March 2008.
13. ALIS Deliverable D4.2: Description of the framework. Available via https://www.myndsphere.com/gm/document-1.9.32640/ALIS_WP5_D5.1a.doc. Accessed 8 March 2008.
14. Bench-Capon T.J.M, Coenen F.P.: Isomorphism and legal knowledge based systems. Artificial Intelligence and Law 1(1), pp. 65–86 (1992).

# A systematic innovation case study: new concepts of domestic appliance drying cycle

**S. Graziosi[1], D. Polverini[2], P. Faraldi[3], and F. Mandorli[4]**

[1] Università Politecnica delle Marche, Mechanical Engineering Department, Italy,
s.graziosi@univpm.it
[2] Università Politecnica delle Marche, Mechanical Engineering Department -
Indesit Company, Innovation & Technology division, Italy,
davide.polverini@indesit.com
[3] Indesit Company, Innovation & Technology division, Italy,
paolo.faraldi@indesit.com
[4] Università Politecnica delle Marche, Mechanical Engineering Department, Italy,
f.mandorli@univpm.it

**Abstract:** While incremental innovation is for most companies a well assessed process, radical product innovation is often handled with difficulty, mainly due to myriad obstacles in the idea-to cash process which limits company's ability to innovate. As a typical approach, engineers firstly try to find innovative solutions only inside their technological product space, basically thinking accordingly to their commonly assessed know-how. In this paper an industrial case is analyzed, showing how TRIZ methodology offers to technicians a systematic way to solve problematic contradictions and find effective ideas.

**Keywords:** Radical Innovation, Concept Design, TRIZ, Idea Generation.

## 1. Introduction

Innovation is a complex process, of dramatic importance for organisational success. Due to international competition intensification and product development process shortening, the pressure to innovate has continuously been heightening since the last decades.

The enterprise need for innovation is clearly expressed by Porter and Stern [1] considering innovation as "the transformation of knowledge into new products, processes, and services - involves more than just science and technology. It involves discerning and meeting the needs of the customers". The terms "innovation" has been deeply analyzed in scientific literature, mainly focusing on the difference between incremental innovation and radical one. Kim and

*Please use the following format when citing this chapter:*

Graziosi, S., Polverini, D., Faraldi, P. and Mandorli, F., 2008, in IFIP International Federation for Information Processing, Volume 277; *Computer-Aided Innovation (CAI)*; Gaetano Cascini; (Boston: Springer), pp. 181–192.

Mauborgne [2] consider incremental innovation as a sort of "imitation" while companies should focus on proactive strategy aiming at creating new customers and markets as well as sustaining the existing ones. On the contrary, author such as Harrington [3] argue that continuous improvements are the major driving forces without which the gains for radical improvements are not sustainable. Our point here is that both incremental and radical innovations are really fundamental for company growth. More than in incremental innovations, in radical ones engineers and technicians should extend their creativity on finding the best technical solutions to drastically and positively change product day-life image. However, in some cases all the attempts at finding these solutions are really stressful and not always successful because of "psychological inertia" which persuades engineers on reasoning only inside their own paradigm or "enterprise area". As S.D. Savransky said [4], psychological inertia "leads us away from the solution of the problem, impedes problem recognition and clarification, creates barriers during the search for step to solution, complicates decision making, and makes other stage of the problem solving difficult". New methodological approaches are needed [5], allowing to effectively start designing process from a general model of the problem, efficiently converging towards the best technical solutions.

In this regard, the present paper aims at showing how TRIZ theory implementation allows the access to the best methodologies and instruments to stimulate and discipline thinking activity leading to really effective problem solutions. An industrial case has been analyzed, where a standard, assessed technology needs to be renewed to comply with emerging boundary conditions in terms of customer needs and regulations: this study case is the drying phase of domestic appliances such as dishwashers, dryers and wash-and-dryers. The experimental tests have been carried on in collaboration with Indesit Company, an important European company, leader in the domestic appliances market. Over the last years, a strong focus on innovation has been performed by this company: a dedicated technical area, the Innovation&Technology Direction, has been built up, whose specific aim is to constantly bring innovation into the industrial products: new technologies, new materials, breakthrough product concepts are continuously being investigated, in order to assess their technical feasibility on the domestic appliance environment.

In this article, we firstly overview which are the main driving innovation forces in modern enterprises, focusing on household appliances, and how firms try to enrich these outcomes. Section 3 describes the drying cycle and the company need for innovation. In Section 4 we discuss our approach to the problem using TRIZ Contradictions Matrix.

## 2. Driving innovation forces in modern enterprises

Product innovation in industrial process and design of consumer goods is nowadays increasingly achieving more and more importance: continuous strengths are held in order to maintain product competitiveness at top level, to efficiently face competitors' actions and increase the market share. Systematic methods to be used in the day-by-day activity are still not present in standard product life cycle management, but a continuously increasing number of innovation projects, aimed to generate new product concepts, are now common also in this industrial sector. "Market-driven projects" and "technology-driven projects" are two typical cases of new concepts projects. In both cases, two basic instruments are used: brainstorming sessions among researchers, designers, marketing people, and consumer tests.  Two are the key points for innovation: a clear identification of customer and market needs and the transformation of these requirements into innovative technical solutions. Preliminary actions shall be mainly focused in correctly understanding the real likes and dislikes of potential customers, and also in assessing the added value they would be ready to charge in the new product. The problem here is that consumer test results are often unclear, and the more innovative is the concept, the harder is to obtain an immediately enthusiastic answer among all consumers. Leaving out these marketing aspects, in this paper we focus on engineering ones, or better we implement a methodology useful to translate marketing aspect into technical solutions.

As above mentioned the first technical idea came out during brainstorming sessions, being these ones a method of creativity activation, in order to overcome psychological inertia [6]. Developed by Alex Osborn in the 1940's, brainstorming consist of an initial analysis of the situation by means of a list of central questions, and a  work phase during which technicians generate an idea and than critique it, as recommended by classical philosophical theories. This method, as A. Orloff said [7], has some advantages because is easy to learn and use, and relatively little time is needed to prepare a session; also idea generation process usually ends with positive results, even if it is not well structured. As assessed by technical and scientific literature, the higher the problem difficulty, the less effective is the solution by using this method, which in the end seems not to be capable of stimulating inspiration. The results are often long and helpless searching: considerable material and intellectual effort, weak and useless ideas and useless deviations from potentially useful goals. In this regard there is a need for the enterprise to introduce new methods of idea generation which can "help control thinking for solutions to construction-technical problems with extreme physical and technical contradictions. Concrete constructive navigators are needed for concrete problematic situations." [6].

To overcome all these drawbacks, the company is willing to experiment another strategy of work in household appliances innovation projects: TRIZ theory has been chosen. The firm interest for TRIZ is due to its ability on carrying on idea generation in a well-framed way and stimulating inventiveness: "the primary goal of TRIZ is to help thinking become talented and intuition become controllable, structured, and functioned well" [7]. TRIZ theory can help companies on eliminating typical mistakes deriving by incorrectly structured inventing sessions, such as extreme concreteness of problem description or lack of a general model as a starting point to analyze a specific industrial problem. Engineers would be hopefully supposed to change their usual approach to technical problem solving, being able to easily "sketch" a general model as an abstraction of the original technical issue. It equips the "user" with a clear understanding of the initial situation and of all the problem solving and idea generation stages, giving a wider vision of all the aspect involved. Moreover company interest is also focused on achieving a better and effective use of patent literature analysis because nowadays, it is usually performed at further project steps, to assess if a specific technical solution can be patented or if other inventors have already developed similar ideas.

## 3. The household appliances innovation forces: the drying cycle

Drying process today represents a typical phase of domestic appliances cycles standard sequence, mainly dishwashers, wash-and-dryers and dryers; the aim is to dewater humid items like clothes or crockery, which underwent previous washing phases, to targeted values of residual in order to restore initial conditions. Different technical solutions can be implemented to reach this target, having always basically in mind item care on one side, and process duration on the other. Potential improvements on drying phase could be very appealing for final consumers; the following list shows the most common features, parameters, criticisms:

1. Energy consumption, up to 40-50% of total cycle for wash-and-dryers;
2. Up to 40% of total cycle duration of dishwashers;
3. Handling operations of garments load to be repeated twice for a consumer that washes clothes in a washing machine and dries the same ones in a dryer;
4. Inhomogeneous distribution of dried load final humidity;
5. Undesired effects for consumers, e.g. the "fog" coming out of the dishwasher tub when door is open at the end of the cycle;

The focus of the present analysis has been the energy consumption reduction and the decrease of the drying cycle duration as primary issues, having taken as a basic reference the results of preliminary consumer tests, specifically held to deeply understand final user's point of view. Another interesting and surprising advice, emerged from the study, is that "ready for use" clothes are not so appealing for the majority of consumers: always having in mind garments care, a specific cycle aimed to eliminate further ironing operations would be perceived as a "niche" function to be used only on low quality garments.

Another important issue, which then reflects in further constraints, is the design and engineering of the appliance. More in details, it means that any innovation to be implemented on the product to satisfy the target (time decrease, energy consumption decrease and "ready to use" garments) shall not: dramatically increase product industrial cost, heavily affect currently assessed industrial process and decrease product reliability. It is anyway evident that the more innovating and performing is the concept, the heavier modifications will be accepted on the design and on the production process. For a completely breakthrough concept, a brand-new design and process could be hypothesized, but a trade-off between new performance and product changes is usually reached. No trade off is accepted on product reliability: first of all, on large-scale industrial production "low quality costs" are already an important issue to control both, from the financial and brand image point of view, so that no unreliable product, even if genial in its innovation, would be accepted. Moreover, people's health and safety while using the appliance is a "must" to be respected in any case.

In the paper test case, traditional abovementioned drivers such as cost, quality or process optimization are not suitable driving forces, because something more radical is needed: a significantly increase on current product performance, new performance and new product design and styling, in order to better fit the desired target of creating totally new products.

# 4. Test Case

## 4.1 The approach

By considering a generic tool, designed to clean items, whether they are garments or crockery, it can be easily acknowledged that one of the most common technical approach is based on using a solution of water and detergent, with which items are put in direct contact. As a brief description of the process, stain removal is mainly due to detergent action, whilst water results in being the carrier of the stain particles, from the item to the waste system (a deeper analysis of chemical and physical phenomena would not be consistent with the target of the present paper). In any case, the target of the dedicated tool can be set as "restoring the initial conditions" of a clean and dry item. Accordingly to this hypothesis, two basic operation modes will be identified: a detergent water activation mode (washing or rinsing) and a water extraction mode. From the TRIZ point of view, for domestic use washing machine (the *technique*), the product *primary function* is related to the first operation, while the water extraction can be considered as *auxiliary* because it ensures the accomplishment of the primary one. It is not worthless to underline that in other household appliances like dryers, the washing operation does not exist and the primary function is represented by the water extraction itself. Dryers are mainly used to perform clothes drying phase in countries whose weather conditions can not ensure an appropriate environment. It is not a case that the implemented drying phase technical solution reflects what happens in nature, using hot flow hair which circulates inside the tank. Thanks to the thermal convection and heat conduction the water changes its physical state and can be removed from clothes. In a washing machine the elimination of water is achieved only by mechanical centrifugal forces, due to drum rotations. Obviously the clothes final humidity level is higher than a dryer: typical water content percentage in garments after an high speed rinsing phase is not less than 45% (weight percentage), whilst in dryers load humidity is lowered down to room humidity values (for the most common fibers, a typical range is 3-8%)

Same year later after the dryer market introduction, everywhere the need to reduce as much as possible the time between the washing phase and the ironing one has led to the introduction of wash-and-dryer machines, briefly indicated as WD. The possibility to combine both the washing action of a typical washing machine and the drying action performed in a dryer seemed to be consumer-appealing mainly because of space availability in modern houses and ease of use. In these specific washing machines, water extraction operation has become a primary function as well as the washing one, as clearly defined by their name. The technical solution implemented in common WD is the same that we can find inside a dryer, the air circuit being optimized to the internal space availability of a washing machine. WD can be considered as a typical example of an already known solution optimizing based approach: the final result is obtained adapting a previously experienced one. This is a really common strategy in industry and even if it could seem to be effective, it does not help researchers and engineers to burst their well assessed framework in order to find other successful solutions out if it.

In this context the use of TRIZ models has been seen as a way to ensure goal-oriented result, to discipline action for solutions to problems and to help in developing the capability to quickly recognize real possibilities or limitations during generation phase. The company main purpose was to find other technical solutions to dry clothes, in order to realize a more energetically efficient cycle and to obtain the improvements listed in chapter 3. To pursuit these objectives, we have followed two building boxes of TRIZ theory: *contradictions* and, *the maximal use of resources* [8]. We have started our tests from a general model of the problem, considering as a main purpose, the introduction of "dry module" inside a commercial washing machine. The final output should be an energy efficient product in which both drying and washing function are considered as primary ones. The analysis has been carried on discussing about clothes and washing machines, but always taking into account company targets: finding a universal technical solution applicable to all household appliances which implement a drying cycle. For this reason, to find the best technical solution, we have firstly evaluated any possible resources present in the *system* (the washing machine), in its surrounding, or in the environment: before introducing new components or complications into the system, it is better to optimize already available resources. For each resource founded during the analysis, characteristic parameters have been identified. The marketing analysis previously discussed has been useful to define the "initial situation" of the problem enabling the identification of some system disadvantages that should have to be eliminated or the requirements through which improve the technique. The "Contradiction Matrix" use has been as a really useful tool to overcome these drawbacks and find the most effective solution instead of making usual engineering trade-offs. Patent literature analysis has been helpful both in the first both in last phase of our test. Several interesting results have been obtained, involving not only the household appliances area but also other correlated industrial activities showing the potentiality of TRIZ theory and its methodologies. Different processes and appliances have been considered as a single concept, which is, as already mentioned, "restoring the initial conditions" of a clean and dry item: TRIZ evidently demonstrated that clothes washing phase and crockery drying phase can be efficiently analyzed as specific situations of a more general model.

## 4.2 The Resources analysis

Being a washing machine the starting point of our test, the first resource is represented by the water itself, which can be classified as a natural or environmental one in accord to [7, 8]. In this case the most important identified variables are: quantity of water and temperature. Water quantity is now, in modern washing machine, the optimal value for the washing phase both from energetic and clothes cleaning performance point of view. Also temperature is a crucial parameter, being straightly correlated to several factors: detergent activation, bacteria elimination, garments care. Such as for water, another important resource is represented by clothes, or material as a general meaning. Also in this case we have found two characteristic parameters: the amount of material to be washed (kilograms) and the fiber typology. In this case we can stand that these two parameters are really random and unknown during design phase because they dramatically depends upon customer needs and specific habits.

An additional resource is represented by the detergent, which has to perform the complex chemiophysical actions of removing stains from clothes. Regarding this resource the most representative parameters are the physical state (powder or liquid) and the chemical composition; both of them can significantly affect washing efficiency. Analyzing the system from an energy point of view, we can identify the electrical field which is used to turn on all the electrical equipment. For the electrical field the representative parameter is the power consumption, in terms of kW. Other incoming energies can be used, such as natural gas, but electric power is today the most adopted solution. All the parameters identified are listed in table 1. Obviously during this analysis we have considered only resources which are already present inside the system after the washing phase because our main objective is to introduce an additional primary function inside an already existing system. The fact of considering only these resources it is not reductive for the methodology, because one of the possible technical solution could consist in giving auxiliary function to existing resources: it is only when all resources have been exhausted or it is impractical to utilize, that the consideration for additional design elements comes to play a crucial role. Technical solutions that use empty space or voids, waste products, byproducts, or harmful substances and fields, as well as available and very cheap energies and substances, can be significantly efficient.

Table 1. The Resource Analysis: parameters identification.

| Resource | Parameters |
|---|---|
| Water | - quantity (liters) |
| | - temperature (°C) |
| Clothes (Material) | - quantity (kilograms) |
| | - fiber typology |
| Soap | - chemical compositions |
| | - physical state |
| Electrical Energy | - Power (kW) |

## 4.3  Technical problem solving: the Contradiction Matrix

Once having defined the main system parameters we have applied contradictions analysis using "The Contradictions Matrix" (CM): a simplified CM has been built, by considering the reduced range of engineering parameters previously identified, and assuming the most suitable inventing principles. The decision of using this tool has been taken according to TRIZ theory which stands that the most effective inventive solution of a problem is the one that overcomes contradictions. To apply this tool we have considered the drying phase as the TP (technical process), and then we have analyzed contradictions among these parameters and the ones, that we have considered the most interesting for the case, selected by Altshuller between the late 1940s and 1970s [6, 11]. To select these ones we have made a point of the results obtained from marketing researches already discussed in chapter 3 from which it clearly stood out that the waste in term of time, energy and power, together with harmful effects in general were the most relevant for customers.

The parameter "quantity of water" can be easily identified with "Amount of substance", the 26th EP. In order to facilitate the water extraction, the amount of this substance should be as less as possible. The problem is that reducing the water could cause harmful effects, (31 EP) because the amount of water is optimized in order to have the best washing conditions. Another important contradiction came to light considering full-load washing cycle which needs a bigger amount of water. In this case this amount has negative effects on the power (21 EP) consumption as well as the energy spent by the subsystem (19-20 EP) and the time (25 EP) to perform the drying action. As well mentioned above, water temperature value (17 EP) is strictly connected to clothes fiber type and to the detergent chemical formulation. The increasing of this value, while can give to water more energy to came out from clothes fiber, can cause harmful from the fiber care point of view and requires a huge amount of power (21 EP). Contradiction analysis results are summarized in table 2.

Table 2. Water analysis: the inventive principles.

|                          | Power (21)    | Energy (19-20) | Spent Waste of Time (25) | Harmful Effects (31) |
|--------------------------|---------------|----------------|--------------------------|----------------------|
| Amount of substance (26) | 35            | 3, 35, 31      | 35, 38, 18,16            | 3, 35, 40, 39        |
| Temperature (17)         | 2, 14, 17, 25 |                |                          | 22, 35, 2, 24        |

Several interesting technical solutions have been identified by means of the inventive principles analysis. Once having analysed these ones we found out that the most interesting ones could be classified in three different approaches: a better use of resources during the drying phase, the application of different physical fields (mechanical vibration or thermal phenomena) and the waste resources reuse after the drying phase.

For the first group of solutions we have:
1. Change the degree of flexibility (35)
2. Use only the necessary part (or property) of an object (2)
3. Using a multy-story arrangements of objects (17)
4. Using "slightly less" or "slightly more" of the same method (16)

Principle 35 suggests modifying the amount of water in relation to the amount and fibers typology of clothes in order to reduce power consumption: accordingly to this approach, the water to be eliminated is the only one useful for washing. This solution is already applied in common washing machine using special load sensors. The multi-story arrangements (17) and the use of only necessary part (2) could mean the creation of special drying cycle in relation to special washing ones that the consumer can choose. This is due to the fact that the clothes fibers type heavily influences both cycles: natural fibers like wool or cotton absorb a bigger quantity of water than synthetic ones and need a different water temperature value. For example another possible solution is to separate during drying phase the clothes already dried from the ones that still need additional treatment. The last inventive solutions (16) suggest precisely identifying the target humidity level to pursuit.

For the second group (mechanical vibration or thermal phenomena) we have:
1. Change an object's physical aggregate state (35)

2. Go from linear to rotary motion, use centrifugal forces (14)
3. Tilt or re-orient the object (17)
4. Used combined ultrasonic or electromagnetic field oscillations (18)

Also inside this group of solutions we can find new ones and others nowadays applied. The solution already present in the market can be associated to the $35^{th}$ principle, due to the water physical aggregate state change realized by the hot flow. About this thermal phenomenon, a possible solution to facilitate water extraction could be the realization of a vacuum atmosphere inside the tank in order to reduce the energy spent by the system. Also the $14^{th}$ principle is already applied in washing machine as the classical mechanical solution, and it could be only optimized by developing specific rotating cycles. The last technical solution (18) has been considered as the most interesting and really innovative one. This solution principle is to transmit vibration energy to water molecules in a more efficient way than today, in order to facilitate the water extraction from clothes. Moreover, the $17^{th}$ principle could be read as a suggestion to optimize garments position at the beginning of the drying phase: being able to "unwrap" washed clothes and increase garments external surface would significantly improve drying process efficiency.

Finally in the third group has been classified these principles.
1. Use harmful factors to achieve a positive effect (22)
2. Make an object serve itself by performing auxiliary function (25)
3. Use waste resources, energy, or substances (25)

In this case technical solutions point an accent into the reuse of waste resources, e.g. extracting hot water by condensing it from the hot air flow, whose humidity value is usually extremely high, and reusing it to warm up cold one.

For clothes, detergent, and electrical energy parameters we do not have applied contradiction analysis. Clothes quantity value and fibers type can be considered as random variables because they depend on human needs. In reality there is a way through which enterprise can reduce this variability, to be more precise, identifying lots of specific washing and drying cycles as above mentioned in the first group of inventive solutions. Regarding to detergent, the possibility to facilitate the water physical aggregate state change could be realized with exothermic reactions. In this case the technical solution involves another market product which is not developed inside the company. Regarding to electrical field, this resource can be included into the technical solutions previously identified.

In conclusion, three possible problem approaches stand out from our analysis which can also be implemented concurrently. Identified solutions are based on a general approach so that they could be developed not only for a specific domestic appliance, like a washing machine, but also for all the ones which implement a drying cycle. Moreover the contraction analysis has seemed to be really effective in managing kick-off project meetings giving a well framed way to cope with technical problems.

## 4.4  The use of patent literature during concept design

The strong advantage of TRIZ [12], in comparison with the other approaches, lies in Altshuller's choice of the right source for acquiring knowledge — the patent search and analysis. Patent information was the work basis, not only to create and introduce new procedures for the elimination of technical contradictions but also to examine general laws for the development of technical systems.

The Contradiction Matrix and the Principles do not work by themselves; they only suggest the most promising directions for engineers to search for a solution. The problem solver has to interpret these suggestions and determine how apply them to any particular situation. Nevertheless, TRIZ heuristics are very valuable because a problem solver does not have to study all patents from all disciplines, if he or she can reformulate the problem in the format of the Contradiction Matrix, thereby increasing the efficiency of solving. Regarding this, after having identified a sufficient number of possible contradictions solutions, we have started patent literature search. In particular we have focused our attention into microwave and ultrasound solutions.

Two different patent literature researches have been performed; the first at the beginning of the analysis considering a list of key-words like: to dry, water removing evaporation and humidity reduction.  They have been generated only focusing on the product primary function. Obviously this research has lead to a big amount of patents because too generic but it has been useful to limit the research area. The second patent test has been conducted after the matrix contradictions analysis. Using words come out during technical contradictions solutions we have been able to limit progressively the analysis. A strong company commitment has given to pursuit a deeper involvement of patent literature analysis, also during the preliminary phases of innovation project: by systematically introducing specific TRIZ-based methodologies, significant and helpful outputs from patent analysis could be obtained in idea generation.

## 5. Conclusions

Problem solving lies at the heart of a new methodology for innovation. Innovators solve problems by focusing both upon the useful parameters of a system that, if increased, would enhance it substantially, and upon the harmful aspects that, if left unchecked, would lead to a contradiction. Contradictions are significant, because they contribute to the development of a breakthrough solution: avoiding compromise is central to innovation.

In this paper we present an industrial case study, whose beginning phase has been carried out to show TRIZ theory potentialities. By means of TRIZ Contradictions Matrix, interesting solution directions have been displaced. After evaluation, a set of innovative and feasible concepts have been obtained to solve the initial problem, the drying phase energy efficiency improvement of household appliances. In particular three different types of solution approaches have been identified which represent three different points of view to address the problem. The potentiality of identified solutions lies in the possibility to develop them for all the domestic appliances which have a drying cycle.

The suggested technical solutions have been deeply evaluated by company technical division, being two of them now under evaluation: specific internal projects are being developed to assess the technical feasibility of the proposed concepts. Furthermore, thanks to the interesting results obtained Indesit Company is now evaluating, on one side, the initiative of organizing idea generation meetings, in order to achieve a more effective involvement of all its innovation division engineers, not only middle and top management, and to maintain employee interest levels and participation rates, aligned to company innovation values. On the other side, further in-depth examinations will be carried out about patents search. In order to reach these purposes a deeper analysis of this theory and its methodology is fundamental because its potentialities in industry also depend on the personal properties of individuals and on their experience in applying it. For this reason several additional case studies will be implemented and analyzed.

# References

1. Porter M. E. Stern S.: The New Challenge to America's Prosperity: Findings from the Innovation Index, Council on Competitiveness, Washington, DC (1999).
2. Kim W. C., Mauborgne R.: Strategy, value innovation, and the knowledge economy. Sloan Management Review, pp. 41-54, Springer (1999).
3. Harrington H. J., Continuous versus breakthrough improvement: finding the right answer. Business Process Reengineering & Management Journal, vol. 1(3), pp. 31-49 (1995).
4. Savransky S. D.: Introduction to TRIZ Methodology of Inventive Problem Solving, CRC Press, New York (2000).
5. Cascini G.: State of the art and trends of Computer Aided Innovation tools, towards the integration within the Product Development Cycle. In Building the information society, Kluwer Academy Publishers (ISBN 1-4020-8156-1) (2004).
6. Altshuller G. S.: Creativity as an Exact Science: The Theory of the Solution of Inventive Problems, Gordon and Breach Science Publishing, New York (1984).
7. Orloff M. A.: Inventive Thinking through TRIZ. A Practical Guide, pp 28-45, Springer (2006).
8. Mc Munigal J., Ungvari S., Slocum M., McMunigal R.: Mechanical Engineers Handbook: Materials and Mechanical Design, vol. 1, John Wiley & Sons, Third Edition (2006).
9. Pevzner L. Kh.: ABC of Invention, Sredne-Ural'skoe Publishing House, Ekaterinburg (1992).
10. Sklobovsky K. A., Sharipov R. H.: Theory, Practice and Applications of the Inventive Problems Decision, Protva-Prin, Obninsk (1995).
11. Altshuller G. S.: 40 Principles: TRIZ Keys to Technical Innovation, TIC, Worchester (1998).

# Towards a Framework for Collaborative Innovation

Heiko Duin[1], Jacob Jaskov[2], Alexander Hesmer[1], and Klaus-Dieter Thoben[1]

[1]BIBA – Institute for Production and Logistics GmbH, Hochschulring 20, D-28359 Bremen, Germany, E-Mail: {du, hes, tho}@biba.uni-bremen.de

[2]Learning Lab Denmark, Copenhagen, Denmark, E-Mail: jacob@jaskov.dk

**Abstract:** This paper presents the Unified Collaborative Innovation Framework (UCIF) developed in the European Integrated Project Laboranova (Collaboration Environment for Strategic Innovation). The Framework aims at the support of the early stage innovation process by means of collaborative working environments. As implied by its name, UCIF is a framework, which by definition is a conceptual construct acting as the skeleton and boundary upon and within various entities and concepts are integrated, outlining a proposed solution.

**Keywords:** Innovation Framework, Collaborative Innovation, Laboranova

## 1. Introduction

Open Innovation as a concept has been coined by Henry Chesbrough who is a professor and executive director at the Center for Open Innovation at Berkeley [1]. The central idea of Open Innovation is that in a world consisting of widely distributed knowledge, organizations like enterprises can not afford to rely entirely on their own research. Instead they should buy or license processes or inventions (e.g. patents) from other companies. In addition, internal inventions which are not used in business could be taken outside the enterprise (e.g. by licensing or joint ventures). In contrast, closed innovation refers to processes that limit the use of internal knowledge within a company and make little or no use of external knowledge.

The integration of end users and other stakeholders into innovation projects has proved to reduce business risks such as the invention and acceptance of products, services and applications. However, the integration of the end-users remains a difficult task. Thus a new methodological approach is required to cope with this problem. One solution is the concept of European Living Labs which offer a unique opportunity for organizations to include end-users and other stakeholders

*Please use the following format when citing this chapter:*

Duin, H., Jaskov, J., Hesmer, A. and Thoben, K.-D., 2008, in IFIP International Federation for Information Processing, Volume 277; *Computer-Aided Innovation (CAI)*; Gaetano Cascini; (Boston: Springer), pp. 193–204.

in new product development or other innovation processes. This enables the user to be a co-creator in the innovation process [2]. Living Labs need support by CAI (Computer Aided Innovation), e.g. the collaborative tools of Laboranova [3].

This paper presents the Unified Collaborative Innovation Framework (UCIF) which – as implied by its name – is a framework, which by definition is a conceptual construct acting as a skeleton and boundary. Upon and within UCIF integrates various entities and concepts, thus outlining a proposed solution. As such, UCIF is expected to simplify the works in user centered open innovation, help in aligning them, remove scientific, linguistic obstacles and obstacles stemming from different backgrounds and perspectives that inhibit people involved to flawlessly exchange ideas and collaborate.

UCIF is presented using a constructive approach. This means that one piece of information (regarding one constituent part of UCIF) will be given at a time, and it will be added to those already presented. Each step of the description is supported by a diagram adding relevant comments. With the last step the whole framework should have become apparent and clear.

Using this approach it is easier to comprehend UCIF, understand the reasons for including each comprising part and allowing the following of the underlying storyline, which outlines the higher-level workflow of UCIF. That is: Influences from the environment lead an individual or team to realize of a new opportunity for innovation (idea, problem, issue, feedback etc); this opportunity is called Innovation Experience Opportunity (IEO). Then an innovation process starts seeking to generate knowledge and ideas that will exploit the new opportunity. During that process several knowledge objects (corporate or external) are sought and used, and furthermore new knowledge assets are created and added to the existing ones. Of course the impact of the innovation process might influence back the environment (closed loop), but this out of scope of this paper.

## 2. Knowledge and Ideation Circles

According to UCIF point of view there are two important, iterative and convoluting processes that take place during innovation, one regarding knowledge-related activities and one regarding idea-related activities. The former is called **Knowledge Circle** and the latter **Ideation Circle**. These concepts trace their origin to knowledge management perspectives such as Gartner Group KM model [4].

**Knowledge Circle** involves activities related to the knowledge life cycle and knowledge management. When referring to the knowledge circle in UCIF, the following tasks are implied:

- Initial definition of process goals and strategy
- Knowledge exploration or seek
- Knowledge retrieval or extraction

- Knowledge use, exploitation, leveraging
- New knowledge capture, modeling and storing
- Knowledge sharing or dissemination
- Reframing and redefinition of exploration purpose or of point of view
- Other knowledge management activities

These activities occur repeatedly as an iterative process. In each process-iteration more knowledge is extracted from knowledge sources and further knowledge is created.

**Ideation Circle** involves activities related to the idea life cycle and idea management. When referring to the idea circle in UCIF, the following tasks are implied:

- Initial definition of process goals and strategy
- Existing idea search, reuse and leveraging; existing idea will then be used as the starting point for further innovation
- Idea generation or ideation. Leveraging of existing knowledge assets
- Idea elaboration or development. Leveraging of existing knowledge assets
- Idea capturing, modeling and storing
- Idea sharing or dissemination
- Reframing and redefinition of ideation purpose
- Other idea management activities

As with knowledge circles, these activities occur repeatedly (iterative process). In each process-iteration more ideas are created. Since idea generation and elaboration (in Ideation Circle), as mental processes as they are, they heavily rely on knowledge exploitation and situation reframing (in Knowledge Circle). The two circles are constantly interacting, convoluting and influencing each other. More specifically, the knowledge creation and modeling activities can influence and provide stimuli for inspiration, thus causing idea generation and elaboration.


## 3. The UCIF Sections

The first part of UCIF to present is **Sections**. Sections are used to distinguish and separate the three major parts of UCIF storyline, which are:

- The **Influences Section** that depicts influences from the environment that might lead to realization of new IEOs,
- The **Innovation Section** that focuses on ways to exploit IEOs and produce ideas, and
- The **Knowledge Objects Section** that depicts Knowledge Objects as these are sought, used or created during the innovation process.

One thing that must be stressed is the entry point from the Influences to Innovation section. That is the realization from an individual or team of a new need that came up, or business opportunity or problem or insight, which needs to be solved or exploited or to further be investigated. It is usually created from stimuli and influences originating from the sources that will be described in the Influences Section, or in some cases from individual inspiration. Realization means the point where the influences section ends and the Innovation section begins.

The innovation process will typically be an iterative process, which includes several knowledge exploration and exploitation activities, new knowledge creation and modeling, which subsequently leads to ideation and new idea generation. Here, ideas are considered as knowledge (or knowledge objects) that have been identified to introduce innovative attributes to products or services or processes or methods etc, with regard to the context.

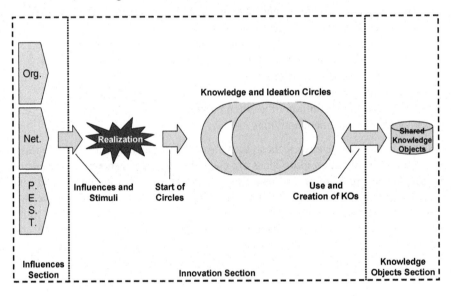

Figure 1 Sections and Storyline of UCIF.

The three UCIF Sections and the basic storyline of innovation in shown in Fig. 1. The storyline includes the following steps:

- Influences from the environment provide stimuli on people inside the organization
- Realization occurs and a knowledge exploration, modeling and ideation circle starts
- This circle which is a high-level business process includes several mid-level business processes
- During this circle many knowledge objects are retrieved and used and some are new created

## 3.1 The Influences Section

The **Influences Section** captures all sources of stimuli that might have some impact on the innovation process. It is the source of new IEOs. In UCIF, three types of influences have been identified depending on their origin (See Fig. 1, left side):

- Influences from inside the company or **organization**
- Influences from the external company or **organization network**
- Influences from the **broader environment** (P.E.S.T. – Politics, Economy, Society, Technology)

The **influences from the company** or organization originate mainly from the corporate strategy, policies, rules and operational tactics, as well as from the corporate culture and value system. It is worth mentioning that the procedures, structures (explicit or implicit), hierarchies (formal or informal), and social networks, have a great impact on the innovation process as they might control access to valuable knowledge resources and furthermore provide the necessary context needed for innovation to take place and propagate to the decision makers.

Another important source of **influences is the company's network** of partners, suppliers, and of course customers. Partners and suppliers can help in improving and rationalizing the organization's business processes and structures in order to increase efficiency. Customers are the users of company's products and/or services, and therefore they can provide valuable feedback about product and service functioning, characteristics, suitability for purpose, as well as provide insights on their own actual needs that must be met by new products and services.

The third source of **influences is the broader** political, economical, social and technological (P.E.S.T.) **environment**, within which the company or organization exists and operates. Technology in the last few decades has proven to be a quite versatile environment and simultaneously a driving factor for innovation. It has provided, and still provides, numerous stimuli and IEOs.

## 3.2 The Innovation Section

The **Innovation Section** captures the essence of the Framework, which is the innovation process that takes place within a company or organization. For this reason it is the core part of UCIF.

In real world, innovation can occur as a result of several interacting and interrelating business processes. Not all of them aim to the generation of new ideas, but they might lead to innovative results as a by-product. In UCIF however the focus is on processes that explicitly seek new idea generation (e.g. knowledge modeling) as well as considering idea management.

The Innovation Section is comprised from several business processes, which are parts of the higher-level, strategic innovation process. They span many scientific domains and areas of interest and involve people, roles and structures at various corporate levels. Business processes are usually executed in the context of projects launched within a company or in some cases in projects that span many companies and organizations. The following paragraphs describe in more detail this section and its comprising parts: Areas of Interest (Management, Knowledge, Ideas), Levels (Top Management, Network, Team, Personal), Innovation Business Processes and their interactions, and Teams and Projects.

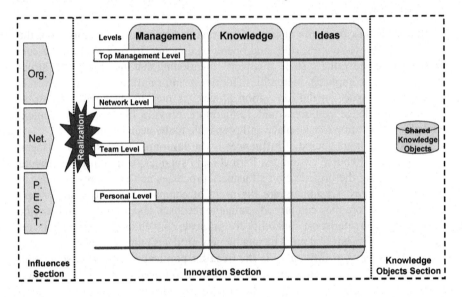

Figure 2 Structure of the Innovation Section

The realization of a new IEO is the entry point from Influences Section to Innovation Section. Fig. 2 shows the Areas of Interest (vertical) and Levels (horizontal) structure of the Innovation Section.

## 3.3 Knowledge Objects Section

The **Knowledge Objects Section** includes all entities and media containing or conveying knowledge. These entities are generally referred to as **Knowledge Objects**. Technically speaking Knowledge Objects can be a Database or Knowledge Base, a folder of documents, a single document, a software package etc. The knowledge and information contained in Knowledge Objects can be represented in various different formats (e.g. database records, plain text, rich text, XML, voice recordings, pictures, drawings etc). The following **Knowledge Object Types** have been identified so far (see also Fig. 3, right side):

- Knowledge Objects residing in knowledge stores
- Idea models
- Idea portfolios
- Knowledge Objects residing in collaboration workspaces
- Evaluation reports

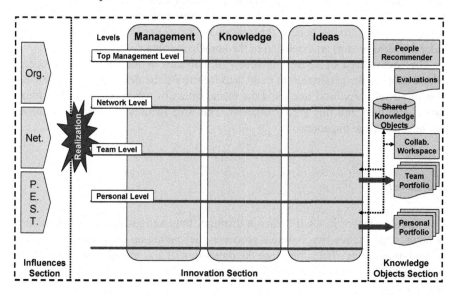

Figure 3 Knowledge Objects Section

# 4. Innovation Section Analysis

## 4.1 Areas of Interest

The **Areas of Interest** identify three domains (areas) that are involved in the innovation processes and innovation management. These areas are:

- Idea generation and management
- Knowledge exploration, exploitation, capturing and management
- Management of people, structures (e.g. teams) and resources

The **Management Area** of interest includes the activities of the strategic innovation process, which relates to the decision-making and management of people, teams, projects and resources. These activities do not generate new knowledge or ideas but provide the necessary operational environment that enables innovation to take place.

The **Knowledge Area** of interest includes the activities of innovation process, which relate to knowledge exploration, exploitation, leveraging, creation, modeling, and knowledge management. The Knowledge Circle falls into this area of interest. The activities of this area are usually providing the necessary influence, context and background needed for ideation to occur. For this reason we can consider the ideas area as an extension of the knowledge area.

The **Ideas Area** of interest includes all activities of the innovation process, which relate to the generation of new ideas (ideation), the development and evolution of already proposed ones, and the management of proposed ideas. The Ideation Circle falls into this area of interest. This area focuses specifically on ideas not on knowledge in general.

## *4.2 Levels*

The **Levels** concept in UCIF helps in distinguishing and grouping the interacting structures and the relating business processes, depending on the level of complexity and/or authority. They introduce the dimension of size and escalation in UCIF. Four levels have been identified: Individual, team, network or open team and top management level.

Each organization or company that might use CAI products and UCIF can adapt these levels to their specific corporate environment and needs. A short explanation of these levels is given next:

- **Individual**: regards the processes, methods, tools or any other related concepts used by a single individual.
- **Team/Group**: regards the processes, methods, tools or any other related concepts used by (planned) teams. Such teams do not necessarily have a formal internal structure.
- **Network or Open Team**: regards the processes, methods, tools or any other concepts used by networks formed from interacting and collaborating teams.
- **Top Management**: regards the processes, methods, tools or any other concepts used by the top management of the company and their assistants, both for managing the whole innovation process as well as making knowledgeable decisions on innovations and ideas.

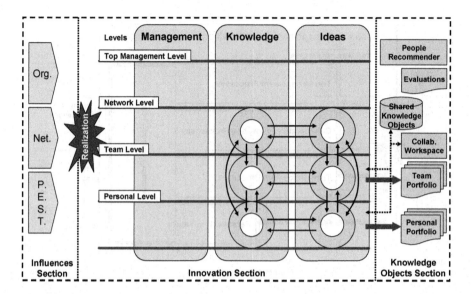

Figure 4 Ideation and Knowledge Circles in Areas and Levels of the Innovation Section

As shown in Fig. 4, the Knowledge and Ideation Circles can be broken down to several smaller circles that reside at different levels. These circles can interact both across areas of interest, across levels or even within the same level and area.

## 4.3 Business Processes

The business process concept is used in UCIF to represent the business processes that take place within a company or organization and which explicitly aim to idea generation and management. Business Processes exist at every level of the organization and span several areas of interest. Furthermore, interactions occur among them both within the same area and level, as well as across areas and levels.

According to [5] "a business process is a set of linked activities that create value by transforming an input into a more valuable output. Both input and output can be artifacts and/or information and the transformation can be performed by human actors, machines, or both".

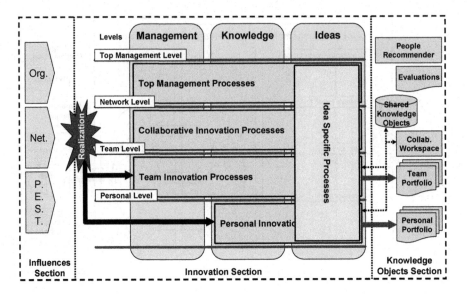

Figure 5 UCIF Business Processes

A business process can be decomposed into several sub-processes, which have their own attributes, but also contribute in achieving the goal of the super-process. The analysis of business processes typically includes the mapping of processes and sub-processes down to activity level. Activities are parts of the business process that do not include any decision-making and thus are not worth decomposing (although decomposition would be possible). In UCIF there have been identified and captured 5 types of business processes: Personal innovation-related processes, team innovation-related processes, collaborative innovation-related processes, top management innovation-related processes, and vertical, ideation-specific processes.

The first four types are horizontal (see Fig. 5), span all areas of interest and reside to one level of UCIF. On the other hand, the fifth process is vertical; it resides in the Idea area of interest and can span all levels.

The meaning of the horizontal processes is that an innovation-related business process includes activities residing in many areas of interest, i.e. knowledge-related, innovation-related and management-related activities. Furthermore, business processes at different levels have different attributes, as the goals, tools and practices used at each level differ.

The vertical business process in the Ideas Area of Interest focuses on the activities and workflows that take place across levels but within the Ideas area. These processes are of special interest because they focus on pure innovation activities (ideation, idea development, idea management, prediction markets etc.).

## 4.4 Business Process Interactions

As stated above, interactions occur among business processes and their activities. These interactions can be of many different types, such as workflow or activity sequencing (next activity), decision points, influences or other implicit impact etc.

Fig. 6 outlines the possible interaction combinations. The true interactions will be detailed later when we will present the processes in more detail. As shown in the diagram, the management activities tightly interact with knowledge activities to enable them produce and disseminate new knowledge. This basic interaction leads to the generation and evolution of new ideas, thus starting and influencing the innovation activities.

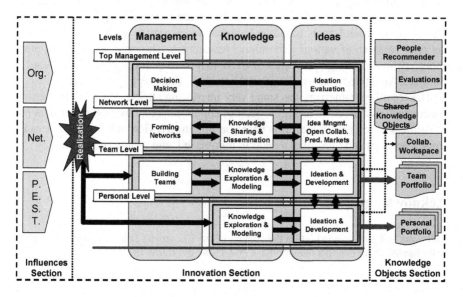

Figure 6 UCIF Business Process Interactions

More specifically, at the Personal Level it is expected the knowledge-related tasks to be the predominant type of activities. Ideation and idea development activities are also happening to some extend. The individual has the ability to share his/her new knowledge with other individuals, or teams, or disseminate it to open projects or networks, or publish it to Knowledge Bases.

## 4.5 Teams and Projects

In fact, humans put business processes and their interactions in practice, either individually or in teams who work on certain projects. Teams can be started for many reasons but in most cases this happens when there is a clear need for a new project, for example research for a new idea after the realization of a new customer need. Then teams, or in some cases individuals, work on the projects following certain, usually predefined, business processes. Teams and projects are created and executed at various levels; they span many areas of interest and participate in several business processes.

## 5. Conclusions

Much effort has been put in identifying the vast majority of collaborative innovation related concepts, as well as of concepts related to many supportive activities. This work has been largely based on Laboranova case study analysis as well as on the prior research of various Laboranova researchers. The result is a concept map and guidelines or design principles of UCIF that trace their origins in theories such Complex Adaptive Systems, Situational Analyses, Emergent Systems etc.

The resulting framework has some very interesting attributes: UCIF focuses on the conceptual and technological aspects of collaborative innovation rather than on scientific and research issues. It is based on literature review and broad consensus among partners and thus gives a neutral, non-biased, and well-accepted view.

## Acknowledgements

This work has been carried out in the context of the EU project Laboranova which is partially funded under contract number IST-FP6-035262 in Priority IST.

## References

1. Chesbrough H.W.: Open innovation. Harvard Business School Press, Boston, MA, (2003).
2. Schumacher J, Feuerstein K.: Living Labs. The User as Co-Creator in: Pawar K.S., Thoben K.D., Pallot M. (eds): Proceedings of the 13th International Conference on Concurrent Enterprising: Concurrent Innovation. An Emerging Paradigm for Collaboration and Competitiveness in the Extended Enterprise. Centre for Concurrent Enterprise, Nottingham University Business School, Nottingham, (2007).
3. Hesmer A., Hribernik K.A., Baalsrud Hauge J., Thoben, K.D.: Supporting the Sytematization of Early-Stage-Innovation by Means of Collaborative Working Environments in Trends in Computer Aided Innovation. pp. 57-64, (2007).
4. Gartner: Using technology to create and capture knowledge, http://www.gartner.com. Accessed 10 March 2006, (2006).
5. Wikipedia Business Process, http://en.wikipedia.org/wiki/Business_process. Accessed: 07 May 2007.

# Communication and Creative Thinking in Agile Software Development

**Broderick Crawford[1, 2], Claudio León de la Barra[1], and Patricio Letelier[3]**

[1] Pontificia Universidad Católica de Valparaíso, Chile, cleond@ucv.cl
[2] Universidad Técnica Federico Santa María, Chile, broderick.crawford@ucv.cl
[3] Universidad Politécnica de Valencia, España, letelier@dsic.upv.es

**Abstract:** This paper describes and analyses how a eXtreme Programming (XP) team work can use some ideas from Psychology and Computer Science fostering creativity and innovation in Software Development. The roles for creative team in order to have a chance for creative thinking, communication, innovation, collaboration and knowledge sharing are addressed to Agile Software Development teams.

**Keywords:** Creativity, Software Development, Agile Methodologies, eXtreme Programming.

## 1. Introduction

Psychology and Computer Science are growing in a interdisciplinary relationship mainly because human and social factors are very important in developing software and hardware. Software is developed for people and by people [1], but surprisingly, most of software engineering research is technical and deemphasizes the human and social aspects. By other hand, the traditional development process of new products that is a fundamental part in marketing has been recently criticized by Kotler and Trías de Bes [2]. They point out that fundamental creative aspects are not considered at all and as a consequence this development is not useful, viable or innovative. In this context, it is interesting to consider the new proposals of agile methodologies for software development in order to analyze and evaluate them at the light of the existing creative expositions, mainly considering the teamwork practices.

The agile principles and values have emphasized the importance of communication, collaboration and interaction in the software development and, by other hand, creative work commonly involves collaboration in some form and it can be understood as an interaction between an individual and a socio-cultural context. In relation with the joint work between users and agile software

*Please use the following format when citing this chapter:*

Crawford, B., León de la Barra, C. and Letelier, P., 2008, in IFIP International Federation for Information Processing, Volume 277; *Computer-Aided Innovation (CAI)*; Gaetano Cascini; (Boston: Springer), pp. 205–216.

developers, there are very interesting cases in the work of Jeff Sutherland, the inventor of the popular Scrum Agile Development Process [3-7]. The most notorious agile methods: Scrum and eXtreme Programming XP [8], had attained worldwide fame for its ability to increase the productivity of software teams by several magnitudes through empowering individuals, fostering a team-oriented environment, and focusing on project transparency and results [9-13].

We believe that the innovation and development of new products is an interdisciplinary issue [14], we are interested in the study of the potential of new concepts and techniques to foster creativity in software engineering [15]. This paper is organized as follows: in section 2 we explain the motivation of this work fixing the relevance of Creativity in Software Development. Section 3 is about central aspects in Creativity. Section 4 gives a brief overview of XP and its phases and roles. In Section 5 we show how the XP Creative Team Can Operate. Section 6 presents a comparison between roles in creative teams and roles in XP teams. Finally, in Section 7 we conclude the paper.

## 2. Creative Thinking in Software Development

Software engineering is a knowledge intensive process, this underlies the need for communication, collaboration and knowledge sharing support to share domain expertise between the customer and the development team [16]. Since human creativity is thought as the source to resolve complex problem or create innovative products, one possibility to improve the software development process is to design a process which can stimulate the creativity of the developers. There are few studies reported on the importance of creativity in software development. In management and business, researchers have done much work about creativity and obtained evidence that the employees who had appropriate creativity characteristics, worked on complex, challenging jobs, and were supervised in a supportive, non-controlling fashion, produced more creative work. Then, according to the previous ideas the use of creativity in software development is undeniable, but requirements engineering is not recognized as a creative process in all the cases [17]. In a few publications the importance of creativity has been investigated in all the phases of software development process [18,15,19] and mostly focused in the requirements engineering [20-22]. Nevertheless, the use of techniques to foster creativity in requirements engineering is still shortly investigated, it is not surprising that the role of communication and interaction is central in many of the creativity techniques. The importance of creative thinking is expected to increase over the next decade [23]. In [20, 24] very interesting open questions are proposed: Is inventing part of the requirements activity? It is if we want to advance. So who does the inventing? We cannot rely on the customer to know what to invent. The designer sees his task as deriving the optimal solution to the stated requirements. We can not rely on programmers because they are far away from the work of client to understand what needs to be invented. Requirements analysts are ideally placed to innovate. They understand the business problem, have updated knowledge of the technology, will be blamed if the new product does not please the customer, and know if inventions are appropriate to the work being studied. In short, requirements analysts are the people whose skills and position allows, indeed encourages, creativity. In [25] the author, a leading authority on cognitive creativity, identifies basic types of creative processes: exploratory creativity explores a possible solution space and discovers new ideas, combinatorial creativity combines two or more ideas that already exist to create new ideas, and transformational creativity changes the solution space to make impossible things possible. Then, most requirements engineering activities are exploratory, acquiring and discovering requirements and knowledge about the problem domain. Requirements engineering practitioners have explicitly focused on combinatorial and transformational creativity. In relation with the active participation of the users in software development, Holzinger has very valuable work making usability practitioners first-class citizens in the process [26-29].

## 3. Creativity in the Development of New Products

The creativity definitions are numerous [30-32], therefore, considering the object of analysis in the present paper: a software development teamwork responding to the requirements of a specific client for a particular problem, a suitable definition is the one raised by Welsch [33]: *Creativity is the process of generating unique products by transformation of existing products. These products, tangible and intangible, must be unique only to the creator, and must meet the criteria of purpose and value established by the creator.*

More specifically, and from an eminently creative perspective, it is possible to distinguish three aspects at the interior of a group developing new products (purposes, performance and structure):

a) The purposes that the team tries to reach, which demand two scopes of results [34-38]:
- Those related to the creative result that must be original, elaborated, productive and flexible.
- Those related to the creative team, so that it reaches its goals, developing cognitive abilities and presenting an improved disposition to the change. All this in order to obtain a better creative team performance in the future.

b) The performance shown by the team in connection with the main aspects of the complex dynamics that the persons build inside a team. We describe three aspects:

- The personal conditions of the members of the team, in terms of the styles and cognitive abilities, the personality, their intrinsic motivation and knowledge [32,39,30,34].
- The organizational conditions in which the creative team is inserted, and that determines, at least partly, its functioning. These conditions, in the extent that pre-sent/display certain necessary particular characteristics - although non sufficient- for the creative performance. They emphasize in special the culture (communication, collaboration, trust, conflict handle, pressure and learning) [32,40,41]; the internal structure (formalization, autonomy and evaluation of the performance) [32,40,41,39]; the team available resources (time disposition) [32,40,30] and the physical atmosphere of work [31].
- The conditions of performance of the creative team, mainly the creative process realized, which supposes the set of specific phases that allow assure the obtaining of a concrete result (creative product) [31, 42].

c) The structure of the creative team, particularly the group characteristics, such as norms, cohesiveness, size, diversity, roles, task and problem-solving approaches [32].

Of the mentioned aspects, we deepen in those referred to the structure and performance of the team for the development of new products, specially considering: the creative process and the roles surrounding this process.

## 3.1 The Phases of the Creative Process

The creative process constitutes the central aspect of team performance, because it supposes a serie of clearly distinguishable phases that had to be realized by one or more of the team members in order to obtain a concrete creative result. Considering the creativity as a "nonlinear" process some adjustments are necessary including feedbacks whose "destiny" can be anyone of the previous phases. The phases, on the basis of Wallas [42] and Leonard and Swap [31], are the following ones:

- Initial preparation: the creativity will bloom when the mental ground is deep, fertile and it has a suitable preparation. Thus, the deep and relevant knowledge, and the experience precedes the creative expression.
- Encounter: the findings corresponding to the perception of a problematic situation. For this situation a solution does not exist. It is a new problem.
- Final preparation: it corresponds to the understanding and foundation of the problem. It's the immersion in the problem and the use of knowledge and analytical abilities. It includes search for data and the detailed analysis of factors and variables.
- Generation of options: referred to produce a menu of possible alternatives. It supposes the divergent thinking. It includes, on one hand, finding principles, lines or addresses, when making associations and

uniting different marks of references and, on the other hand, to generate possible solutions, combinations and interpretations.

- Incubation: it corresponds to the required time to reflect about the elaborated alternatives, and "to test them mentally".
- Options Choice: it corresponds to the final evaluation and selection of the options. It supposes the convergent thinking.
- Persuasion: closing of the creative process and communication to other persons.

## 3.2 The Roles in a Creative Team

Lumsdaine and Lumsdaine [43] raise the subject of the required cognitive abilities (mindsets) for creative problem resolution. Their typology is excellent for the creative team, and the different roles to consider. These roles are the following ones:

- Detective. In charge of collecting the greatest quantity of information related to the problem. It has to collect data not making judgements even when it thinks that it has already understood the problem exactly.
- Explorer. Detects what can happen in the area of the problem and its context. It thinks on its long term effects and it anticipates certain developments that can affect the context (in this case, the team). The explorer perceives the problem in a broad sense.
- Artist. Creates new things, transforming the information. It must be able to break his schemes to generate eccentric ideas, with imagination and feeling.
- Engineer. Is the one in charge of evaluating new ideas. It must make converge the ideas, in order to clarify the concepts and to obtain practical ideas that can be implemented for the resolution of problems.
- Judge. Must do a hierarchy of ideas and decide which of them will be implemented (and as well, which ones must be discarded). Additionally, it must detect possible faults or inconsistencies, as well as raise the corresponding solutions. Its role must be critical and impartial, having to look for the best idea, evaluating the associated risks.
- Producer. In charge of implementing the chosen ideas.

Leonard and Swap [31] have mentioned additional roles, possible to be integrated with the previous ones, because they try to make more fruitful the divergence and the convergence in the creative process:

- The provoker who takes the members of the team "to break" habitual mental and procedural schemes to allow the mentioned divergence (in the case of the "artist") or even a better convergence (in the case of the "engineer").

- Think tank that it is invited to the team sessions to give a renewed vision of the problem-situation based on his/her expertise and experience.
- The facilitator whose function consists in helping and supporting the team work in its creative task in different stages.
- The manager who cares for the performance and specially for the results of the creative team trying to adjust them to the criteria and rules of the organization (use of resources, due dates).

Kelley and Littman [44], on the other hand, have raised a role typology similar to Lumsdaine and Lumsdaine [43], being interesting that they group the roles in three categories: those directed to the learning of the creative team (susceptible of corresponding with the detective, explorer, artist, provoker and think tank roles); others directed to the internal organization and success of the team (similar to the judge, facilitator and manager roles); and roles whose purpose is to construct the innovation (possibly related to the role of the engineer and judge).

## 4. Agile Software Development with eXtreme Programming

Extreme Programming is an iterative approach to software development [8], the process is shown in Figure 1.

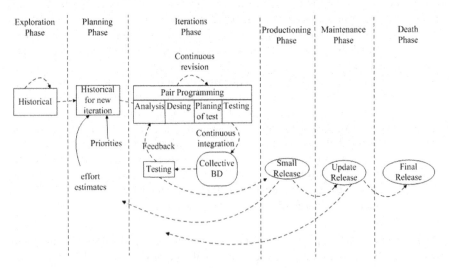

Figure 1 The eXtreme Programming Process.

The methodology is designed to deliver the software that customer needs when it's needed. This methodology emphasizes team work. Managers, customers, and developers are all part of a team dedicated to deliver quality soft-ware. XP implements a simple, yet effective way to enable groupware style development. XP improves a software project in four essential ways; communication, simplicity, feedback, and courage.

## 4.1 The Roles in a XP Team

XP defines the following roles for a software development process [8]:

- Programmer. The programmer writes source code for the software system under development. This role is at the technical heart of every XP project because it is responsible for the main outcome of the project: the application system.
- Customer. The customer writes user stories, which tell the programmer what to program. "The programmer knows how to program. The customer knows what to program".
- Tester. The tester is responsible for helping customers select and write functional tests. On the other side, the tester runs all the tests again and again to create an up-dated picture of the project state.
- Tracker. The tracker keeps track of all the numbers in a project. This role is familiar with the estimation reliability of the team. Whoever plays this role knows the facts and records of the project and should be able to tell the team whether they will finish the next iteration as planned.
- Coach. The coach is responsible for the development process as a whole. The coach notices when the team is getting "off track" and puts it "back on track." To do this, the coach must have experience with XP.
- Consultant. Whenever the XP team needs additional special knowledge, they "hire" a consultant who possesses this knowledge. The consultant transfers this knowledge to the team members, enabling them to solve the problem on their own.
- Big boss. The big boss or Manager provides the resources for the process. The big boss needs to have the general picture of the project, be familiar with the current project state, and know whether any interventions are needed to ensure the project's success.

## 5. How the XP Creative Team Can Operate

In relation with the structure dimension it's important to considerate how the team can operate. In order to implement the functionality of each role, we must considerate two aspects: basic organizational conditions and the pertinent creative process.

## 5.1 Basic Organizational Conditions

The creative team performance is determined by the organizational conditions in which it's inserted [39, 31, 32, 40, 41]. Some conditions are necessary - although not sufficient - for the creative performance. We are interested in explore the influence of autonomy, communication, cooperation and learning, the handling of possible conflicts, pressure, formalization, performance evaluation, available resources (time) and the physical atmosphere of work.

The team member's communication, cooperation and learning are fortified since the client is present and there exist opened spaces to work together and in a pair programming mode. The work dynamics is based on a game of planning and metaphors involving all the participants from the beginning (client and equipment developer).  Also, the use of codification standards, the small deliveries, the collective property of the code and the simple design, allow that the person has clear performance codes and rules about what is expected and acceptable (internal culture) in order to establish the required communication and cooperation.

The handling of possible conflicts between the client and the development team, and internally at team level is favored by XP practices handling it (presence of the client, pairs programming, planning game, continuous integration, tests, collective property), or to reduce it and to avoid it (small deliveries, simple design, 40 hour a week and codification standard). Cooperation and trust are associated to this issue.

The pressure (that in creativity is appraised as favorable until certain degree, favoring the performance, and detrimental if it exceeds this degree), is susceptible then to favor in XP through the client in situ, the programming by pairs, the planning game, the tests and continuous integration. It's possible to avoid, or at least to reduce, the pressure through the refactorization, the small deliveries, the collective property, and the fact that surpassing the 40 weekly working hours is seen like an error.

The formalization gives account of all those formal aspects (norms, procedures) defined explicitly and that are known, and even shared, by the members of the team. It's assured in XP through planning game, metaphors, continuous integration, the collective property, the 40 hours per week and the codification standards guiding the desirable conduct and performance of the team.

The evaluation of the performance is made in XP through pair programming (self evaluation and pair evaluation), frequent tests and even through the 40 weekly hours (as a metric indicating limit of effectiveness), all at the light of the planning (including the standards). Finally, the presence of client constitutes the permanent and fundamental performance evaluation of the team and the products. The evaluation characteristics empower the learning process.

The time dedicated has fundamental importance in XP team respecting the avail-able resources. This aspect is strongly stressed in creativity. The pair programming and the developer multifunctional role allow optimize the partial working-times, as well as the whole project time, ensuring a positive pressure.

The physical atmosphere of work, referred in creativity to the surroundings that favor or make difficult the creative performance (including aspects like available spaces, noise, colors, ventilation, relaxation places) are assured only partially in XP through the open spaces, as a way to assure the interaction between members of the team.

## 5.2   The Creative Process

The team performance is directly determined by the creative process [31, 42]. It's important to correlate the phases defined in XP with the phases considered in a creative process.

The initial preparation and "finding" defined in the creative process correspond to the exploration phase in XP, where the functionality of the prototype and familiarization with the methodology are established.

The final stage of preparation is equivalent with the phases of exploration and planning in XP, defining more in detail the scope and limit of the development.

The option generation phases, incubation and election of options defined in the creative process correspond to the iterations made in XP and also with the liberations of the production phase (small releases). In XP there is not a clear distinction of the mentioned creative phases, assuming that they occur to the interior of the team.

The feedback phase (understanding this one as a final stage of the process, and not excluding that can have existed previous micro - feedbacks since the creative process is nonlinear) it could correspond in XP with the maintenance phase.

The persuasion phase is related to the phase of death established in XP, constituting the close of the development project with the final liberation.

## 6. The Roles in Creativity and XP Roles

Regarding to the structure dimension of a new product development team (in particular software), it is possible to relate the roles in creativity to the roles defined in the XP methodology distinguishing: base roles, that is, those directly related to the creative processes and software development; and support roles, whose function is to support or lead the other roles for a better performance. As previously mentioned in the creative process there are base and supporting roles. The base roles are directly related to the creative and software development process and the supporting roles support or lead the base roles to a better performance. The following is the correlation between creative and XP roles:

- The detective function consisting in collecting information related to a problem is made by the client himself in XP, because this one generates the first contact with the software development team.

- The function of explorer consisting in defining completely the problem is made in XP as much by the client as the manager of the team, all together they appreciate the reach of the identified problem, as well as of the possible solutions. The function of the artist consisting in transforming the information, creating new relations, and therefore generating interesting solutions is made by the developer, that in XP methodology is in charge of the analysis, design and programming of software.
- The function of the engineer referred to clarify and to evaluate the new ideas, in terms of its feasibility is made in XP by the tester and the tracker.
- The function of the judge, understood as the definitive selection of the solutions to implant, is made in XP by the tracker and the client.
- The function of the producer, referred to the implementation of the selected ideas (strictly speaking it is working software) is made in XP by the client in his organization, including the processes and procedures that this function implies.

The supporting roles considered are:
- The provoker; creativity demands that the divergence as well as convergence in the solutions be maximum and complete. There is not explicit reference in XP methodology about divergent thinking.
- The think tank who helps the team work "from outside" is equivalent completely to the role of the consultant.
- The facilitator whose function is helping the team, corresponds in XP to the coach role.
- The manager whose function is to lead to the team in terms of its general efficiency and its effectiveness corresponds with XP's big boss or manager.

## 7. Conclusions

The Extreme Programming methodology includes implicitly central aspects of a creative teamwork. The structure that the team adopts and specially the different roles that the methodology advises to define, nearly correspond with the roles at the interior of a creative team. By other hand, the performance that characterizes the team through certain advisable practices, from the perspective of creativity, constitutes the necessary basic conditions, although non-sufficient, in order to favor the group creative performance. We think that XP methodology should have a more explicit reference to the provoker role that is thoroughly described in creativity as a fundamental factor to generate innovation. Furthermore, it is necessary a better distinction and formalization of the creative phases to generate options incubation and option choices (that are fundamental in creativity). It is assumed that they take place in the iterative and production process. Again, XP is not focused in "originality", resulting that the divergence is not so fundamental in XP. A more direct mention to the physical atmosphere of work, that in creativity are considered as highly relevant to enhance the performance, it is recommendable in XP.

# References

1. Maurer J.M., Tessem F.: Human and social factors of software engineering: workshop summary. SIGSOFT Softw. Eng. Notes, 30(1–6) (2005).
2. Kotler P., Trías de Bes F.: Marketing Lateral, Editorial Pearson/Prentice Hall, Spain (2004).
3. Sutherland J.: Agile can scale: Inventing and reinventing scrum in five companies. Cutter IT Journal, 14, pp. 5–11 (2001).
4. Sutherland J.: Agile development: Lessons learned from the first scrum. Cutter Agile Project Management Advisory Service: Executive Update, 5, pp. 1–4 (2004).
5. Sutherland J.: Recipe for real time process improvement in healthcare. 13th Annual Physician Computer Connection Symposium, 2004. In Rancho Bernardo, CA: American Society for Medical Directors of Information Systems (AMDIS) (2004).
6. Sutherland J.: Future of scrum: Parallel pipelining of sprints in complex projects. In: Agile, IEEE Computer Society, pp. 90–102 (2005).
7. Sutherland J., van den Heuvel W.J.: Towards an intelligent hospital environment: Adaptive workflow in the OR of the future. In: HICSS, IEEE Computer Society (2006).
8. Beck K.: Extreme programming explained: embrace change. Addison-Wesley Longman Publishing Co., Inc., Boston, MA, USA (2000).
9. Fruhling A.L., Tyser K., de Vreede G.J.: Experiences with extreme programming in telehealth: Developing and implementing a biosecurity health care application. In: HICSS, IEEE Computer Society (2005).
10. Christensen C., Bohmer R., Kenagy J.: Will disruptive innovations cure health care. Harvard Business Review pp. 102–111 (2000).
11. Dadam P., Reichert M., Kuhn K.: Clinical workflows - the killer application for process oriented information systems. BIS 2000 - Proceedings of the 4th International Conference on Business Information Systems pp. 36–59 (2000).
12. Fruhling A.: Examining the critical requirements, design approaches and evaluation methods for a public health emergency response system. Communications of the Association for Information Systems, 18 (2006).
13. Fruhling A.L., Steinhauser L., Hoff G., Dunbar C.: Designing and evaluating collaborative processes for requirements elicitation and validation. In: HICSS, IEEE Computer Society, 15 (2007).
14. Takeuchi H., Nonaka I.: The new product development game. Harvard Business Review (1986).
15. Gu M., Tong X.: Towards hypotheses on creativity in software development. Bomarius F., Iida H., eds., Computer Science, Springer vol. 3009, pp. 47–61 (2004).
16. Chau T., Maurer F., Melnik G.: Knowledge sharing: Agile methods vs tayloristic methods. Twelfth International Workshop on Enabling Technologies: Infrastructure for Collaborative Enterprises, WETICE, Los Alamitos, CA, USA, IEEE Computer Society, pp. 302–307 (2003).
17. Maiden N., Gizikis A., Robertson S.: Provoking creativity: Imagine what your requirements could be like. IEEE Software 21, pp. 68–75 (2004).
18. Glass R.L.: Software creativity. Prentice-Hall, Inc., Upper Saddle River, NJ, USA (1995).

19. Crawford B., León de la Barra C.: Enhancing creativity in agile software teams. Concas, G., Damiani, E., Scotto, M., Succi, G. eds.: XP. vol. 4536, Computer Science, pp.161–162 Springer (2007).

20. Robertson J.: Requirements analysts must also be inventors. Software, IEEE 22 pp. 48–50 (2005).

21. Maiden N., Robertson S.: Integrating creativity into requirements processes: Experiences with an air traffic management system. In: 13th IEEE International Conference on Requirements Engineering (RE 2005), 29 August - 2 September 2005, Paris, France, IEEE Computer Society, pp. 105–116 (2005).

22. Mich L., Anesi C., Berry D.M.: Applying a pragmatics-based creativity-fostering technique to requirements elicitation. Requirements Engineering, vol. 10, pp. 262–275 (2005).

23. Maiden N., Gizikis A.: Where do requirements come from? IEEE Softw. 18, pp. 10–12 (2001).

24. Robertson J.: Eureka! why analysts should invent requirements. IEEE Softw. 19, pp. 20–22 (2002).

25. Boden M.: The Creative Mind, Abacus (1990).

26. Memmel T., Reiterer H., Holzinger A.: Agile methods and visual specification in software development: a chance to ensure universal access. In: Coping with Diversity in Universal Access, Research and Development Methods in Universal Access. Computer Science, vol. 4554, pp. 453 462 (2007).

27. Holzinger A.: Rapid prototyping for a virtual medical campus interface. IEEE Software 21, pp. 92–99 (2004).

28. Holzinger A., Errath M.: Designing web-applications for mobile computers: Experiences with applications to medicine. In Stary C., Stephanidis C., eds, User Interfaces for All. Computer Science, vol. 3196, pp. 262–267 Springer (2004).

29. Holzinger A., Errath M.: Mobile computer web-application design in medicine: Research based guidelines. In: Springer Universal Access in Information Society (in print) (2007).

30. Amabile T., Conti R., Coon H., Lazenby J., Herron M.: Assessing the work environment for creativity. Academy of Management Journal, vol. 39, pp. 1154–1184.

31. Leonard D.A., Swap W.C.: When Sparks Fly: Igniting Creativity in Groups. Harvard Business School Press, Boston (1999).

32. Woodman R.W., Sawyer J.E., Griffin R.W.: Toward a theory of organizational creativity. The Academy of Management Review, vol. 18, pp. 293–321 (1993).

33. Welsh G.: Personality and Creativity: A Study of Talented High School Students. Unpub. doctoral dissertation, Chapel Hill, University of North Carolina (1967).

34. Csikszentmihalyi M.: Creativity: Flow and the Psychology of Discovery and Invention, Harper Perennial, New York (1998).

35. Guilford J.P.: Intelligence, Creativity and Their Educational Implications. Edits Pub (1968).

36. Hallman R.: The necessary and sufficient conditions of creativity. Journal of Humanistic Psychology, vol. 3 (1963) Also reprinted in: Gowan J.C. et al., Creativity: Its Educational Implications. John Wiley and Co., New York (1967).

37. Hallman R.: Aesthetic pleasure and the creative process. Journal of Humanistic Psychology, 6, pp. 141–148 (1966).

38. Hallman R.: Techniques of creative teaching. Journal of Creative Behavior, vol. I (1966).

39. Amabile T.: How to kill creativity. Harvard Business Review, pp. 77–87, Sept-Oct (1998).

40. Kotler P., Armstrong G.: Principles of Marketing, 10th Edition, Prentice Hall (2003).

41. Isaksen S.G., Lauer K.J., Ekvall G.: Situational outlook questionnaire: A measure of the climate for creativity and change. Psychological Reports, pp. 665–674.

42. Wallas G.: The art of thought, Harcourt Brace, New York (1926).

43. Lumsdaine E., Lumsdaine M.: Creative Problem Solving: Thinking Skills for a Changing World. McGraw-Hill, Inc, New York (1995).

44. Kelley T., Littman J.: The Ten Faces of Innovation: IDEO's Strategies for Defeating the Devil's Advocate and Driving Creativity Throughout Your Organization. Currency (2005).

# Product Lifestyle Design: Innovation for Sustainability

Rinaldo C. Michelini and Roberto P. Razzoli

PMARlab, University of Genova, Italy, {michelini ‖ razzoli}@dimec.unige.it

**Abstract:**     The product lifestyle design is necessary sustainable growth accomplishment, enforced by the enacted eco-regulations. The paper discusses the incumbent restructuring of the manufacturing companies, recalling the innovation at the design phase, by effective product-process-environment-enterprise, 2P2E, integration, supported by suitably detailed modelling and simulation features, *M&SF*, leading to information intensive value chains based on: - net-concerns, gathering and enabling business set-ups, from the facility/function market; - service dealers, for the extended enterprise added value operations; - recovery rulers, for reverse logistics accomplishments and tasks overseeing. A short outlook of the topics is sketched, and, for explanatory purposes, example developments are recalled, referred to industrial situations emerging from the recent EU environmental policy.

**Keywords:** Lifestyle design, Modelling & Simulation features, Reverse logistics, Extended enterprise, Lifecycle diagnostics

## 1. Introduction

The product design methodologies and practices are expected to face in the short future important changes, to deal with the lifestyle requirements of the growth sustainability, spurred by the enacted rules of the EU environmental policy. The future to come suggests that competition shall take place, under market regulatory conditions different from now, to grant environmentally more conservative goals [1,2]. In this vision, producers' responsibilities are widened, and products information needs to extend across the supply chain, to cover lifecycle and recovery. The changes aims at granting visibility at the points-of-service, in connection with the on-duty conformance-to-specification tests, and at the end-of-life, to comply with the enacted recovery (reuse, recycle) rules.

The innovation develops along paired lines, where competitiveness will depend on entrepreneurship founded on economies of scope, ruled by *extended* enterprises, offering product-service combinations. Combined modelling and simulation are the winning tools, to expand the supply chain visibility, keeping unified accountability of the lifecycle properties. The materials, process, operation, maintenance, dismissal and recycling figures are tested and assessed by virtual prototypes, during the design phases. As compared to earlier industrial habits, when competition was won by the off-process presetting and optimal production plans, today enhanced decision support is required to run on-process, aiming at [3]:
• product quality for customised requests and minimal environment impact;

---

*Please use the following format when citing this chapter:*

Michelini, R. C. and Razzoli, R. P., 2008, in IFIP International Federation for Information Processing, Volume 277; *Computer-Aided Innovation (CAI)*; Gaetano Cascini; (Boston: Springer), pp. 217–228.

• manufacture choice for process robustness, to preserve the throughput quality;
• service schedules for conformance-to-use maintenance, as supply chain option;
• end-of-life take-back, with recovery rules, within the enacted mandatory targets.

The growth eco-sustainability charges, brought on by (passed or visibly declared) acts are thought troubles to defer to the future to come, by short-sighted companies. The worldwide competitors have consciousness of the above prospects, and arrange information intensive value chains, incorporating:
• off-process condition knowledge data-bases, caring for products lifestyle design;
• real-time diagnosis and decision tools, designed as on-duty service complements;
• recovery functions and facilities, assuring compulsory reverse logistics duties.

The paper offers a bird-eye overview of these lines, to address the design practice requirements, by multi-disciplinary approach, with concern of on hand CAD tools that embed algorithmic and heuristic blocks to offer mixed mode simulation-and-emulation, and product lifecycle management aids that look at service engineering and reverse logistics, to tackle with the on-duty and recovery tasks provision.

## 2. Integrated Design for Lifestyle Innovation

The industrial economy exploits the manufacture efficiency for the wide trade of low cost goods, obtained transforming raw materials into waste and pollution. The growth sustainability requires deep changes, for better resource exploitation by recovery and remediation practices. This means restructuring the companies' businesses, moving the producers/sellers responsibility, from the point-of-sale, to the points-of-service, and to the take-back of end-of-life items. The corporations' competition has to turn from the product suitability (by scale-economy) and the process fitness (by simultaneous engineering), to the environmental protection (by ecology stability) and the enterprise aptness (by function/facility trimming). The change requires dramatic up-dating, with the new scope-economy, quickly moving from the shop internalities of the conventional «firm theory» (the make-or-buy dilemma), to the supply chain externalities of the product life and call-back duties [4,5,6].

The world-class companies are compelled to re-orient the business value chain on trading products-services, with the latter extension object, in some case, of extra voluntary agreements, drawn up with the clients, in other case, of fixed mandatory targets, enacted by the governs. Indeed, the technical choices, allowing to put in the market a product, are, always, manufacturers' responsibility, with decisions taken at the design phase. Thus, the winning innovation, assuring the competitive advantage to one or the other company, has to played at the lifestyle levels, by warranting utmost on-duty performance and recovery abilities to the offers, the all to be proved out of the conventional productive shops. These new scopes request:
• to preset product lifecycle management, PLM, tools, as standard design out-fit;
• to provide the service engineering, SE, for diagnosis, decision and maintenance;
• to fulfil the reverse logistics, RL, when compulsorily enacted at the end-of-life.

The business widening, around the whole product-service, is sought with resort to enhanced PLM tools, with *federated* architecture, assuring unified access to the lifecycle data. The integration of all the lifecycle *views* (structure and function layout, fabrication process, quality certification, maintenance policy, dismissal duties, etc.) into a *super-model* is competitive plus, for value chain up-grading.

More specifically, addressing the product design phase as off-process decision support, four domains need to be in-progress tackled by the pertinent integration steps [7,8]:

• product specification, leading to proper performance, selecting, by CAD, CAM, etc. tools: producibility figures, operation constraints, dismissal requests, etc.;

• process specification, leading to better manufacturing value by simultaneous engineering practice of the product-and-process mutual pace-wise up-grading;

• eco-consistency specification, leading to establish regulation, maintenance, restoring, etc. plans, for on-duty conformance-to-use, and to call-back plans;

• enterprise specification, leading to adapt the supply chain with resort to the facility/function integration, matching the in-progress requested externalities.

The design develops, embedding the major modelling and simulation features, *M&SF*, to cover the four spheres of the product, the process, the environment and the enterprise. The consistent product description through the pertinent *M&SF*, assures adequate lifestyle characterisation by means of effective *virtual* checks, fulfilled on relatable digital mock-ups, timely, related to the *vitual* prototypes of the product or enterprise under test. The cross-linked description permits hierarchical inquiry, giving consistent views of given aspects (operation performance, manufacture goals, eco-conservativeness figures, etc.) at different levels of abstraction and/or lifecycle steps, so that the item designers (and the enterprise managers) readily verify the actually achieved properties, they need to make decisions. The issued *super-model*, collecting functional models, structural lay-outs, constituent materials, fabrication processes, quality certification, up-keeping policy, recovery requirements, etc., becomes the basic means, to build up the competitiveness of the product-service provision activity [9,10,11].

The four *M&SF* ranges expand the conventional PLM tools reaches, to include the *service engineering*, SE, data into the PLM tools, creating SE-oriented-PLM, or PLM-SE, and to further expand the *reverse logistics*, RL, figures in the same tools, creating RL-oriented-PLM, or PLM-RL. The *M&SF*-driven picture is nice reference of integrated design knowledge frames, with extension towards the eco-sustainability challenges, to reach the *product-process-environment-enterprise*, 2P2E, design, where the lifecycle *externalities* are dynamically accounted, in-progress adapting the *enterprise* functions and facilities, whenever new *environment* requirements appear.

The *product-process-environment-enterprise* 2P2E design becomes best practice, once the all lifecycle, dismissal included, duties are standard responsibility of manufacturers. This shows the way to the *extended* enterprises, and the *M&SF* description shall evolve to include the business and operation management areas, so that the supply chain *externalities* are dealt with by simultaneously adapting the enterprise data (taking in the timely useful facilities) to the environmental requests (mandatory targets or voluntary agreements). The task is here more problematic, since the physic-based frames of engineering and manufacture are replaced by economic transactions, human and intellectual activities, social and legal constraints. Objects and events are specified by texts, frames, spreadsheets or graphic trends; model validation and simulation testing quickly lead at data reduction in terms of cost propagation and due dates. This provides effective way to acknowledge business and operation functions, and to help providing full visibility for reliable prediction and on-process control and steering actions. The incorporation of appropriate *extended* enterprise M&SF is domain open to new developments, where the PLM aids option shall play strategic role, with large resort to declarative and procedural knowledge, and extensive exploitation of the networked infra-structures. At the *enterprise-environment* integration steps, the use of the net-concern or *virtual* enterprise options provides enhanced efficacy, especially if the market of productive facilities/functions exist, and the assembling of the co-operating entrepreneurial setting can operate on it [12].

The sketched design metods explain how to deal with the sustainable growth demands, and show how innovation is strictly connected with new information flows, the PLM-SE and PLM-RL, to be established at the design phase, to make effective the service engineering, SE, expanding the business through voluntary agreements, and the reverse logistics, RL, whenever enacted through call-back requirements. The emerging business lines profit of co-operative networked organisations, according to different approaches: on one side, manufacturers could be spurred to keep in charge the all *service*: artefacts supply, lifecycle conformance and dismissal incumbents, so that the trade regulation would depend on single indentures; on the other side, independent enterprises could profit by safety rules and environment acts expansion, to become *service* dealers, with technology oriented qualification and infrastructure-based organisations.

Both approaches require to focus on the design phase, built on significant modelling and simulation features, M&SF, moving the enterprise profitability to be critically dependent on the value chain choices, by on-going *product-process-environment-enterprise*, 2P2E, adaptive enhancement.

## 3. Extended-Enterprise for Lifestyle Innovation

The joint 2P2E approach allows to deal with the product-service externalities at the design phase. The *environment-enterprise* data integration is tough option (not existing in the traditional manufacture practice) progressively required with the expansion of the eco-regulations. In terms of the manufacturers' participation, one has two lifestyle frames [3]: technical responsibility of the on-duty and recovery tasks, even when the points-of-service and -take-back assessments are managed by end users; full (forward and backward) supply chain responsibility over the product-service eco-consistency, to lawfully put in the market of new offers.

In the first case, the producers and the buyers are jointly liable, face to the enacted environment directions. A given offer, of course, has different values at the point-of-sale, depending on the expected lifecycle and end-of-life charges, so that the eco-costs need to be included, when weighing competing proposals. In the second case, the visibility of the eco-fees is not only (implicit or explicit) merit, rather necessary accomplishment to be carried, at the design phase, when assessing the given delivery profitability. The trend is consistent with using the 2P2E frame as constant reference, [8]. An example development is recalled hereafter, [13], for explanatory purposes of *extended* enterprise's decision support, for the lifecycle pro-active maintenance, ruled through *voluntary* agreements, [14], with the clients.

The idea is to grant lifecycle diagnostics and maintenance of widespread durables, with primary goal in conformance-to-use warrantee of the product, and secondary goal in the reliability data collection for reuse and redesign duties. The service engineering, SE, provision is centralised at the manufacturer shop, making use of distributed intelligence and structured communication aids. The lifecycle visibility is initial step, allowing the ensuing decision-frame, to select effective recovery policy in front of the finally privileged EU position. The example deals with the critical situation, in the automotive areas, of the plastic components, which are used, also, for structural items, with strength and reliability requisites so that recycled stuffs are not allowed. The EU policy foreshadows four tracks: - reuse of reconditioned items, once verified safe operation and reliability; - recycle of warn-out pieces, with secondary-material certification; - thermal recovery of chosen stuffs, assuring emission eco-compatibility; - reduction to ASR, if the previous options are not met.

The first, only, belongs to the forward supply chain, delaying the item's life end. It deals with the product-service delivery, using embedded and ambient intelligence. The former assures the local knowledge build-up; the latter, its communication management by outer outfits. The recovery by condition monitoring up-keeping aims, [2,3], at:

• proactive regeneration: embedded ability establishes zero-defect on-duty plans;
• reactive restoration: the anomalies are removed at detected/programmed stops.

The embedded diagnostics is of no help, unless suitable regeneration outfits are forecast at the design steps, with additional cost and sophistication. The proactive maintenance complexity and price advise against fully autonomous solutions, and efficient alternative is reactive up-keeping, with remote diagnostics and restoring planning. The concept behind is to have information when you need it, and to plan the service provision by lean rigs. The knowledge-base (e.g., system assumption, reasoning abilities) has remote location, where the process data are transmitted and processed, for inferring diagnoses and feed-forward plans. This facilitates managing the decision for maintenance, trims the charges and lowers the wastes. Remote diagnostics is consistent with reactive restoring, after provisioning the repair equipment, but, also, with basic proactive actions, if the nominal state is brought back to the original conditions by the embedded redundancy, so that the renovation is enabled by 'switching-and-play' options. With focus on condition monitoring, [13,3], the basic actions are:

- to detect/identify the abnormal situations, shown by operation features or drifts;
- to assess crash situations, defective components, fault level, failure type, etc.;
- to troubleshoot, assessing restoring policy and replacing/maintenance duties.

The development of the central diagnostic knowledge demands big efforts. The profitably depends on each situation, with scenarios belonging to one company and with the tools to be used in other contexts.

The example investigation deals with the automotive domain, where, the EU eco-policy distinguishes severe on duty demands, to be achieved through voluntary agreements with the users, and mandatory recovery targets, under total carmaker's responsibility. The idea is to assign tags to the components, in view to record the cumulated damage, for on-duty maintenance and end-of-life evaluation, Figure 1. In terms of cost, the in-progress technology evolution and the extended versatility, the resort to Radio Frequency Identification Device, RFID, is privileged, as ideal means for the component traceability by history, use modes/styles and cumulated issues storing. At the moment, the amount of inscribed data in RFID is small; to remove the limitation, a remote on-board intelligent module ought to be added, with the capability: - to acquire the data from the on-the-field sensors; - to process the measurements, obtaining characterising signatures, assessing operation modes, severity indices, etc., writing pertinent message on the label; - to read/write the information, for subsequent up-dating or completion.

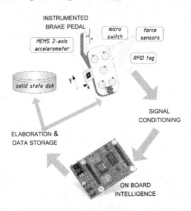

Figure 1 The brake pedal intelligence and communication set-up.

On the remote module, a virtual instrument is programmed, having in charge to compute and to store two different kinds of knowledge: the short-term data, providing more details on the on-duty conditions and on the operation modes of the components, which, due to their redundancy, need to be vaulted into external archives and saved at regular time intervals; the long-term data, giving synthetic features of the item overall life, which are written on the *RFID*. Looking, for example purpose, to the car braking pedal, Figure 1, the on-process information frame exploits the front instruments, monitoring [15]:
- the number of pedal actuations, shown by a counter driven by micro-switches;
- the averaged pedal stroke, combining micro-switches and timers;
- the averaged pedal stroke variance, computed in parallel with the said data;
- the actuation law, given by MEMS accelerometers and subsequent processing;
- more specific operation «styles», such as high/weak strokes, long-lasting/iterated features, etc., reckoned by detecting and coding the signatures corresponding to the singled out drivers' habits.

The module is integrated in the car computer: the short-term data are collected and checked during the standard maintenance and conformance assessment operations. This way, fully transparent information flow is created, assuring process visibility to the different stakeholders: car-makers, users, car-repairing shops, car-breakers and certifying/controlling bodies.

The healing/restoration features are fulfilled with regard to the specific product-service delivery. One distinguishes the embedded, for knowledge build-up, from the ambient intelligence, for communication help. The ambient intelligence is above all

relevant for the processing frame (not the component itself), and for the friendliness of the information flow, Figure 2. The main benefits are the following [15]:
• to concentrate information on supplied functions and to create lifestyle mind;
• to enable information sharing, and easier eco-consistency data management;
• to fulfil in real-time and intelligent ways the conformance-to-specification tests;
• to automatically manage the product lifecycle and service provision checks;
• to exploit the supply chain product/process carried/acquired/computed data.

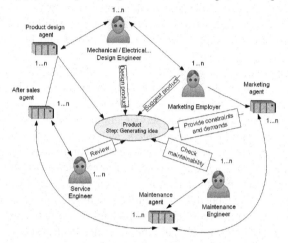

Figure 2 The PLM-SE set-up, with Ambient Intelligence aids.

The ambient intelligence empowers the PLM-SE, once large, heterogeneous, distributed frames, built on multiple-function platforms, support the delivery of value added services to clients. The ambient intelligence authorises easy interaction, with plain language or any other means a non-computer specialist uses to communicate. The remote service is built on standard blocks, Figure 2, equivalently given by operators or computer agents, typically, split into:
- the *common knowledge-base*, with the product-process-environment-enterprise data, the design up-dated reference, combining product lifecycle management PLM and service engineering SE frames;
- the *set-up module*, or data-base manager, with graphic interface to help the user to follow and understand the process under observation, with related diagnostics frame, and to make the best use of it, by supporting the definition, modification, storing, deletion, etc., of the common knowledge-base elements;
- the *information processing module*, to map the input (supplied by the distributed sensors) into the common knowledge-base elements, following the idea that the ambient data can be expressed into any format and the detection/transmission is operated automatically, without explicit peripheral concern;
- the *diagnostic engine*, providing the interactive problem-solving support to the users with resort to heuristic rules, case-driven reasoning, etc. and connects, by means of the shared broker architecture, to the common knowledge-base, to make decisions and to friendly acknowledge diagnostics signatures;
- the *client support module*, core of the remote diagnostics with the products data

(operation, maintenance, disassembly, etc.), for process instantiation, assuring that the operation unit sees the *virtual* image of network (this allows protected access to the certification/supervision bodies);
- the *knowledge analysis module*, doing data the restitution and reporting, by spot entries (database query, etc.), statistical outcomes (Pareto charts, etc.), lifestyle analyses (on-duty reports, etc.), etc., with link to the common knowledge-base, through the client support module.

The example case shows how the *extended* enterprises, with domain proprietary technologies, turn into handy product-service dealers, fulfilling lifecycle support, provided that information/communication aids specialise into PLM-SE tools, fully developed at the design phase [8].

The instrumental set-up, according to above sketched lines, is developed with in mind the emerging demands in terms of the carmakers' extended responsibility, with unequivocal involvement in the reverse logistics and in the re-engineering tasks, and relevant engagement in the service engineering, as the explicit origin of the product data, or, with higher commitment, as the direct provider of the lifecycle backing. These new facts require rethinking the competition paradigms of the automotive industry, and, of course, object of special concern among the world-wide carmakers. The instrumental set-up, moreover, is also worthy help in assessing the users' behavioural accountability. The lifecycle monitored data supply objective checks whether or not the driver has operated with full compliance of the manufacturer's notices or warnings and the law rules or instructions. The achieved transparency is important for the contractual bonds and the third-people protection, providing clear access to the users' liability, in case of accidents, when, e.g., the assurance is required to have objective reports on the elapsed occurrences, with resort to the records that document, in the present example, if, when, how long and by which trend the pedal is actuated.

## 4. Virtual-Enterprise for Lifestyle Innovation

The EU eco-policy tends to expand the carmakers' responsibility, imposing the eco-rules for new deliveries and the free take-back of end-of-life items, subdued to compulsory recovery targets. This was declared with over ten years advance, but apparently only in Germany the 2P2E approach coherently leads to lean structured *extended* enterprises that guarantee the *free* take-back duties. Elsewhere, the *virtual* enterprise solution seems factual issue, and the recovery (reuse, recycle) compulsory targets are ruled by governmental agencies or steered by collaborating brokers. The EU targets are strict:
▪ from 01.01.2006: 85% by weigh of the vehicle has to be recovered or recycled; the 10% can be dumped to landfills (after suitable neutralisation), and the 5% can be used as auxiliary fuel;
▪ from 01.01.2015: the figures are modified, allowing 10% for fuel use, but only 5% to landfills.

The reverse logistics, Figure 3, develops with unified information flow, with end-of-life recovery ruled by the carmakers PLM-RL data-bases, actually, collected by the automotive [16], covering some 1 000 vehicle types of 25 producers, listing around 46 000 pieces, with ample visual and analytical data. The EU acts require involving properly authorised treatment facilities, ATF, which guarantee the backward process under the three parties scheme [3]:

• purveyors, covering the *supply-chain*: materials provision, items manufacture, lifecycle up-keeping, backward recovery; the eco-responsibility is dealt with by clustering several firms in alliance of co-operating multi-sectional interest units;

• users, purchasing *products-services*, to profit of provided *functions* with reliability figure close to one; the payments include conformance certification at the point of service, after tax collection against tangibles depletion and pollutants release;

• supervisors, assuring *third party* checks of environment and society protection; the certifying bodies report to governmental authorities and use standards, having access to the *extended* artefacts life-cycle data-bases.

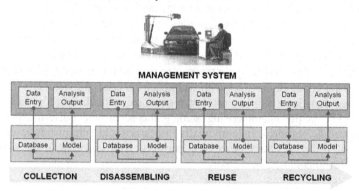

Figure 3 The knowledge build-up in end-of-life vehicles recovery.

The ATF are, surely, out of the core business of usual carmakers, and *extended* enterprises, with explicit mind on reverse logistics effectiveness, [17,18], are substituted by:

- governmental agencies overseeing the recovery (reuse, recycle) duties, through deposit-refund schemes, so that the reverse logistics is (top-down) financed by taxing each new car put in the market;

- specialised 'recovery rulers', who replace the carmaker, having broker's activity to select the reverse logistics facilities/functions, collecting from the users, the (bottom-up) visible fees.

The UE rules accepts these different set-ups, and only the German carmakers tend to become *extended* enterprises. The agency scheme is used in Sweden; the broker alternative, in the Netherlands. The first set-up is winning, but assumes pioneering work with coherent 2P2E issues, by feeding back the *design-for-recovery* scopes. On the short span, the return on investment is not easily assessed, in terms of the individual manufacturer and country. The Netherlands solution is highly efficient (today recovery visible fees, as low as 15 €, [19]). Anyway, the domain knowledge build-up, Figure 3, needs to consider the *M&SF*, addressing the PLM-RL tools, up to the suited details. The *virtual* enterprise solution, thereafter, could result especially efficient, replacing the German 'firm theory' (the *make-or-buy* paradigm), by the 'enterprises creation' alternative, assuming:

• to trade facilities, functions, technologies and related integration protocols, with helpful access, negotiation, assembling and management abilities;
• to establish the selection, acquisition and merging brokerage area, wide enough to grant competitive choices, and efficiently ruled to keep steadiness.

The reverse logistics typifies by like information flows, but differs on value chain. The *extended* enterprise incorporates in the offer all demands necessary to put the car on the market (call-back included). On the opposite side, the governmental agency manages economic incentive (deposit/refund), to finance the recovery, fulfilled under permission ruling. In between, the *virtual* setting builds, using:
• a logistic network, with collecting and transport means, storage points, handling and inspection devices, joined to information flow for acquisition and recording;
• dismantling shops for safe parts recovering and storing, with forwarding of left hulks to suitably located shredding facilities, for grinding to tiny pieces;
• sorting plants, to pull out metals (ferrous alloys, stainless steels, aluminium alloys, brass, etc.), different plastics, glass, etc., and safe incineration plants;
• parts-reuse and materials-recycle tracks, for service engineering maintenance and design and manufacture practices with secondary materials provisioning.

The listed functions/facilities are heterogeneous, with the authorised treatment facility, ATF, as the characterising step, gathered around buffering/dismantling shops, Figure 4. The brokerage alternative does not add administrative costs, and only assemble the necessary processing partners, with visibility of the mandatory targets achievement [12,20].

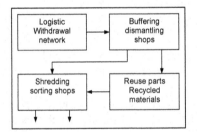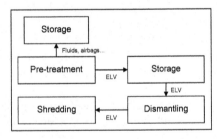

Figure 4 The reverse logistics flow and example dismantlig shop.

The authorised treatment facility, ATF, is node of the networked concern, built, with broker help, from the function/facility market. The *virtual* enterprise ruler, devising business projects, and demanding the gathering of qualified partners, has, just, intermediation duties. The assembly allows the facilities/functions collection, with varying goals and technical heterogeneity, but capable of efficient provision in the given business. The all implies the advanced features of net concerns. This does not lead to a corporation and is better identified by a manufacture/service cluster, possibly, time-varying, so that the 'recovery rulers' is identified by the supply chain, and is the legal entity, having up-dated below architectures of facilities/functions providers. It happens that the car user interacts at the point-of-sale with a dealer linked to a given partners' set, and at the end-of-life, the entitled 'recovery rulers' corresponds a to modified partners' set [21].

The *virtual* enterprise solution does not lead to completely different set-ups. The related issues, moreover, are not even new, as they simply separate the 'brand', from the production/service facilities. The difference comes out from the lifecycle obligation, engaging the firm by respect to the society, notably, for the eco-duties. In the facility/function market, the brokerage helps building alliances, having the skill and competency in the reverse logistics only, while the *extended* enterprise is involved in the integrated 2P2E design, for everything that concerns the *business* decision-making (choice, negotiation and integration) operation all over the supply chain. The broker role has, instead, bottom-up value, enhancing the organisation effectiveness, strengthening the trust between partners and assuring the supply chain stability (also in legal terms). The sketched frame is consistent outcome of knowledge-driven entrepreneurial assets, where access to suited net-concerns is factual prerequisite. If the industrial context cannot afford the 2P2E issues up to *extended* enterprises, the 2E issues permit to combine recovery facilities/functions, which are able to fulfil the environmental acts, by bottom-up ATF deployment.

## 5. Conclusion

The *product-process-environment-enterprise*, 2P2E, practice is deemed to extend the *product-process*, 2P, simultaneous engineering, turning the value chain on the lifestyle *externalities*. The new PLM tools distinguish by the addition of on-duty service engineering, and reverse logistics, with the pertinent *M&SF* supplements. The design-for-manufacturing, *DfM*, design-for-assembly, *DfA*, etc., scopes shall expand over the *new* design-for-disassembly, *DfD*, design-for-recovery, *DfR*, etc., ones, which need to establish since the early product ideation steps. The business idea shall include recovery, reuse and recycle of products, parts and materials, to minimise the tangible resources spoil and to maximise the supply chain efficiency. The full *M&SF* identification shall enable the designers to explore and to analyse the reverse logistics as worthy option, to enhance the tangibles productivity and the environmental protection, for company liability and profitability. The issue brings to the *extended* enterprise organisation, specialised in product-service. Today, the EU eco-regulation has enacted mandatory recovery (reuse, recycle) targets within the manufacturers' responsibility. The rules apply to the automotive industry, but not all carmakers have the *extended* enterprise in mind. In default, the *virtual* enterprise goal might result effective, specialising the *environment-enterprise*, 2E, design whether the proper PLM-RL aids allow the 'recovery ruler' brokerage to integrate the right functions/facilities. The product lifestyle design is, once again, the enabling option, supporting the innovation.

In general, proper exploitation of *M&SF* description will be the way of improving the effectiveness of the manufacture businesses, to reach the best balance of all constraints in designing, developing, producing, supporting, servicing, recovering and recycling products. Cost and time reduction, customer satisfaction, lifecycle responsibility, environmental protection and resources conservativeness have to be part of super-models, with algorithmic and heuristic blocks, balanced by captured knowledge, virtual tests, on-line analyses and designer's decision making. The PLM aids will support the best practice, from the ideation, up to operation and call-back, with waste handling and remediation. Every requirement is shown to the users, and transparent to the authorities, so to assess the resource productivity. The federated modelling approach becomes dynamic, with learning a bit at step issues and training the design teams to combine views and integrate functions.

# References

1. Michelini R.C., Razzoli R.P.: Product-service for environmental safeguard: a metric to sustainability. Intl. J. Resources Conservation and Recycling, vol. 42(1), pp. 83-98 (2004).
2. Michelini R.C., Razzoli R.P.: Product-service eco-design: knowledge-based infrastructures. Intl. J. Cleaner Production, vol. 12, n° 4, pp. 415-428 (2004).
3. Michelini R.C.: Knowledge entrepreneurship and sustainable growth, p. 390, Nova, Hauppauge (2008).
4. Michelini R.C., Acaccia G.M., Callegari M., Molfino R.M., Razzoli R.P.: Artefact integration by concurrent enterprises and productive break-up. Jacucci G., Olling G.J., Preiss K., Wozny M. Eds.: 'Manufacturing Globalisation in the Digital Communication Era, pp. 221-234, Kluwer, Boston (1999).
5. Michelini R.C., Kovàcs G.L.: Information infrastructures and sustainability. In: Camarinha Matos L., Ed., Emerging Solutions for Future Manufacturing Systems, pp. 347-356, Springer (2005).
6. Michelini R.C., Razzoli R.P.: Collaborative networked organisations for eco-consistent supply-chains. In Putnik&Cunha, Eds., Virtual Enterprise Integration, pp. 45-77, IGI Press (2005).
7. Michelini R.C., Acaccia G.M., Callegari M., Molfino R.M., Razzoli R.P.: Shop controller-and-manager for intelligent manufacture. S. Tzafestas Ed.: 'Management and Control of Manufacturing Systems', pp. 219-254, Springer (1997).
8. Acaccia G.M., Kopàcsi S., Kovàcs G., Michelini R.C., Razzoli R.P.: Service engineering and extended artefact delivery. In: G.D. Putnik M.M. Cunha Eds., Knowledge Management in Virtual Organizations, IDEA Group Pub., pp. 24-68, IGI Press (2007).
9. Acaccia G.M., Michelini R.C., Penzo L., Qualich N.: Automotive systems: end-of-life vehicles dismantling facilities. 8th ESDA ASME Conf., pp.1-8, Torino July 4-7 (2006).
10. Anufriev A., Kopàcsi S., Kovàcs G., Michelini R.C.: Ambient intelligence as enabling aid for modern business paradigms. J. Robotics Comp. Integr. Man., n. 2, pp. 242-256 (2007).
11. Borg J.C., Farrugia Ph.J., Camilleri K.P.: Knowledge-intensive design technology. Springer, IFIP Series, pp. 1-200 (2004).
12. Cunha M.M., Putnik G.D.: Agile virtual enterprises: implementation and management support. IDEA Group Pub. Hershey (2006).
13. Belotti V., Michelini R.C., Razzoli R.P.: Remote overseeing of car brake pedal for reuse/recycle and pre-collision history investigation. Intl. Conf. Remote Engineering and Virtual Instrumentation REV2007, Intl. Assoc. of Online Eng., Porto, June 24-27 (2007).
14. Kovàcs G., Kopàcsi S., Haidegger G., Michelini R.C.: Ambient intelligence in product lifecycle design. J. Eng. Appl. of Artificial Intelligence, vol. 19, n. 8, pp. 953-965 (2006).
15. Michelini R.C., Razzoli R.P.: Ubiquitous computing and communication for product monitoring. M. Khosrow-Pour, Ed.: Encyclop. Information Sci. and Techn., 2nd Ed., IDEA Group (2007).
16. IDIS, International Dismantling Information System. http://www.idis2.com, (2008).
17. Acaccia G.M., Michelini R.C., Qualich N.: Sustainable engineering management: end-of-life vehicles with recovery in mind. World Review Sci., Techn. and Sustain. Dev., vol. 4, n. 4/5 (2007).
18. Acaccia G.M., Michelini R.C., Penzo L., Qualich N.: Reverse logistics and resource recovery: modelling car dismantling facilities. World Review Sci., Techn. and Sustain. Dev., vol. 4, n. 2/3 (2007).
19. ARN, Auto Recycling Nederland. http://www.arn.nl/ (2008).
20. Dickhoff H., Lackes R., Reese J.: Supply chain management and reverse logistics. Springer Verlag, pp. xviii-426, Berlin (2004).
21. Blumberg D.F.: Introduction to management of reverse logistics and closed loop supply chain processes. CRC Press, pp. 1-296 (2004).

# Web-based Platform for Computer Aided Innovation

## Combining Innovation and Product Lifecycle Management

**Nora Dörr[1], Edda Behnken[2], and Dr. Tobias Müller-Prothmann[3]**

[1] Pumacy Technologies AG, Germany, nora.doerr@pumacy.de
[2] Pumacy Technologies AG, Germany, edda.behnken@pumacy.de
[3] Pumacy Technologies AG, Germany, tobias.mueller-prothmann@pumacy.de

**Abstract:** Innovation is one of the main drivers of business success. Using computers and special software applications in support of innovations cannot only shorten the whole process of bringing an initial idea to life, but it can improve the overall decision making process. Moreover, aligning innovation management and product life cycle management (PLM) helps organizations in gaining and reusing important knowledge to be one step ahead of the competitors. This chapter provides a practitioner's view on the current situation, deployable solutions, current trends and future developments in the field of computer aided innovation (CAI) and product lifecycle management. A web-based Platform will be illustrated as an example of computer aided innovation.

**Keywords:** innovation management, collaboration, documentation, organization, knowledge management

## 1. Introduction

During the last decade, innovation and the management of innovation have become industry buzz-words. Following Lueke and Katz [1], "[i]nnovation ... is generally understood as the successful introduction of a new thing or method ... Innovation is the embodiment, combination, or synthesis of knowledge in original, relevant, valued new products, processes, or services". Don Sheelen, former CEO of Regina Co., placed innovation at the forefront of modern business stating that: "Innovation is the lifeblood of any organization". He emphasizes, "[w]ithout it, not only is there no growth, but, inevitably, a slow death". And management guru Peter Drucker [2] described it in a quite similar way: "Not to innovate is the single largest reason for the decline of an existing organization".

*Please use the following format when citing this chapter:*

Dörr, N., Behnken, E. and Müller-Prothmann, T., 2008, in IFIP International Federation for Information Processing, Volume 277; *Computer-Aided Innovation (CAI)*; Gaetano Cascini; (Boston: Springer), pp. 229–237.

But how does a modern way to innovation look like? What is appropriate for today's business life? Which challenges lie ahead and how do we intend to face these challenges?


## 2. Background

Computed aided design (CAD) is already a very well known and highly respected way to work among engineers, architects or designers. Computer aided innovation (CAI) in contrast is a relatively new way to gain a relevant advantage in the market. According to Schumpeter's definition, innovation is a significant, sometimes even radical improvement; either in products, processes or services offered to an internal or external customer of an organization [3].

Some of the most common reasons for failure of innovations are according to O'Sullivan [4]:

- poor leadership,
- poor organization,
- poor communication,
- poor empowerment,
- poor knowledge management.

While the above mentioned reasons are barriers in the cultural infra-structure, other failures happen within the innovation process. These include:

- poor goal definition,
- poor alignment of actions to goals,
- poor participation in teams,
- poor monitoring of results,
- poor communication and access to information.

By taking these failures into account, CAI does not mean the simple use of personal computers within the innovation process. Neither should it imply the use of a computer aided TRIZ-tool nor other models such as provocative word or picture. Rather, it is the goal-oriented adoption of advanced information and communication methods and tools that describes CAI in its current state of development. Major functions of these methods and tools must focus on integration and virtualization as well as interdisciplinary, multi-scalable and multicultural team collaboration. All of these functions are meant to avoid or overcome the innovation barriers described above.


## 3. Knowledge management platform

A web-based platform for knowledge management is an example of software designed to facilitate collaboration and perform specific knowledge management tasks. This platform should provide support to knowledge sharing, communication within and across different types of organizations such as teams, departments, or inter-organizational networks. It shall promote active knowledge management of the organization's members to develop new ideas, document existing knowledge, and integrate all aspects of innovation processes. A platform for knowledge and innovation management must provide a basic framework to develop, capture, share, preserve, apply, and evaluate knowledge as presented in Figure 1.

| DEVELOP | Creative processes are fostered, ideas emerge, |
|---|---|
| CAPTURE | personal experiences may be stored, and |
| SHARE | shared with colleagues. |
| PRESERVE | For later access, knowledge components are archived, |
| APPLY | integrated in working processes, and |
| EVALUATE | validated. Core knowledge has been identified. |

Figure 1 Knowledge Management Framework (www.kmmaster.com)[1]

## 3.1 Concept

An ideal platform is based on three central concepts that provide the core of a holistic knowledge management approach and the fundament of a modern innovation management: documentation, organization, and collaboration. Every approach combines these three concepts in a single solution (Figure 2). The precise implementation of these concepts is based on individual characteristics that may vary depending on existing requirements within an organization.

Organization is related to processes, people, roles and the formal organization as presented in an organization chart. Here, the web-based platform supports mapping of organizational and knowledge management processes.

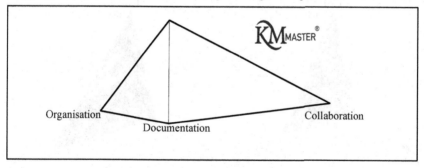

Figure 2 Central Concepts of the KMmaster (www.kmmaster.com)

---

[1] The KMmaster is a web-based platform developed by Pumacy Systems GmbH. The main goal of the tool is the support of organizations in knowledge based processes (e.g. innovation management). The approach of integrating different fields of interest makes it a unique solution in the area of computer aided innovations. Nevertheless it represents a broader range of tools dedicated to support organizations along the innovation process.

Documentation is related to structures, documents, data, and classifications. The platform aims at the construction of knowledge components to capture codified knowledge as well as tacit experiences, competencies, and networks.

Collaboration is related to communities of practice, individual motivation, and groupware. The tool supports knowledge and new ideas developed and shared within specialized communities of practice.

## 3.2 Task-driven View

Given a typical task concerning the management of innovations within an organization, the three concepts outlined above can be combined into different approaches. An approach presents a strategy to solve a certain problem. Figure 3 illustrates two approaches to the development of knowledge, competencies, and ideas. They are possible examples from the six knowledge activities introduced in Figure 1. In both approaches the documentation is reduced to a minimum in advantage of the dimension collaboration. The peculiarity of the parameter organization varies.

| Approach 1 | Approach 2 |
|---|---|
| If collaboration becomes more intensive and formalised, do you believe that the innovation process could be improved and extended? | If knowledge was not documented and made accessible, an innovation process in combination with an intense exchange of experiences might support a reuse of knowledge. |
| | |
| 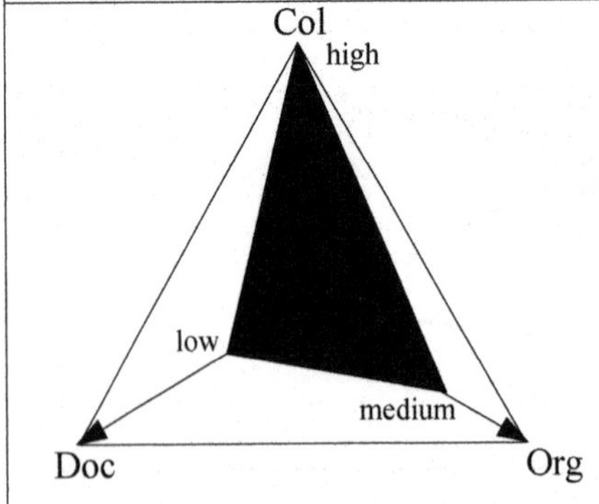 **Col:** Collaboration<br>**Doc:** Documentation<br>**Org:** Organization<br>**low, medium, high:** Specification | |

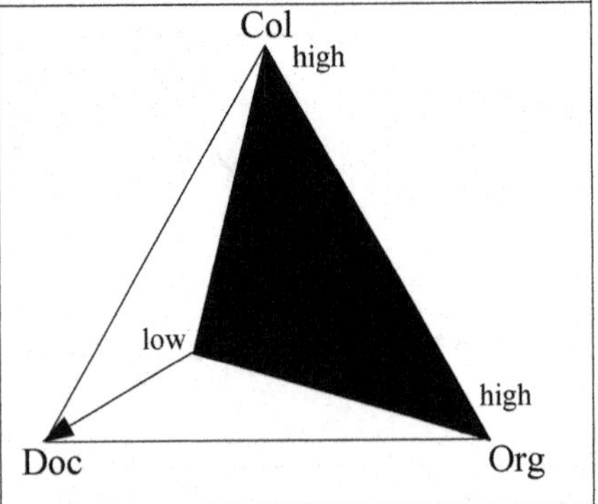

Figure 3 Approaches of a web-based platform - KMmaster-examples (www.kmmaster.com)

These examples show only two different ways in which the general platform might evolve, always according to the specific needs of the utilizing organization.

## 3.3 Functions

The web-based platform should support internal and external communication as well as virtualization of knowledge, visualization of decision making processes and the ability of teams to cooperate. These functions are connected to a concrete technical level. For each of the three concepts, the framework of the platform shall provide the following functions:

- Documentation of knowledge and experiences:
  - flexible templates to capture knowledge components,
  - software system integration,
  - classification by community and taxonomy,
  - full text search including attachments, meta-data and timeframes.
- Organization of processes and knowledge:
  - modeling of innovation and knowledge processes,
  - assignment of user rights and roles,
  - process-based validation of documents.
- Collaboration in knowledge communities:
  - community-based document management,
  - individually configurable workflow management,
  - support of distributed teams and sites,
  - collaborative desktop.

## 3.4 Innovation Management Edition

Every generalist platform must provides specialized editions to meet the requirements within different environments and their individual approaches. These editions must be designed with regard to specific applications (lessons learnt, reporting), processes (innovation management) and industries (life science). Though the editions are standalone solutions, they might be adapted and combined according to the requirements of the deploying organization.

An Innovation Management Edition supports the entire idea management process. From generating ideas, their evaluation, up to their documentation, all people, processes, and organizational levels can be included through highly flexible workflows.

As a result from the analysis of the innovation management process concerning the different roles (idea provider, experts, management), this edition provides a functional tool which practically supports de-centralized creation, share, and use of ideas effectively.

In addition, an ideal Innovation Management Edition provides functionalities to communicate and interact. Teamwork is supported with interchangeable language files, interdisciplinary teams are united via highly flexible community concepts.

The generation of ideas is supported as well as their contribution. Collaborative workflows back the development and enrichment of the generated ideas, while the anonymity of organization members is guaranteed if they wish so. Nevertheless, detailed ratings and assessments filter the relevant and promising ideas from the one with less good prospects. The latter one might be kept in an archive to inspire others and the former will be fostered and enriched.

Systematic analysis, statistics and reporting allow detailed information of management and other stakeholders.

## 4. Product Lifecycle Management (PLM)

Knowledge is one of the most important factors regarding profit realization in innovation management. For instance, companies who pursue to be "first to market" with their products, have the advantage to realize the profits in the initial phases of PLM until the imitators come to the market. PLM is a strategy which enables the companies to bring better products to market faster and provide better support for customers [5]. Therefore, PLM should be integrated in a whole added value of the company.

Crossan et al. [6] predicted the urgent need to enable feed-forward and feed-backward knowledge sharing between the product lifecycle phases. Their framework points out three levels of organizational learning and knowledge management: individual, group and organization. A knowledge management platform affiliates the exchange of all these levels and allows consequently feed-forward and feedback processes. The feed-forward process is embedded in the tool itself, as the system and structures are represented. The institutionalized knowledge affects groups and individuals within the organization (feedback process). However, forward and backward learning does not only affect the different levels of learning but might be seen as a suggestion how to use knowledge gained in different projects and products (Figure 4). Forward and backward knowledge sharing across different products illustrates how knowledge might be used across different product lines.

Forward knowledge sharing is already established in many organizations and the learning curve represents the improvements in costs and benefits. Backward knowledge sharing, however, is also of importance as new solutions or new knowledge gained by the development team is given back to management, sales, and support.

The different states of a product should not be seen as autonomous and self sufficient tasks. Rather, each of them is an important share of the wheel. Only with interaction between the different parts the organization will run smoothly. The knowledge gained by idea owner and developers is important not only for themselves as the turn to new projects, but it is important for the people working later with the product, and vice versa.

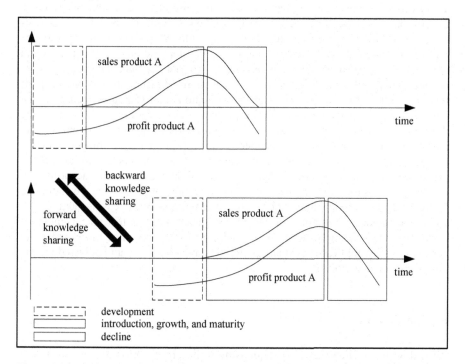

Figure 4 Forward and backward knowledge sharing across different products

Therefore, it is extremely important to integrate the different stakeholders and harvest their knowledge, their ideas, and the successful innovations. A computer based tool which combines organizational, documentary, and collaborative tasks presents a successful approach. According to the organization's needs, it will be modulated with its highly flexible background.


## 5. Future Trends

Commonly, only the individual construction engineer, developer or decision-maker has the knowledge, why a potential solution has been adopted or abandoned. The goal of every future orientated application must be the externalization of this knowledge and the ac-companying information. The overall view over a product lifecycle is mostly exclusive for the people working on the very project. Nowadays, the reuse of information and knowledge mainly depends on informal networks and communication between the employees [7]. Therefore, it becomes necessary to use specific tools and methods to reuse information throughout the whole PLM process.

It should be a strategic goal to optimize the process of implementing an innovation, the innovation pace. The quality should be improved and supported by a universal engineering system along the product development process. Innovations must be described formally and systematically and their stage of maturity should be measurable. This will help to improve the quality of innovations and reduce the overall costs. For a systematic innovation process and requirements resulting in reference models, appropriate methods and strategies are needed. This will contribute to make innovations measurable and enable their implementation. The development of these methods and strategies focuses on an integrated risk management to identify product and process risks early on in the development and prepare and plan preventive quality strategies and measurements. Moreover, a dedicated innovation maturity model and an integrated measurement of static and dynamic process parameters to control the processes must be considered. Methods to validate innovations according to quality gates within the innovation implementation process must be gathered. Current trends as Open Innovation and the continuously increasing demand for collaboration lead to additional factors of uncertainty in the management of innovations [8]. Though the decision making process becomes more and more complex, easily applicable evaluation methods must be found and adjusted for the deploying organization [9].

## 6. Conclusion

According to Davila et al. [10] "[i]nnovation, like many business functions, is a management process that requires specific tools, rules, and discipline". An ideal web-based platform shall provide an organization with an easy to use tool. Depending on the specific necessities, it can be implemented as idea or innovation management solution; or even more future orientated using the tool along the whole process of managing a product lifecycle. The necessary rules are integrated into the application and display its backbone. Discipline is supported by special features implemented in the software.

Nevertheless, it is the people of an organization who make the system run. Therefore, it is extremely important to combine not only methods and theories, but to integrate employees and partners as early as possible in the process of deploying a system for computer aided innovation – especially if it is meant to accompany the whole product lifecycle management.

# References

1. Luecke R., Katz R.: Managing Creativity and Innovation, Harvard Business School Press, Boston (2003).
2. Drucker P. F.: The Essential Drucker: Selections from the Management Work of Peter F. Drucker, HarperBusiness, New York (2001).
3. Schumpeter J.: The Theory of Economic Development, Harvard University Press, Boston (1934).
4. O'Sullivan D.: Framework for Managing Development in the Networked Organisations. Computers in Industry, 47(1), pp. 77-88 (2002).
5. Scheer A. W., Bozsanki M., Muth M., Schmitz W. G., Segelbacher U.: Prozessorientiertes Product Lifecycle Management. Springer, Saarbrücken (2005).
6. Crossan M.: An Organizational Learning Framework: From Intuition To Institution. Academy of Management Rev., 24(3), pp. 522-537 (1999).
7. Müller-Prothmann T.: Leveraging Knowledge Communication for Innovation. Framework, Methods and Applications of Social Network Analysis. In Lang P., Research and Development, Frankfurt (2006).
8. Behnken E.: The Innovation Process as a Collective Learning Process. ICE 2005 Proceedings, pp. 219-226, München (2005).
9. Dörr N.: Entwicklung und Implementierung einer Methode zur anwendungsorientierten Bewertung von Ideen im Rahmen des Ideenmanagements der T-Systems Multimedia Solutions GmbH. HTW Dresden, Dresden (2006).
10. Davila T., Epstein M. J., Shelton R.: Making Innovation Work: How to Manage It, Measure It, and Profit from It. Wharton School Publishing, Upper Saddle River (2006).

# A Conceptual Framework of the Cooperative Analyses in Computer-Aided Engineering

Min-Hwan Ok[1] and Tae-Soo Kwon[2]

[1] Korea Railroad Research Institute, Korea, mhok@krri.re.kr
[2] Korea Railroad Research Institute, Korea, tskwon@krri.re.kr

**Abstract:** The role of this framework of cooperative analyses is to build a foundation for higher quality analysis in large work of CAE. The distributed vaults are constituted in peer to peer manner. A large scale analysis can be conducted in higher quality by cooperative analyses with the dividing and unifying process.

**Keywords:** computer-aided engineering, cooperative analysis, distributed vaults

## 1. Introduction

Computer-Aided Engineering, CAE, is nowadays a common method for analysis of some phenomena in many engineering area. Some of the CAE advantages are the cost-effectiveness, the time-efficiency, and the capability-efficacy of the worker or the working team. The capability efficacy, in this paper, is similar to the productivity of a worker or a team but dissimilar in focus on the quality than the quantity of the work produced. However this capability is intrinsically dependent on the ability of the worker or the working team, and the efficacious field or the specialty is differ between the workers or the working team.

For large work of CAE, it is desirable to divide the object into partitions and they are distributed to the workers along the person's efficacious field and then collected and unified into the entire object. In this paper we call these distributed analysis tasks *cooperative analyses* between the dividing and the unifying of the object. Among the partitions divided, some may have deep relevancy among them thus should be analyzed exchanging results. There have been a number of works related to cooperation including computer-aided acquisition and life-cycle support(CALS), product data management(PDM), knowledge management or etc., but none of them was suitable to this specific cooperation of analysis tasks.

Most of developments on CAE have been focused on one specific field, such as dynamic analysis, structural analysis, or fatigue analysis for example. Their interests are to pursue higher accuracy in simulations approaching to measured

Please use the following format when citing this chapter:

Ok, M.-H. and Kwon, T.-S., 2008, in IFIP International Federation for Information Processing, Volume 277; *Computer-Aided Innovation (CAI)*; Gaetano Cascini; (Boston: Springer), pp. 239–245.

values in the experimentation. However, in real world a machine is a composite of many fields from various branches. For instance, a railway system is a synthetic one of multi-body vehicle from mechanical engineering, railroad construction from civil engineering, electric power supply from electrical engineering and the other adjunct fields. In railway system, several parts have interactions between each other, for example, the wheel and the rail contacts each other and they have influences in their analyses conducted. In this work the objective of the analyses is conducted in size to be processed separately, so different from multiphysics or multidisciplinary system design optimization. After processed separately, the influencing values are exchanged and the analyses are conducted again in their sizes until some criterion is satisfied.

The role of this framework of cooperative analyses is to build a foundation for higher quality analysis in large work of CAE, in which the specialists or experts in their efficacious fields are participating. The process and system schematics are described in the next sections.

## 2. Distributed Vaults of the Analysis Files

The partitions in the cooperative analyses are distributed to, and collected from each specialist or expert. One central vault could be adequate however, for quick access of large files frequently, it is better to use local storage subsystems of experts or specialists who may be geographically dispersed. Distributed PDM contains replicated/fragmented metadata and user data since it has vaults inherent from the concept of one central vault as classified in [1].

```
struct partition_file {
Object-title
 partition-name, number,
 ownerID,
 description,
 file-pwd,
 file-name,
 file-state,
}

□ File State
     1. Draft
     2. Ready to check
     3. Pass / Fail
     4. Approved
```

**Figure 1** File organization and states.

The file of the distributed partition is most accessed by the worker dealing with the partition. A local storage contains all the versions of the worker or the working group data, as one is shown in Figure 1, in the framework proposed in this paper.

The distributed vaults are constituted in peer to peer manner. There is no replication and thus no actions for file state change such as check in/out or release/obsolete, required by one central vault. The owner only is able to create, modify and remove the file and it is stored in the person's local storage only. A remote worker may access a cached file of the original in the person's local storage, but the cached file does not remain after the person's logout.

This distributed vaults is dissimilar from the other distributed vaults evolved from one central vault. The vaults also have one service point in which metadata is located but there is no particular server for vaulting. The original files locate only in the owner's local storage. The one service point does not have any stored file but exits for the view of conceptually one vault, which is congregated local storages in reality. The reason behind this composition of file locations is human concerns. The specialists or experts don't agree on the exposure of their know-how by files of versions in several steps. Participating workers could endeavor to conduct more-skilled analysis concealing their know-how. In the guarantee of concealing person's know-how, the person might play an innovative role.

The cooperative analyses proceed by changing the states of files associated with partitions. After the completion of an analysis for a partition, the files appear to other remote workers indicating Ready to check. When analysis files of a relevant partition appears with Ready to check, the cooperating workers conduct larger analyses combined with files of relevant partitions and make the report of each result. The result is messaged including Pass or Fail to the owner. If the larger analysis produces the result does not satisfy a prescribed criterion, the result is messaged with Fail and additional memo describing the reason.

Only if all the results of relevant partitions are messaged with Pass, the files state is changed into Pass. Only if every file state of the relevant partitions is changed into Pass, then those files are all marked Approved.

## 3. Dividing the Object into Partitions and Unifying from the Partitions

Basically cooperative analyses proceed with the unanimous passes in peer-to-peer manner. However dividing the object, the entire work, and unifying into the entire work are processed in top-down and bottom-up manner, respectively. The dividing and unifying process is shown in Figure 2. A few partitions could be overlapped on one functional block according to the specialty of interest. Some functional blocks become partitions to be structural analysis, and some other functional blocks become partitions to be fatigue analysis. In the cooperative analysis, analyses on those partitions are conducted concurrently. Partitions the influencing values need be exchanged should Pass analyses again with the exchanged values.

When structural analyses on every partition Pass, all the partitions are unified into one total view, the object. When every partition Passed the fatigue analysis, those are unified into another total view. With the two total views overlapped, partitions of some functional blocks may need another round of analyses due to their interactions by related features. This cross-field analysis is conducted by related teams under the co-operation of the two team leaders and the head analyst. By modified criteria after the cross-field analysis, further analyses could be necessitated in each team. In the case the object is a car, for example, an axle shaft can be a functional block. The partitions of structural analysis and the partitions of fatigue analysis may overlap on the wheel block. In Figure 3, the partition S2 and the partition F3 may overlap on some functional block, for example.

The continuation modifying the criterion involves non-deterministic rounds of analyses. This continuation is analyses in progress toward higher accuracy in simulations approaching to measured values in the experimentation. In this continuation the team leader can be replaced with a team worker, with respect to the specialty of interest. The new team leader takes over only the authority to access the metadata, and it is another reason why the files are locally stored.

1. The object is fragmented in functional blocks by the head analyst. The leaders of analysis teams is assigned in accordance with their specialties.
2. Each leader divides the object into partitions with respect of his specialty. The partitions are distributed to the team workers.
3. The leader may adjust the prescribed criterion to coordinate the cooperative analyses when it is not expected that the Failed partition would satisfy the criterion. After the partitions are marked Approved, they are collected by the leader.
4. The partitions in respect of each specialty are overlapped with ones of other specialty to form the blocks. The head analyst produces an analysis report of the object out of the functional blocks in cooperation with the leaders.

**Figure 2** The dividing and unifying process.

## 4. Cooperative Analyses

The analysis results of the Approved partitions are collected and unified into the object. As each partition has partial information of the object, parametric conditions are properly prescribed. This is the *prescribed criterion* and settled while dividing the object by the leader and workers. The source data for analysis, such as CAD files, could be delivered via the database like described in [2]. The input data for analysis is created from the source data. It may be stored in the database but produced output data may not necessarily be stored in the database in this framework.

Since the prescribed criterion may not be properly settled in the first time, dividing, cooperative analyses and unifying could be repeated several times.

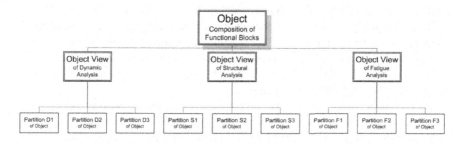

**Figure 3** Dividing the object into partitions by multiple views of respective analyses.

Many of metadata structures should be required to maintain the output files, and input files as shown in Figure 1, of each partition. However those are not defined in this paper as they are application-specific. A subset of sample user interfaces is displayed in Figure 4 and 5, which are of the database for source data distribution for the analysis of a partition. The input data is created and stored at the worker's local storage.

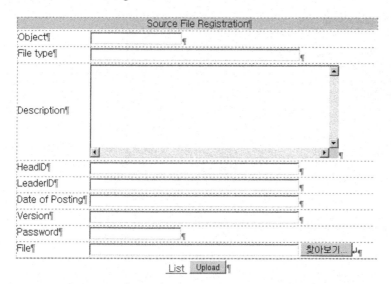

**Figure 4** Source data registration for distribution.

## 5. Summary

A peer-to-peer mannered data exchange and the process are proposed for cooperative analyses. The peer-to-peer manner eliminates tedious file check in/out and the file state field replaces the release/obsolete markings. A large scale analysis can be conducted in higher quality by cooperative analyses with the dividing and unifying process. Although this framework presents a foundation of cooperative analyses, the target of the framework is knowledge management such like [3]. However it should be avoided a complex usage from complicated process in the system. The data exchange method would evolve, in the peer-to-peer manner, for the knowledge management.

By the cooperative analyses the development of a product, with parts in higher quality, is prospective. When the knowledge management is realized in evolution of this framework, the users could derive a new technology, which is innovative, not only a better product from the knowledge management system. In this work we presented a way to collaborate on CAE with teams. In this collaborated CAE we are seeking for a practical method to derive a system for Virtual Engineering. The knowledge management would be a part of the system and the processes are refined and synthesized to be generalized ones against each sort of the analysis. While building and upgrading the cooperative analysis system, the system would develop into one for Virtual Engineering resolving the issues arising from the collaborated CAE.

**Figure 5** Search of the source data from a Web DB.

# References

1. Abramovic M., Gerhard D.: A Flexible Web-Based PDM Approach to Support Virtual Engineering Cooperation. Proc. Hawaii Int. Conf. System Sciences, USA (2000).
2. Kriegel H.-P., Müller A., Pötke M., Seidl T.: DIVE: Database Integration for Virtual Engineering. Demo. Proc. Int. Conf. Data Eng., pp. 15–16, Germany (2001).
3. Yoo S.B., Kim Y.H.: Web-based knowledge management for sharing product data in virtual enterprises. Int. J. Production Economics, Elsevier Science, vol. 75, pp. 173–183 (2002).

# TRIZ-Based Patent Investigation by Evaluating Inventiveness

**Daniele Regazzoni[1] and Roberto Nani[2]**

[1]University of Bergamo, viale Marconi, 24044 Dalmine (BG), Italy
[2]Scinte Srl, Ranica (BG), Italy

**Abstract:** Among TRIZ users the importance given to patent resources is far behind the mere protection of R&D results. Patents represent a starting point for new inventions and a huge resource for collecting information on the way contradictions have been solved and in which different field such solutions may be adopted. Moreover the worldwide patent database contains information about the technology evolution that can be extracted so that the level of maturity of a product or process can be evaluated towards TRIZ laws of technical evolution. The contribution of this paper is to provide a step by step procedure, partially automatic, to perform TRIZ oriented patent search. The procedure, while determining the level of innovation of patents, allows defining a sharp set of patents responding to a structured query. The procedure has been applied to several case studies of different fields (e.g. mechanical, medical, and electronics) and a significant example referring to X-rays technology is shown in the paper.

**Keywords:** patent investigation, TRIZ, level of inventiveness, patent clustering

## 1. Introduction

This paper presents a systematic approach to search and classify world patents in groups according to their degree of novelty and inventiveness. TRIZ methodology has been used to define the criteria to discriminate patents describing a small inventive step or optimization from real breakthrough inventions and discoveries. TRIZ literature presents a large number of papers referring to the subject of level of innovation [1-3] as it is part of basic concepts of the methodology, and patent search methods according to TRIZ are widely known as well. By the way usually the focus is put on the way patents can be exploited to innovate more while the previous step, finding the right set of patents, is less considered. This may cause the whole work to fail because some information are missing, or not enough time is available to perform manual analyses.

*Please use the following format when citing this chapter:*

Regazzoni, D. and Nani, R., 2008, in IFIP International Federation for Information Processing, Volume 277;
*Computer-Aided Innovation (CAI)*; Gaetano Cascini; (Boston: Springer), pp. 247–258.

The goal of the overall research is to provide the inventor with a procedure to perform better and quicker patent search. Then the results obtained could be used for several purposes, such as:

- Defining the state of the art of technologies from emerging to mature;
- Assessing the degree of inventiveness of a patent or concept;
- Building quantitative curves describing main drivers trends of a technology;
- Forecasting future evolution of technology and products.

Ikovenko et al. [4] define five steps to enhance Intellectual Property (IP) strategy taking advantage of TRIZ tools: evaluate goals and area to protect, evaluate company assets, develop a defensive patent strategy, implement it to build broad patents and, finally, manage your patent portfolio. TRIZ together with problem analysis and semantic tools are powerful instruments for patent strategies development. It is necessary to further sharpen algorithms and recommendations on using specific TRIZ tools for specific strategic IP objectives.

TRIZ practitioners are familiar with using patent resources to perform innovation in addition to protection and circumvention. Generally patents are required to be classified by the Contradiction they solved and Inventive Principles they used instead of the fields in which they are involved. Most of the currently available general purpose patent classification systems, such as International patent Classification or European Classification, are based on technology-dependent schemes and they hardly satisfy TRIZ users' requirements. TRIZ-oriented automatic systems to identify Contradictions and Principles have been developed and notable enhancements have been obtained in the last years [5,6] but they are not yet mature for a wide diffusion.

## 2. Methodology

The methodology presented in this paragraph has not the goal to obtain better results in terms of patent found compared to other TRIZ based patent search method. What is claimed is a better usability and short timing in gathering the desired set of patents. This goes through a less iterative procedure in which there is almost no need to read the content of any considered patent. The methodology takes into consideration Souchkov's works [7] on the classification of five Levels of Invention and on the differentiations of solutions according to such classification. Souchkov distinguishes novelties of solutions on the base of three criteria:

1. Function: Any man-made system is designed to fulfil a certain purpose, which, in turn, is provided by a certain main function of the system;
2. Principle: This is a basic scientific effect, principle or phenomenon that enables function to be delivered.

3. Market: Any man-made system delivers its function within a certain context, which meets a certain need of a specific market.

The methodology developed determines a model capable to (a) classify every man-made system on a function-principle combination and (b) individuate the systems and sub-systems that materialize such function-principle combination. For what concerns market no information are retrieved by patent database and market issues will not be taken into consideration.

The step by step procedure explained in the followings is based on an intensive use of Delphion [8] patent search engine capable of:

1. Browsing Codes according to International Patent Classifications, using keyword searching to find relevant IPC classes going down through the entire hierarchy. At each level of the hierarchy the number of child classes is identified, along with the number of patents associated with each class.
2. Clustering Texts to examine search results using linguistic technologies to explore relationships among patents creating a more targeted analysis of patent data and analyzing similarities to focus on what's most relevant.

## 2.1 Patent Investigation and Analysis Procedure

The procedure is composed of five steps as shown in the scheme of Figure 1. Starting from a research context or general interest in a technology the procedure gives back small and precise sets of patents depending on specific objective of the research project, such as cost reduction, elimination of a device or change in the product layout. In the following each step is explained in details while the next paragraph shows step by step the application to the X-ray technology and results are discussed.

### 2.1.1 Step 1: Boolean search

On the base of a given subject or field of research the first step consist in performing a Boolean search using few and generic keywords defining the technology, and no restriction on the IPC (International Patent Classification) classes are imposed. The search results consist in a wide set of patents describing several different aspects of the technology and commonly distribute over several different fields of application. After the search algorithm has been defined and results are given from the patent database some simple statistical elaborations are made. Starting from the date of the first patent of interest some trends are plotted over time to describe:

- The number of patents filed per year;
- The cumulative number of patents filed per year
- The number of IPC 4 digit classes in which patent have been classified per year

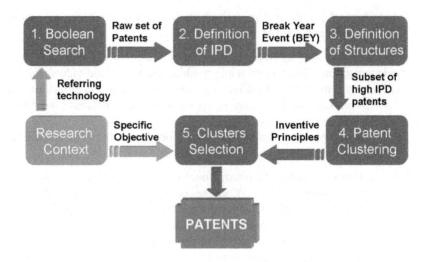

Fig. 1 5 steps scheme of the patent investigation and analysis procedure

Although data are still to be refined and analyzed according to TRIZ tools, the shape of the cited graphs is a preliminary raw indicator of the level maturity of the technology searched. In particular the cumulative number of patents may resemble to a complete or partial S curve and hypothesis on the stage of evolution can be done.

### 2.1.2  Step 2: Definition of Intellectual Property Density (IPD)

The second step consists in the definition of the Intellectual Property Density (IPD) given by the ration of number of patents over the number of IPC 4 digit classes per year. The IPD indicator shows the concentration of patents of the given technology according to the IPC classification. Plotting the cumulative graph of the Intellectual Property Density the Break Year Event (BYE) can be defined. The cumulate IPD is a simple but effective tool to discriminate low and high level innovation patents on the base of the stage of evolution. Actually, as it is commonly recognized that inventive level of patents applications decreases along the S curve, we can roughly divide patents before and after a specific year named BYE. Finding the BYE is necessary for the following steps but its determination cannot be performed universally by means of an automatic algorithm. A technician with some expertise in patent analysis may recognise the BYE by observing the graph cited before. It may correspond to the change of concavity in the cumulative density of IP, or to specific small signals. For emerging technology the last stages of evolution are not been reached and all patents may belong to the first group. Anyway, a mistake of a few years can be generally tolerated since it does not impact dramatically on the overall results.

### 2.1.3 Step 3: Structures of Novelty

A direct result of the definition of the BYE is the creation of two subset of patents that will be addressed as Structure A and B. Structure A is made by the patents filed before the BYE that are characterized by a low level of intellectual property density. Patents of Structure B on the contrary are subsequent to the BYE and belong to several different IPC classes. According to TRIZ classification of level of invention we can assume inventions of level 1-2 belongs to Structure B while inventions of level 3-4-5 belong to Structure A. The subset of patents of Structure A and B can be easily obtained by opportunely adding a time frame to the search algorithm of step 1.

### 2.1.4 Step 4: Clustering

In step 4 a clustering algorithm is applied to patents of Structure A. Analyzing the text of patents terms are grouped in order to obtain the minimum number of cluster having almost no cross connections. The result can be automatically shown by a graph. Each cluster is composed by a number of terms, describing both devices and actions that for Structure A are quite homogeneous for meaning and field. A quick scan of the terms is enough to associate TRIZ Inventive Principles to each cluster. By the way there no need to go through all the clusters if in the working context a specific goal is defined. Actually, the goal can be directly associated to one or a few clusters and further analysis can be focused on those ones.

### 2.1.5 Step 5: Functions and Systems

The last step has the goal to identify a small set of highly interesting patents of the given technology responding to the specific goal of the research project. Once one or a few clusters of Structure A have been identified, Inventive Principles are used as keywords in a new search on Structure B. This allows highlighting critical components and interactions focused on the specific research goal. The overall output of the procedure consists in a list of patents strictly related on the research issues, together with a sharp indication on devices and functions involved.

## 2.2 Application to X-rays technology

X-rays technology has been chosen to demonstrate a real application of the procedure described so far. According to Step 1 the Boolean text search by words or phrases (alphabetical or numeric), using up to four designated patent fields, is performed. The search criterion (1) is:

$$((x\text{-rays}) <in> (TITLE, ABSTRACT, CLAIMS)) \tag{1}$$

Collections searched: European (Applications - Full text), European (Granted - Full text), US (Granted - Full text), WIPO PCT Publications (Full text), US (Applications - Full text), 15,601 matches found of 11,254,955 patents searched

The patent data base gives the information (plotted in Figures 2-4), distributed on the Field Years, valid for European (Applications - Granted), US (Applications - Granted) and WIPO PCT Publications.

In the second step the distribution of patents in respect to the branches of technology is considered. In particular the Intellectual Patent Density is defined and plotted in Figure 5 and 6.

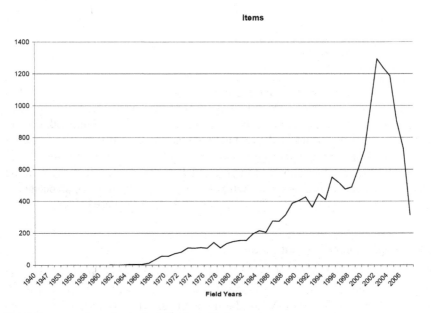

Fig. 2 Items: number of patent applications filed every year

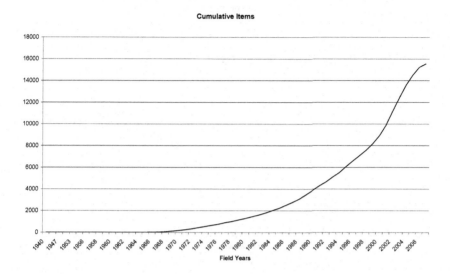

Fig. 3 Cumulative Items: number of the cumulated patents per year

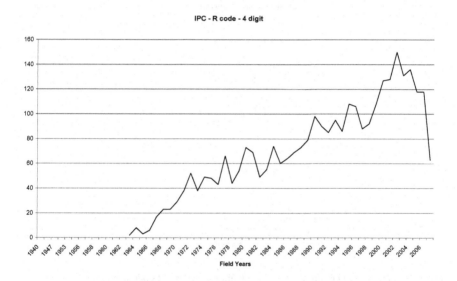

Fig. 4 IPC-R code: number of technological classes (expressed by 4 digit) engaged by the patents

**Items / IPC**

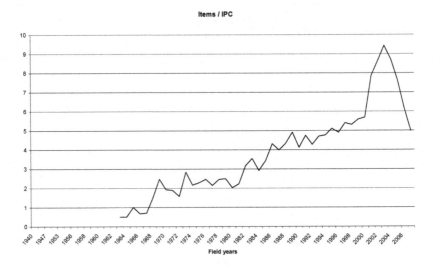

Fig. 5 IPD per year (Patents/IPC 4 digit per year)

**Cumulative Items / Cumulative IPC**

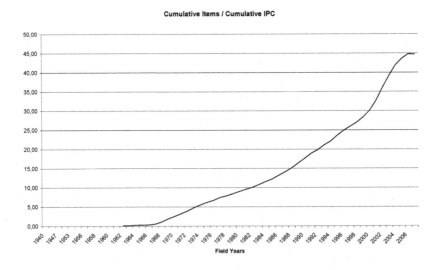

Fig. 6 Cumulative IPD (Cumulative Items/Cumulative IPC-R code per year)

In this case the Break Event Year (BYE) is simply determined as the year corresponding to the average value of the cumulative density of intellectual property. Thus, being 16 patents per IPC class the cumulative IPD average the BYE correspond to year 1989.

Third step is aimed at classifying the whole set of patents into two Structures:

- Structure A comprehend solutions of level 3,4 and 5: discovery, pioneering, radical creation of news functions and new systems;
- Structure B involves Level 1 and 2: relatively simple modification on the existing function/principle combination, relatively simple modifications of the existing subsystems, no new functionality, improving or merging existing solutions.

Structure A is characterized by a low density of intellectual property.

In fact, every new patent application - regarding a discovery of a new principle (Level 5), or a creation of a radically new function/principle combination (Level 4), or the extending a function/principle combination (Level 3) – involves news IPC code, maintaining a low value of Density of Intellectual Property (IPD) and/or Cumulative Density of intellectual property.

Structure B is characterized by a high density of intellectual property. In fact, every new patent application - regarding a qualitative (Level 2) or quantitative (Level 1) improvement within existing function/principle/market – does not involve new IPC code. The two subsets of patents can be obtained by adding a time constraint to the Boolean algorithm used in step 1. Structure A is defined by:

(X-rays) <in> (TITLE,ABSTRACT,CLAIMS) AND (DP>=1960-01-01) AND (DP<=1989-12-31)                                                                  (2)

Patents of Structure B are defined analogously.

Step 4 has to goal to create clusters and associate them with Inventive Principles. We take into consideration a number of clusters capable to involve only the principles avoiding or minimizing the number of connection of descriptive words between different clusters. A Text clustering of Structure A results to be optimized for 20 clusters for which there are only three combined clusters (6←10→8) as shown in Figure 7.

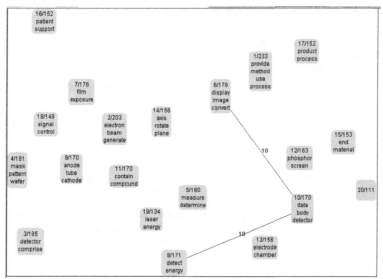

Fig. 7 Graphical representation of Clusters of Structure A and their limited interactions

Table 1 Results of text clustering on Structure A

| Cluster | Items | Descriptive words |
|---------|-------|-------------------|
| 1 | 233 | provide, method, use, process, disclose, comprise, form, invention, radiation (38), material |
| 2 | 203 | electron, beam, generate (25), target, electron beam, apparatus, mean, focus, produce, source (25) |
| 3 | 185 | Detector (3), comprise, source (25), detect, system, device, plurality (1), apparatus, radiation (38), dispose |
| ... | ... | ..., ... |
| 18 | 149 | signal, control, (23) voltage, current, value, output, tube, include, produce, predetermine |
| 19 | 134 | laser, energy, target, focus, use, produce, emit (38), beam, obtain, high |
| 20 | 111 | Image (26), display, enable, use, provide, scan, film (30), control (23), cause, mean |

Step 5 prescribes the Boolean combination of items of structure B and principles extracted by the clustering texts of items of structure A. This allows to define the matching system and sub-system designed to fulfil a certain technical purpose. We consider for example the principles characterizing cluster 20 of structure A. We consider 10 clusters as optimized structure.

Table 2 Final set of clusters defining systems and subsystems of a technology

| Cluster | Items | Descriptive words |
|---------|-------|-------------------|
| 1 | 20 | comprise, carry, relate, form, process, move, invention, film, method, use |
| 2 | 17 | correspond, apparatus, first, light, method, receive, response, describe, capable, portion |
| ... | ... | ..., ... |
| 9 | 12 | patient, move, first, position, calculate, subject, detector, combine, tube, disclose |
| 10 | 11 | utilize, object, display, radiation, source, digital, electronic radioscopic imaging system use, portable, pulse, self-contained |

We can observe that every cluster obtained is constituted by concatenated sub-clusters. Figure 8 shows cluster 1 that is formed by concatenated sub-clusters. The main sub-clusters contain the main function of the system.

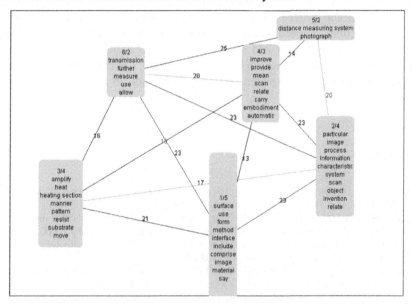

Fig. 8 Graphical representation of sub-Clusters of Structure Band their strong interactions

At last to each sub-cluster a small amount of highly focused patents are identified. For sub-cluster 1 five patents are found with a high level of similarity.

Table 3 Set of papers resulting from the patent search

| Publication | Similarity | Title |
|---|---|---|
| WO09930486A2 | 59% | FORMING AN **ASSEMBLED IMAGE** FROM SUCCESSIVE X-RAY IMAGES |
| WO00243856A2 | 55% | ORDERED TWO-AND THREE-DIMENSIONAL STRUCTURES OF AMPHIPHILIC MOLECULES |
| US26032433A1 | 51% | Rapid X-ray diffraction method for structural analysis of a nano material [...] |
| US26131669A1 | 49% | Thin film transistor for imaging system |
| WO09821625A2 | 49% | WIDE LATITUDE FILM |

## 3. Conclusions

The contribution of this paper to the state of the art of TRIZ oriented patent search is to provide a step by step procedure, almost automatic, based on level of invention. The described procedure allows to define a narrow set of patents responding to a structured query taking into account both general definition of a technology and a specific objective of research. The procedure is based on the advanced use of a patent search engine together with some TRIZ tools to gather results suitable for innovation means.

## References

1. Gibson, N.: The Determination of the Technological Maturity of Ultrasonic Welding, The TRIZ Journal, http://www.triz-journal.com/archives/1999/07/a/index.htm (1999).
2. Leon, J., Martinez, C. Castillo: Methodology for the Evaluation of the Innovation Level of Products and Processes, proceedings of TRIZCON05, Brighton MI USA, April 2005 (2005).
3. Slocum, M. S., Lundberg, C. O.: Case Study: Using TRIZ to Forecast Technology, The Triz Journal, http://www.triz-journal.com/content/c070507a.asp (2007).
4. Ikovenko, S., Kogan, S.: TRIZ Application for Patent Strategies Development, Proceedings of TRIZ Future Conference p. 427-434, Graz, Austria, Nov. 16-18 (2005).
5. Han Tong Loh, Cong He and Lixiang Shen: Automatic classification of patent documents for TRIZ users World Patent Information, vol. 28, pp. 6-13, Issue 1, March 2006 (2006).
6. Han Tong Loh, Cong He: Grouping of TRIZ Inventive Principles to facilitate automatic patent classification Source. Expert Systems with Applications: An International Journal, vol. 34, Issue 1 (January 2008), ISSN:0957-4174 (2008).
7. Souchkov, V.: Differentiating Among the Five Levels of Solutions. The Triz Journal, http://www.triz-journal.com/archives/2007/07/02/ (2007).
8. www.delphion.com